ISBN 978-1-330-31650-4
PIBN 10024715

English
Français
Deutsche
Italiano
Español
Português

www.forgottenbooks.com

Mythology Photography **Fiction**
Fishing Christianity **Art** Cooking
Essays Buddhism Freemasonry
Medicine **Biology** Music **Ancient
Egypt** Evolution Carpentry Physics
Dance Geology **Mathematics** Fitness
Shakespeare **Folklore** Yoga Marketing
Confidence Immortality Biographies
Poetry **Psychology** Witchcraft
Electronics Chemistry History **Law**
Accounting **Philosophy** Anthropology
Alchemy Drama Quantum Mechanics
Atheism Sexual Health **Ancient History**
Entrepreneurship Languages Sport
Paleontology Needlework Islam
Metaphysics Investment Archaeology
Parenting Statistics Criminology
Motivational

A History of Events in
Egypt from 1798 to 1914

" With antecedents,
    With Egypt . . .
    With the fading kingdoms and kings,
    With countless years drawing themselves onward
    And arriving at these years—
    O, but it is not the years : it is I, it is You . . .
    We stand amid time beginningless and endless,
    We stand amid evil and good . . .
    I know that the past was great and the future will be great,
    And that where I am or you are this present day
    There is the centre of all days, all races,
    And there is the meaning to us of all that has ever come
    Of races and days, or ever will come."
                                —WALT WHITMAN.

THE SULTAN OF EGYPT.

H.H. PRINCE HUSSEIN PASHA KAMEL.

A History of Events in
Egypt from 1798 to 1914

BY

ARTHUR E. P. BROME WEIGALL

LATE INSPECTOR-GENERAL OF ANTIQUITIES TO THE EGYPTIAN GOVERNMENT

AUTHOR OF
'THE LIFE AND TIMES OF CLEOPATRA, QUEEN OF EGYPT,' 'THE
LIFE AND TIMES OF AKHNATON, PHARAOH OF EGYPT,'
'THE TREASURY OF ANCIENT EGYPT,' ETC., ETC.

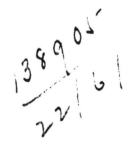

William Blackwood and Sons
Edinburgh and London
1915

TO

MY MOTHER

PREFACE.

My fellow-workers may ask why an Egyptologist, deserting for a while his temples and his mummies, should meddle with modern affairs and politics. I must, therefore, give my reasons for having turned my attention to these nineteenth- and twentieth-century studies in Egyptian history.

It has lately been definitely proved that the ancient and modern Egyptians are one and the same people. Anthropologically there is no real difference between them, and it would seem that neither the Arab nor any other invasion materially affected the purity of their blood. They have suffered a certain nervous deterioration, and have perhaps lost some of their initiative and strength of purpose, just as any individual in his lifetime may, after a long illness, find himself not so energetic as once he was; but physically and mentally the modern Egyptians are not different from their ancestors of the days of the Pharaohs.

This being so, I do not see how an Egyptologist

can hope to understand the ancient inhabitants of the Nile Valley unless he make some study of their modern descendants. The antiquarian will reply that modern politics are of too transitory a nature to interest him; but in answer, I would point out to him that all historical episodes are transitory, and yet in bulk they serve to define the only permanent quality by which a people may be judged—namely, the national character. The antiquarian must remember that in his archæological work he is dealing with a people who are still alive, still contributing their strength to the labours of the world. The affairs of bygone times must be interpreted in the light of recent events, just as modern conditions can be rightly appreciated only by those who know what has gone before. There must be a constant interchange of suggestion between the past and the present, and both in the study of the distant ages and in that of modern days, we must not lose sight of the fact that the long road of Time stretches in one unbroken line from the far past into the far future, and that the traveller upon that road is indeed a lost wanderer if he sees not from whence it comes and into what direction it seems to go.

Egypt has recently passed under the Protection of the British people, and it is therefore incumbent upon those . who take their national responsibilities with seriousness to understand how it comes about that we are in any way concerned with the people of the Nile. Lord Cromer once remarked to me that no statesman could hope to understand the Egyptian Question unless he had made some study of ancient history ; and with equal reason it may be said that no antiquarian can expect to interpret rightly the events of Egypt's mighty past unless he has been an interested spectator of Egyptian actions in modern times.

Such is my excuse for spending many of my spare hours in the preparation of the following chapters, which, as far as I am concerned, have served to enlighten me very considerably upon certain remote episodes, and have produced in my mind an unbounded confidence in the ability of the Egyptian nation to re-establish its great-ness under our very eyes, and, by England's high-minded aid, to become, as the new Sultan has said, " a centre of intensive cultivation, both moral and material."

Some of the following chapters have been published as papers in ' The Fortnightly Review,' and others have appeared in ' Blackwood's Maga-zine.' I have to thank the editors for allowing them to be reproduced here.

CONTENTS.

PART I.

MODERN EGYPT BEFORE THE BRITISH OCCUPATION.

PART II.

EGYPT DURING THE BRITISH OCCUPATION.

ILLUSTRATIONS.

PART I.

MODERN EGYPT BEFORE THE BRITISH OCCUPATION

"Then will this consecrated land, the abode of shrines and temples, be densely filled with graves and corpses. O Egypt, Egypt! of thy worships only rumours will be preserved, and even these will seem incredible to thy coming generations; only words will be preserved on the stones to tell of thy pious deeds, and Egypt will be inhabited by the Scythian or Indian or other such from the neighbouring barbarian land." — *Attributed to* APPULEIUS.

CHAPTER I.

In 1515 the Turks declared war upon Egypt, which at that time was governed by independent Mameluke Sultans, and on January 20, 1517, Cairo was captured. The Sultan Selîm I. of Turkey was declared Sultan of Egypt, and when he returned to his own country he left a viceroy who should rule in his name, with the advice of twenty-four Mameluke chieftains.

In 1750 a certain Mameluke, named Ali Bey, rose into prominence, and when, in 1769, the Porte ordered him to send 12,000 Egyptians to serve against the Russians, he felt himself strong enough to revolt. Shortly afterwards, therefore, he proclaimed himself Sultan of Egypt and *Khakan* of the Two Seas, and came to an understanding with Russia. In 1773, however, he was defeated, and Egypt passed once more under the rule of the Porte. A period of anarchy ensued, and at length, in 1782, a Turkish force marched into Egypt to restore order. The government then passed into the hands of the two Mameluke chieftains, Murad and Ibrahim, who ruled as the vassals of the Porte; and it was during their tenure of office that Napoleon Bonaparte conceived the idea of invading Egypt.

The extraordinary personality of Bonaparte, and the bold manner in which he created and dominated the European situation during the end of the eighteenth and beginning of the nineteenth centuries, often lead us to forget that he, like most other commanders, made his blunders and suffered his defeats. The available forces of France were not always able to put into execution the grandiose and sometimes fantastic schemes of his fertile mind, and Napoleon's failing throughout his career was his inability to curb his ambitions. The splendid romantic dreams of conquest which were evolved in his brain led him to attempt more than his armies could accomplish, and on three or four occasions he embarked upon enterprises which ended in disaster. Yet so overjoyed is mankind at any display of confident optimism, so tolerant is the world towards any miscalculations in a scheme which is in any way heroic, that it is our custom to judge an enterprise not so much by its degree of success as by the boldness of its conception. The drama of Moscow is laid on so grand a scale that we are pleased to regard the retreat of the French army more as a triumph than as a catastrophe. The abandonment of the project for the

invasion of England is forgotten in the press of
the crowding events of that period. The disasters
which led to the Emperor's exile on Elba are
wiped out in the memory of the stirring "hundred
days." And, in like manner, Bonaparte's Egyptian
campaign, which was a total failure, is dressed by
the historian in the trappings of the projected
Oriental conquests or in the tinsel of the Battle of
the Pyramids; and the prime fact of the break-
down of the entire scheme is steadily ignored.
There is something magnificent in the picture of
Bonaparte pacing the broad avenues of the park of
Passeriano in the glow of the sunset, demonstrating
to his generals his schemes for the conquest of
Egypt and of Asia, "frequently betraying by his
exclamations the gigantic thoughts of his unlimited
ambition," as Lacroix tells us. "Was it not, then,
a noble project," asks that historian, "to reopen
the roadway of the ancient world, to explore a
country so rich in great memories, to go to mark
his place amongst the most illustrious conquerors,
and to plant the tricoloured flag upon the ruins of
Thebes?" Indeed, it was a fine, if a somewhat
sensational, dream; and the mouth of the critic
being stopped by the largeness of its conception,
he is wont to refrain from the cold comment that
a very temporary and quite useless subjection of
little Malta and unwarlike Egypt was all that
came of Napoleon's romantic project. Here, as in
the Peninsula and in Belgium, he collided with

that so often under-estimated factor in international affairs—the persistence of England, which in some irresistible manner slowly sweeps all before it by virtue of a combination of pluck and optimism. His wild plans for making himself Sultan of the Orient, which developed out of the original scheme, were brought to a sudden termination by the Battle of the Nile, in which a small fleet of British ships destroyed his armada, and by the Defence of Acre, where a handful of British sailors turned back his dispirited invading army; and, when he had slipped back to France in disgust, a British expeditionary force caused that same army to capitulate at Alexandria. In Egypt and Syria the great duel between England and the much-dreaded "Boney" opened; and the first bout, like the last, ended in a hard-earned victory for our arms. The events deserve a far greater prominence than they generally receive, not only because they reveal the amazing fighting power of England, but also because they show Bonaparte in a *rôle* which, at first romantic, can only be described in its later phases as that of a lunatic.

The importance to any European power of possessing Egypt had been realised for many years. In 1672 Leibnitz had explained to Louis XIV. that he might best hope to subjugate the Dutch, not by the invasion of Holland, but by an attack on Egypt. "There you will find," said he, "the great Indian commercial route, you will take away the commerce from Holland, and you will assure the eternal domination of France in the Levant." His words, however, were not heeded, and, though the project was proposed by the Duc de Choiseul to Louis XV. and Louis XVI., nothing came of it. In 1781 the Comte de Saint-Priest, the French ambassador at Constantinople, urged his government to consider the scheme. "We must hasten to occupy Egypt," he wrote. "The conquest of the country is easy. It is defended only by 5000 or 6000 Mamelukes, who have never been under fire, and who do not possess a single cannon." This was very true. The Mameluke chieftains who had ruled the country since its conquest by Turkey in 1517, under the Sultan Selîm I., were of foreign extraction, and no affection was displayed towards them by the Egyptians whom they tyrannised. Nor were the Turks, whose Sultan was the nominal sovereign of Egypt, satisfied with the arrogant and independent behaviour of these chieftains. A few years later, at the time of the contemplated French invasion, the Nile valley was ruled jointly by two Mamelukes, Murad Bey and Ibrahim Bey, and Napoleon's agents had told him of the cruelties practised by these two men upon the long-suffering Egyptians, and of the annoyance of the Sultan at their conduct. In August 1797, therefore, Bonaparte wrote to the Directoire telling them that the time was ripe for an Oriental campaign; but the discussion of the subject was interrupted by the attempted invasion of England, and it was not until the abandonment of that rash project that the Egyptian campaign was again considered.   In March 1798 the troops which had been collected along the north coast of France were marched over to the south coast, and *l'armée d'Angleterre* became *l'armée d'Orient.*

The ostensible reason for the invasion of Egypt was provided by a communication received from the French Consul in Egypt, M. Magallon, who pointed out that French commerce was suffering greatly owing to the precarious situation of the French merchants resident in that country, who were always liable to unjust and tyrannical treatment at the hands of the Mamelukes.   Bonaparte, therefore, caused it to be understood by those who were admitted into the secret, that he was about to restore order and security in Egypt by overthrowing the Mamelukes and by upholding the authority of the Sultan.   This was, however, but one of several objects which he had in view. Egypt and Asia suggested all manner of possibilities to his creative brain.   The East had always appealed to him, possibly owing to an Oriental strain in his blood.   As early as August 1795 he had seriously thought of going to Turkey to reorganise the Sultan's artillery, but now this far greater opportunity had presented itself.   He saw himself setting out from the abundant Nile to

conquer Asia and to bring India under his domination. He regarded Egypt as the natural gateway
to the East, through which his armies should
stream out into the unlimited plains of Asia, and
thence over the mountains to the sacred rivers of
India. The Venetian Sanuto had spoken of the
effect on India which must follow from the conquest of the Nile valley; and the Comte Daru had
declared that the possession of Egypt was to be
preferred to that of all the provinces between the
Indus and the Ganges, so essential was it to the
conquest of the far countries beyond. The English
were already making themselves masters of India,
while their trade with the East was very considerable; and thus the French were assured that the
capture of Egypt might lead on to the destruction
of British prestige in Asia.

"There were," says Bonaparte in his Memoirs,
"three objects in the expedition to Egypt. Firstly,
to establish a French colony on the Nile which
would prosper without slaves, and serve France
instead of the Republic of St Domingo and of all
the sugar islands. Secondly, to open a market for
our manufactures in Africa, Arabia, and Syria,
and to supply our commerce with all the produc-
tions of those vast countries. Thirdly, setting out
from Egypt, as from a place of arms, to lead an
army of 60,000 men to the Indies to excite the
Mahrattas and oppressed people of these extensive
regions to insurrection. 60,000 men, half European

and half recruits from the burning climates of the equator and the tropics, carried by 10,000 horses and 50,000 camels, having with them provisions for sixty days, water for five days, and a train of artillery of 150 pieces, with double supplies of ammunition, would have reached the Indus in four months. Since the invention of shipping the ocean has ceased to be an obstacle, and the desert is no longer an impediment to an army possessed of camels and dromedaries in abundance."

This all sounds very well, but it is in actual fact sheer nonsense. It would have been quite impossible to collect 50,000 camels, even supposing that the Arabs would have attempted the task to the best of their ability, which is a highly improbable supposition. The watering of this vast caravan at the shallow wells in the desert, and the feeding of the camels, would have been impracticable; and the carrying of sixty days' rations and five days' water per man would have wanted the assistance of some very black magic.

Bonaparte further conceived the idea of cutting a canal between the Red Sea and the Mediterranean, along the route of the later Suez Canal, and of opening this new passage to none but French shipping. The ancient road to India, travelled by Alexander the Great, and the maritime highway down the Red Sea, would thus be patrolled by the men and the ships of France; and he might hope to found an Oriental Empire

of vast extent. For this purpose he had already
sent his agents posting away over the hills to
spread discontent amongst the peoples of India,
in order that they might welcome the French
army, when it should come, as their deliverer
from oppression; for such preparatory methods
had already been tried with conspicuous success
in Switzerland, Venice, Italy, Ireland, and other
countries. He had, moreover, entered into negotiations with the famous Tippoo Sahib, "the tiger
of Mysore," who was then struggling against the
English advance in India. There can be no doubt
that at this time Bonaparte was honestly impelled
by his desire for the glory of France and for the
destruction of her enemies; but as the scheme
shaped itself in his mind patriotic sentiments gave
way to personal ambitions, and he came to regard
the projected march into Asia not so much as a
French campaign as the fulfilment of his own
destiny. The expedition for the destruction of
British commerce was changed in his mind to an
armed establishment of himself upon that far-
distant throne for which he believed that Providence had ordained him.

As though consciously setting out to found an
Empire, Bonaparte decided to take with the expedition a large staff of artists and savants—
painters, poets, musicians, architects, engineers,
mathematicians, astronomers, archæologists, historians, botanists, entomologists, zoologists, geol-

ogists, and others—who should study the countries
visited, and thus demonstrate to the world that
the Corsican was the pioneer of an advanced and
noble civilisation.   The work accomplished by
these scientists still stands as a record of the
utmost importance.   It served as the foundation
of the science of Egyptology, and to this day the
archæologist is able to regard the monumental
'Description de l'Égypte' as a standard work.
Bonaparte provided his expedition with a fine
collection of mathematical and scientific instruments, and with a good library of books of
reference; while, for the purpose of issuing proclamations and general orders, he took with him
printers and a printing-press stocked with both
Latin and Arabic type.

On April 12, 1798, when all was in readiness,
the army, the fleet, and the transports being
collected at Toulon, Bonaparte received in Paris
his orders from the Directoire, stating that "he
will chase the English from all their Oriental
possessions which he is able to reach, and notably
he will destroy all their stations on the Red Sea.
He will cut through the Isthmus of Suez, and he
will take the necessary measures to assure the
free and exclusive possession of the Red Sea to
the French Republic."   Shortly afterwards he set
out for Toulon, and on May 10, just after his
arrival, he issued a bombastic proclamation to
the troops, telling them that though they had

fought their way over mountains and plains, the
sea yet remained to be conquered. "Soldiers!"
wrote he, "Europe has its eyes on you," and much
else he penned of a similar nature which, owing
to the disparity between the emotional training
of the French and English nations, it were better
here to leave unrecorded.

On May 19 the fleet set sail. Its destination
was an absolute secret from all save the chief
officers The British Government knew nothing,
and the rumours that an Oriental campaign was
pending were discredited as being fantastic and
improbable. Bad weather, and this lack of in-
formation as to the direction in which the French
proposed to move, combined to divert the attention of our English squadron; and though it was
known that Nelson was cruising on these seas,
the chances were small that the two fleets would
meet, while in the event of such an occurrence
the French men-o'-war, commanded by Admiral
Brueys, were considered strong enough to hold
their own and to defend the 300 transports in
their charge. On June 10 the fleet arrived at
Malta, which, after a brief struggle, capitulated
to the invaders, the Knights of St John of Jerusalem who held it being in no mood to fight. On
June 19, a month after setting sail from Toulon,
the great armada put out from Malta, steering
for Crete; but on reaching this island Bonaparte
received news that Nelson was in pursuit, and

therefore gave orders to the Admiral to proceed at once to Alexandria.

Nelson did not know whither Bonaparte was bound; for Spain and Ireland, Greece and Syria, were equally probable goals of his ambition. He therefore had to inquire of passing vessels as to whether they had seen the French fleet. On reaching Naples, on June 19, he was told that the enemy had gone to Malta; but while following them thither he bespoke a passing vessel, which informed him that the French had departed eastwards. Nelson, at once guessing the truth, wrote to his Government saying, "They are going on their scheme of possessing Alexandria and getting troops to India." Immediately he set sail in pursuit, and therewith began one of the finest sea-hunts in history. "I will fight them," wrote Nelson, "the moment I can reach their fleet, be it at anchor or under sail." The keen excitement of the British sailors at having a complete French army as their quarry inspired them to the supremest efforts, and the vessels were kept at top-speed day and night. Nelson had, however, lost some of his frigates which had been disabled in a storm off Gibraltar; and owing to his lack of these "scouts" he passed the French fleet as it was sheltering under Crete, and arrived before them at Alexandria.

The town was at that time a small seaport, with a total population of not more than 8000 souls. The European colony was neither large nor prosperous, and had suffered many indignities at the hands of the native authorities. The governor of the town was an Egyptian who regarded the nations of Europe as the natural servants of the Orient. Like his ancestors of Pharaonic days, he considered only the Egyptians to be "men," and foreigners to be some quaint species of animal; and when Nelson's ships arrived and a deputation was sent ashore to ask for news of the French, the governor treated them with lofty scorn, telling them to be pleased to go away as quickly as possible, since Egypt really had no wish to know anything about either the French or the English. Nelson, seeing that the enemy had evidently not yet reached the country, set sail for Crete with black murder in his heart at this new disappointment. As so often happens in summer, however, a dense haze lay over the water, and during one of the following nights the two fleets passed one another unseen. When Nelson arrived at Syracuse, after a fruitless search, he declared that his heart nearly broke. He had chased the French for 600 leagues, had been within fifty miles of them, and yet had missed them.

After leaving Crete Bonaparte issued a proclamation to the troops, informing them of their destination, which until now had not leaked out. "Soldiers!" he wrote, "you go to undertake a conquest of which the effects upon the civilisation and the commerce of the world are incalculable. You will strike at England the most certain and the most acute blow while waiting to give her the death - stroke. . . . The Mamelukes who favour exclusively English commerce . . . some days after our arrival will exist no more. The peoples with whom we are going to live are Mohammedans; their main article of faith is this : 'There is no God but God, and Mohammed is His prophet.' . . . Have for the ceremonies prescribed by the Koran the same tolerance that you have had for convents, for synagogues, for the religion of Moses, and for that of Jesus Christ."

On July 1 the fleet arrived before Alexandria, and the governor, startled by the number of ships, sent messengers to Cairo saying that French vessels "without beginning or end" were outside the harbour. A council was at once called in the metropolis to decide upon a course of action ; and one deputy, voicing the wishes of the mob, proposed that, as a first step, the Europeans there resident should be massacred. The more temperate judgment of the leading Mamelukes, and of the Turkish representative, Bekir Pasha, however, caused this irresponsible suggestion to be abandoned. Egyptians are by nature kindly and humane. On many occasions, both in Pharaonic days and in recent times, they have shown marked aversion to bloodshed ; and it is a fact, not always recognised, that throughout their history they are very decidedly conspicuous for their gentleness and forbearance. Now, at this council meeting, not only was the thought of massacre put aside, but measures were actually taken for the safety of all Europeans, and Ibrahim Bey went so far as to place one of his palaces, situated in the fashionable quarter at the south side of the Pool of Elephants,[1] at the disposal of the European ladies, who were invited to take up their residence there under the protection of his soldiers.

Meanwhile, Bonaparte received news that Nelson was somewhere in the neighbourhood, and the consequent hurried landing of the army was hardly distinguishable from a headlong flight to safety. He had managed, after some difficulties, to get into communication with the French Consul, Magallon, and from him he had learnt that the defences of the town were insignificant. The disembarkation began soon after the sun had set, but, as is usual in July, the sea was rough and the breakers could be heard thundering upon the rocky coast ahead. The point at which the landing was to be effected was some distance from the town; and under the warm brilliance of the summer moon neither the rolling waters nor the desolate shore offered encouragement to the troops. They were unfeignedly agitated as to the approach

---

[1] Now the Esbekieh Gardens.

of Nelson, whose ships were expected to appear out of the hazy distance at any moment; and they knew not what valiant armies awaited them on land.   In the rough sea some of the over-crowded boats struck the rocks and sank, carrying many heavy-armed soldiers to their deaths.   "My fortune has forsaken me," said Bonaparte gloomily, as he descended into the boat which was to take him ashore.

Some Bedouîn, seeing the troops massed upon the beach, rushed into the town to inform the governor.   He at once sprang on to his horse, and, at the head of some twenty men, galloped towards the invaders.   He took the advance-guard completely by surprise, charged down upon them, whisked off the head of their captain with his curved sword, and galloped back to Alexandria waving his ghastly trophy, leaving the French soldiers with mouths open and knees knocking together.   About 500 Bedouîn horsemen then attacked them, inflicting some losses; but with the coming of day the order was given to advance on the town, and the troops soon steadied them-selves. A short and sharp battle ensued.   General Menou, with seven wounds, was the first over the walls; General Kléber was seriously wounded as he led his men; and Bonaparte was grazed by a bullet which came near to terminating his career. Street fighting continued till noon, by which time most of the town was in the possession of the

NAPOLEON BONAPARTE.

[*By* BARON GROS, Versailles.

French ; and, after some negotiations, the governor decided to capitulate. The French casualties were 40 killed and 100 wounded. The former had the honour of being interred, at the theatrical Bonaparte's suggestion, beneath the famous granite column known as Pompey's Pillar, which stands on the site of the ancient Serapeum, and their names were inscribed upon the sides of this monument.

On July 2, Bonaparte issued a proclamation to the people of Egypt, printed in Arabic characters by his own press. This is the first of a series of most extraordinary documents addressed to the Egyptian people by the audacious Little Corporal. Its insincerity is only less astonishing than the obvious satisfaction with which it was written. It displays Bonaparte at his worst: glib, cunning, a hypocrite, and a liar. It shows, too, how completely he misunderstood the Orient and its peoples in supposing that such a document would influence any of them in his favour.

The proclamation begins by stating that the hour of the chastisement of the Mamelukes has arrived. "For a long time," it continues, "this crowd of slaves bought in Georgia and the Caucasus have tyrannised the most beautiful place in the world ; but God, on whom all depends, has ordained that their empire is finished. People of Egypt, they have told you that I am come to destroy your religion. Do not believe them!

Answer that I am come to restore your rights, to punish the usurpers, and that I respect, more than the Mamelukes, God, His Prophet, and the Koran. Tell them that all men are equal before God : intelligence, talents, and virtues alone differentiate them." (This, of course, was rank blasphemy to Moslem minds, for the Koran teaches that there can be no equality between Mohammedans and Christians.) What virtues or intellectual qualities, he asked in the cant of the Republic, could these tyrants boast that should give them the exclusive right to all that made life worth living? Was there a beautiful piece of land, a beautiful slave, a beautiful horse, a beautiful house : the Mamelukes seized it. "But God is just and compassionate to the people. . . . Cadis, shêkhs, imams, tchorbadjis, say to the people that we are the friends of true Musulmans. Is it not we who have destroyed the Pope who said that he was going to make war on the Musulmans? Is it not we who have destroyed the Knights of Malta, because these madmen believed that God wished them to wage war against the Musulmans? Is it not we who have been throughout all the centuries the friends of the Sultan (whose desires may God fulfil!) and the enemy of his enemies?" Then, bursting into biblical language in order to give his discourse the necessary Oriental touch, he writes : "Thrice happy are those who will be on our side! They will prosper in their fortune and their rank.

Happy those who remain neutral! They will have time to get to know us, and will range themselves with us. But woe, woe threefold, to those who arm themselves for the Mamelukes and fight against us! There will be no hope for them: they will perish." The proclamation ends with an order to the religious leaders of Islam to pray for the French cause. " Each man will thank God for the destruction of the Mamelukes, and will cry: Glory to the Sultan! Glory to the French army, his friend! Malediction to the Mamelukes, and good luck to the people of Egypt!"

On July 9, when the summer was at its height, the advance on Cairo began. A garrison having been left at Alexandria, the bulk of the army took the direct road to the capital, following the route of the present railway line; but General Dugua with a smaller force was sent eastwards to the neighbouring town of Rosetta, which stands at one of the mouths of the Nile, whence he was to make his way up the river to El Rahmanieh, where the two divisions were to meet. The latter force was able to carry its baggage and provisions on native boats, which were towed up the stream with comparative ease; but Bonaparte's division, and more especially its advance - guard, under General Desaix, suffered great hardships, for very insufficient supplies were to be obtained from the impoverished and half-deserted villages along the route, while the wells in many cases had been filled up. Bands of Arabs continuously harassed the weary, sweating troops, cutting off the stragglers by day and sniping at the bivouacs by night. On one occasion Bonaparte himself escaped capture only by the merest chance. The great heat of an Egyptian summer which drenches one in perspiration, the powerful sun which must have caused the heavy uniforms to be a torture to the wearers and the metal appurtenances to become unbearable to the touch, the flies and mosquitos which ceaselessly tormented them, the unquenchable thirst produced by energetic action under the blazing heavens, the lack of food, the constant fear of attack, and the unknown fate which awaited them, must have rendered the march towards Cairo an experience suggestive of nightmare.

After ten days of such distressing conditions the temper of the army became almost unmanageable. "For what had they been sent to Egypt?" the soldiers are said to have asked. "Had the Directoire deported them, wishing to be rid of them?" Many of them drowned themselves in the Nile, considering a rapid death in the muddy waters to be more to their liking than a continuity of miseries such as they had endured since they set out from Alexandria. They were bitterly disappointed at the poverty of the towns through which they passed. They had believed Egypt to be a land of palaces whose walls were studded with jewels and whose floors were paved with gold. They had looked forward to rich booty, and had pictured themselves billeted in splendour and waited upon by fair slave-girls. Instead of all that their imaginations had thus portrayed, they beheld dirty hovels or tumbled-down houses, and miserable, vermin-infested townspeople; while of food there was little to be procured, and that little of mean quality.

Bonaparte, himself low-spirited, must have also experienced something of the disillusionment undergone by his soldiers. Like them, he had dreamed of the riches of the Orient, and had permitted himself to indulge in the very common but very erroneous belief, that Egypt was a land of the Arabian Nights' variety. He now saw around him in the sun-scorched villages and fields of the Delta nothing but ruin, poverty, and distress.

On July 10 General Desaix arrived with the advance-guard at El Rahmanieh, and there he encountered a large force of Mamelukes, who had travelled from Cairo confidently expecting to overthrow the infidels at the first shock of battle; but these warriors were no match for the disciplined troops of France, and in spite of a fiery display of courage they were easily routed. Two days later the flotilla, which was to meet the main army at this place, was suddenly attacked by the Mamelukes and came very near to capture. So serious, indeed, was the situation that one of

the savants attached to the expedition, named
Bertillon, was observed during the course of the
fight to be filling his commodious pockets with
stones taken from the ballast of the boat in which
he was travelling, in order, as he afterwards
explained, that he might drown the more quickly
if capture became otherwise unavoidable. At the
end of the day, however, Bonaparte arrived, and
the Egyptians were driven off. One of the Mameluke chieftains, exasperated by the defeat, and
unaware that the days of Western chivalry were
as good as dead, rode up to the French lines clad
in his Saracen chain-armour and waving his huge
crusading sword. In a loud voice he challenged
any French officer to single combat; and it must
have been with indignant astonishment in his
mind that he fell a few moments later before
the fire of his unimaginative adversaries.

A week's march brought the army in sight of
the capital, and on the 20th it had reached a
spot on the west bank of the Nile almost exactly
opposite to Cairo. The city stood on the east
bank about a mile back from the river, all the
space now covered by the modern European
quarters of Kasr - el - Nil and Kasr - ed - Doubara
being then open fields. On the west bank, barring
the farther progress of the invaders, the Mameluke army was drawn up near the village of
Embabeh. In the far distance, many miles to
the south-west, rose the three great pyramids,

dim upon the horizon and half-hidden behind the groves of palms. The order was given to prepare for battle, and early in the morning of July 21 Bonaparte addressed the troops in the well-known words: "Soldiers, forty centuries are watching you"—words which for some inadequate reason are treasured up by history as though they had something more than a theatrical quality. Actually, however, they were not at all apt. The centuries—much under - estimated—which looked down from the pyramids would have had to have used a telescope to see the battle, and the reminder that these long Egyptian years were keeping an eye on them might well have been somewhat dispiriting to the troops, as meaning that the occult power of Egypt's mighty past was standing sentinel, with a very natural prejudice against all invaders. Bonaparte undoubtedly believed himself to be in for a pretty hard day's work, and thought, therefore, that the occasion demanded a dramatic utterance; but in reality he was faced by no more than a mob of over-wrought children, led by a rabble of dare-devil chieftains without a rudimentary knowledge of modern warfare. 30,000 picked veterans — the army, in fact, which was to have marched on London — were opposed to this ill-armed crowd of no more than 12,000 natives; and the disproportion will be more readily appreciated when it is remembered that an English army of 13,000

men routed the trained Egyptian army of more
than twice that number with the utmost ease
in 1882.

Hearing that the Mamelukes had entrenched
themselves in front of the village of Embabeh,
and had placed forty guns in position, Bonaparte
decided on a flank movement, and, at two o'clock
in the afternoon, advanced in a wide crescent,
each division marching in hollow square. Murad
Bey, the Egyptian leader, seeing the manœuvre,
ordered Ayoub Bey, one of his officers, to charge
General Desaix' division which was swooping round
to the west to attack his left flank. Ayoub and
his reckless cavalry headed straight for the enemy,
and burst their way into the open square, but were
there entrapped and had to fight their way out.
The French central division, under Dugua, meanwhile delivered a frontal attack and captured the
Egyptian trenches at the point of the bayonet.
At the same time the eastern division, commanded
by Bon and Vial, got round between the enemy's
right flank and the river, cutting them off from
escape as they fell back from the central attack.
The fight, or rather massacre, was over in less
than an hour. Murad Bey, badly wounded, fled
to his palace at Gizeh and thence to Upper Egypt,
leaving many thousands dead upon the field or
drowned in the Nile.

The French soldiers, of whom less than thirty
had been killed, at once turned the battlefield into

a vast market. Rich armour, gold-inlaid weapons, gold and silver coins and ornaments, embroidered silks, and much else of value, fell into their hands, and were bought, sold, or exchanged amongst themselves during the remainder of the afternoon. The dead were stripped of their valuables, and even the bodies of those who had been drowned in the river were fished for and similarly treated. The men were in the best of spirits, believing that their troubles were now at an end, and, in the words of Bonaparte, they were at last reconciled to Egypt.

The Mamelukes, meanwhile, begged M. Bandeuf, the leader of the French colony in Cairo, whose safety they had magnanimously secured throughout this dangerous period, to treat with Bonaparte, since they had heard that he only wanted a free passage through to India; but ere these negotiations were commenced Bonaparte was bringing his army across the river to the city. A dreadful panic ensued, and Cairo became for a time a frenzied inferno. The houses of the Beys were plundered by the retreating mob, and precisely those scenes occurred which were repeated during the Egyptian retreat from Alexandria in 1882 after the bombardment. Another French proclamation was issued to the townspeople as the invaders entered the city. It stated that they had come to destroy the Mamelukes, and incidentally to protect the religion of the Prophet whom the French loved.   Bonaparte was soon hailed by the bewildered Egyptians as "The Great Sultan," and within three days he had quieted the city and had begun to organise a government.

But while Bonaparte, delighted with his easy victory, was indulging in dreams of vast conquest, the less imaginative Nelson was still scouring the seas in search of the French fleet, and was once again approaching the Egyptian coast.   It was on August 1 that a middy at the masthead of the *Zealous* caught sight of the French ships lying in Aboukir Bay, and the signal was received by the whole fleet with the utmost joy.   Night was drawing on when the ships came to close quarters, and it was the general opinion on the French side that the inevitable battle would be postponed till the morning.   But Nelson and his men had been living at a high pitch of expectancy for the last few weeks, and in spite of the fact that the French greatly outnumbered them (20 ships and 11,200 sailors being opposed to their 12 vessels and 7400 men), they could brook no delay.   They were sick of this dread of an invasion of England which had hung over them like a dark cloud for so long, and here in these remote waters they felt that they were about to fight for their English homes.   Every man on board was absolutely determined to do his best to destroy Bonaparte's fleet, and the enthusiasm is said to have been most inspiring.   There was the keenest rivalry on the part of Nelson's ships to be first into the bay. The *Goliath* and the *Zealous* had a most exciting race for lead, and the profane language of the officers and men of the latter vessel when they proved to be the loser is said to have been most startling.

The French men-o'-war were anchored in two lines, but Admiral Brueys had made what proved to be the mistake of allowing between each ship sea-room for her to swing round without colliding with her neighbour. By the most daring and skilful manœuvres some of the British ships managed to slip in between the French vessels and the shore and to attack them on both sides. One of Nelson's finest vessels, the *Culloden,* grounded and took no part in the fight. All night long the battle raged, and at one time the sailors upon a certain British man-o'-war were so tired that they were allowed to sleep for twenty minutes beside their guns. The French admiral was cut nearly in two by a shot, dying a few minutes later upon the quarter-deck, saying with his last breath that that was the right place for an Admiral of France to die. Nelson's forehead was grazed by a bullet, and the flap of severed skin falling over his one eye half blinded him. He was dazed by the blow, and was carried below, but soon recovered sufficiently to direct the battle. *L'Orient*, the French flagship, blew up in the thick of the fight, and one by one the other ships were captured or put out of action.

The British victory was complete, and at one blow the French schemes for the conquest of Asia were shattered.

All ignorant of the disaster, Bonaparte remained in Cairo until August 7, when he hurried into the Eastern Delta to attack Ibrahim Bey, who had gathered a small army together and had done some damage to the French garrisons in that part of the country. The Mamelukes, however, were easily defeated at Salhieh on August 10, and Ibrahim Bey was chased out of Egypt. On his march back to Cairo, Bonaparte received news of the disaster at Aboukir. *"Eh bien,"* he said, with no change in the expression of his face, " it will be necessary to remain in these countries, or to make a grand exit like the Ancients." From one point of view the destruction of the fleet fell in with his schemes, for it cut him off from France, and made the advance into the Orient appear far less startling. He was at this time firmly convinced that his destiny lay in the East, and his one desire was to lead his invincible army to India, holding them loyal to him by rich presents of loot, and ultimately to make himself Emperor of the Orient. He believed that in France there was no future for him greater than that of a successful general ; but in the East he felt that his career was without limit. He perceived at once, therefore, that the loss of his ships expatriated himself and his soldiers, and converted

them into a disciplined band of adventurers de-
tached from all authority save his own. Now was
his chance. Now was the opportunity for him to
realise his dreams of self-aggrandisement.

With these thoughts in his mind he began
openly to profess that he was a Mohammedan, for
he felt that since it was evidently his destiny to
conquer Asia and to become the Great Sultan of
the East, it was necessary for him to hold a faith
that would be acceptable to a large portion of
the realms over which he intended to rule. He
headed his proclamations with the words, " In
the name of Allah, the Merciful and Indulgent.
There is no God but God. He has no son, and
reigns without a partner." It was his idea ultimately to create a new religion himself, and to
be the Prophet of an up-to-date Islamism. " I
pictured myself," he said afterwards to Madame
de Rémusat, " on the road to Asia, mounted on
an elephant, with a turban on my head, and in
my hand a new Koran, which I should compose
according to my own ideas." He did his best to
persuade his soldiers to adopt the faith of Islâm,
and was much annoyed at their refusal to do so.
General Menou and several other officers, however, embraced Mohammedanism with sincerity;
and Napoleon is said to have gone so far as to
adopt native dress on certain occasions and to
have performed the rites of Mohammedan prayer.
On August 26 the great caravan which goes each

year to Mecca with the holy carpet set out from Cairo, and Bonaparte took the opportunity of writing to the Sheríf of Mecca assuring him of his goodwill towards Islam. "We are friends of the Musulmans," he wrote, "and of the religion of the Prophet; we desire to do everything that may be favourable to the Religion." At about the same time he sent a letter to Ahmed Pasha Djezzar, the Governor of Acre on the Syrian coast, with a view to arriving at a friendly agreement with this important neighbour, whose state acted something in the manner of a buffer between Egypt and Turkey. "You must know," he wrote, "that my first care on entering Malta was to set at liberty 2000 Turks, who for many years have languished in slavery. On arriving in Egypt I have reassured the people and protected the Muftis, imams, and mosques. The Mecca pilgrims have never been treated with more care and friendliness than I have shown to them, and the festival of the Prophet has been celebrated with more splendour than ever before. . . . The Moslems have no greater friends than the French."

Djezzar, however, had already seen the ships of England patrolling his coast, sailing silently to and fro, day after day, like mighty sentinels; and to Bonaparte he answered never a word.

Meanwhile the French had their hands full in Egypt. Revolts had to be suppressed in the

Delta, and an expedition had to be despatched to Upper Egypt to effect the conquest of that country. In Cairo the Government had to be reorganised, and Bonaparte spent some time in planning and founding a French Institute for the study of the Arts and Sciences. His labours here, however, were rudely disturbed on October 21 by a sudden revolt of the townspeople, who killed General Dupuy, Commandant of the City, and several soldiers; and for two days things were very uncomfortable for the invaders. Bonaparte was furious, and as soon as quiet was restored he issued thoroughly Oriental instructions for the decapitation of large numbers of Arabs. By his orders their heads were placed in sacks which were conveyed to the Esbekieh and there opened in the presence of the crowd. All persons who had escaped from jail and had taken up arms were decapitated, and their headless bodies, by his special orders, were thrown into the Nile. A report was spread that the Prophet Mohammed had appeared to Bonaparte and had promised him his help and assistance; and it was now generally believed that the French were under some sort of divine protection. On December 21, two months after the revolt, Bonaparte was able to issue yet another of his amazing proclamations, this time addressed to the people of Cairo, forgiving them for their naughtiness and granting once more to them certain concessions which he had curtailed.

"Sherîfs, ulemas, preachers in the mosques," he wrote, "make it known to the people that those who light-heartedly declare themselves my enemies shall have no refuge either in this world or the next. Is there a man so blind as not to see that Destiny itself directs all my operations? . . . Make it known to the people that since the world began, it was written that after having destroyed the enemies of Islam and beaten down the Cross, I should go to the end of the Orient to carry out the task which has been imposed upon me. Make the people see that in the sacred book of the Koran, in more than twenty passages, that which has now come to pass has been predicted, and that which shall come to pass is likewise explained. . . . In making their prayers to heaven against us, they solicit their own condemnation: let the true believers pray for the success of our arms. I might demand of each one of you an account of the most secret thoughts of your hearts: for I know everything, even that which you have told to no one. But a day will come when it will become evident to all the world that I am led by orders from on high, and that all human efforts against me are futile. Happy are those who in good faith are the first to place themselves on my side."

Bonaparte was here attributing to himself divine powers, and who shall say that he did so solely to impress a foolish people? Who shall deny that he now had the intention of posing to all men as a prophet of a new era? And yet there can be no doubt that to him this attitude was assumed for purely political motives. At this stage in his career he sank to the lowest level to which at any time his ambitions brought him; for he now boasted of his contempt for our Lord, and, with his tongue in his cheek, professed his devotion to the Prophet Mohammed. To further his personal ambitions he insulted Christianity and attempted to make a fool of Islam. He made the colossal mistake of supposing that to rule the Orient he must pose as an Oriental. He was blind to the fact that the one thing for which the Orient was seeking was an upright ruler. Could he have beheld that future sequence of honest men who obtained the devotion of Hindoo and Egyptian, not by the renunciation of the Cross, but by the straightforwardness of their characters, he would have been filled with astonishment. Could he have seen the God-fearing King of England seated upon that throne of India to obtain which he, the mighty Bonaparte, had schemed and lied and blasphemed in vain; could he have beheld the peoples of India enthusiastically receiving their English Emperor, who stands as the symbol of that quality of quiet integrity which Bonaparte discarded as worthless, he might indeed have hidden his face for very shame.

The Turks, probably encouraged by the English,

declared war against the French early in January
1799, and mobilised their troops at Rhodes and
in Syria.   Bonaparte, having decided to take the
offensive, at once began to organise an expedition
into Syria, and early in February he set out with
nearly his whole army to cross the desert to
Gaza.   He arrived at that town on February 25,
and on March 7 Jaffa was taken by assault—all
the prisoners, between 4000 and 5000, being
taken out upon the beach and there butchered
in cold blood by the express orders of the Corsican "Sultan," who at a later date attempted to
justify his conduct on the plea of expediency.   On
March 19 the army arrived in sight of the seaport
of Acre, and it must have been with the utmost
annoyance that Bonaparte discerned upon its walls
the heavy guns which very imprudently he had
sent by sea to be delivered to him at this spot,
but which had been captured by the ubiquitous
English and landed at Acre.   He learnt also to
his chagrin that the town had been put into a
state of defence by a French Royalist engineer
named Phelippeaux and by Sir Sidney Smith,
the reckless English naval officer who, five years
previously, had set fire to the arsenal of Toulon.
These two men were now in command of the small
Turkish garrison of Acre, and were calmly defying
the whole French army.

Acre was to some extent to be regarded as the
key to Syria, for although it was a town of small

size, it could not be left unsubdued in the rear of an advancing army. "In that miserable fort," said Napoleon at a later date, "lay the fate of the East." "When I have captured it," he told his generals, "I shall march on Damascus and Aleppo. I shall arm the tribes. I shall reach Constantinople. I shall turn the Turkish Empire upside down." And more than this : when Acre fell Bonaparte would begin in earnest his reign as Sultan of the Orient and Prophet of the new Islam. But Acre did not fall. The grimy faces of those few British bluejackets smiled at him from the rotten walls, day after day defying him and enraging him with their light-hearted taunts. With the aid of the men-o'-war in the harbour Sir Sidney Smith kept up an astonishing defence, again and again repulsing the French troops. The sailors fought with a will, thoroughly enjoying their tussle with the great "Boney," patting the Turks on the back with friendly energy, as a certain writer states, and leading them out in one daring sally after another. The little garrison of less than 3000 men all told wrought havoc amongst Bonaparte's mighty army ; and by the time that the siege had lasted a month the French irritation had caused the fighting to be daily of the most desperate character. The enemy often succeeded in obtaining a temporary footing at the very gates of the town, and here they would entrench themselves by erecting walls of sandbags, amongst which the still warm bodies of their fallen comrades were built in.   By the first week in May nearly forty assaults had been made on the town, and Sir Sidney Smith had led over twenty sorties. In some of these the midshipmen rendered valuable service by running forward with an armful of grenades and throwing them like so many snowballs at the exasperated French veterans.   The only disaster on the English side was caused by the over-zeal of a middy who was amusing himself by collecting unexploded French shells, which were to be used against their original owners, and who blew himself and his ship to smithereens in the process.

On May 8 a Turkish fleet approached the port with reinforcements from Rhodes, and Bonaparte therefore made a desperate attack upon the town. The fighting was hand-to-hand, and at one time the very spearheads of the opposing standards were locked.   The enemy, however, was driven back with dreadful slaughter.   The fighting lasted all day, and towards evening a last assault was delivered by General Kléber's famous grenadiers. Bonaparte, standing upon a gun in the nearest French battery, watched the fight with white, expressionless face ; and although members of his staff were killed around him, he was far too desperate and far too angry to move to a safer position.   He watched the gigantic Kléber leading his men up to the breach, he watched the appalling

struggle under the blackened, ruined walls, and
finally he saw his invincible grenadiers pushed
down the hill once more, pursued by Sir Sidney
Smith and his sailors, while Kléber, black with
powder and grime, and voiceless with rage, tried
in vain to rally them.

On May 20, sixty days after the beginning of
the siege, Bonaparte was in full retreat back to
Egypt, leaving behind him 4000 dead Frenchmen,
amongst whom were eight generals. The temper
of his army was sullen, and he himself was in the
lowest depths of depression. His dreams of an
Oriental empire were shattered, and bitterly he
spoke of "that young fool," Sidney Smith, as the
man who had "spoiled his destiny."

Previous to invading Syria, Bonaparte had sent
a letter to Tippoo Sahib at Mysore, saying that he
was coming to relieve him from the iron yoke of
the English, but this letter had fallen into the
hands of these very English, who seemed destined
to thwart him at every point ; and it had served
to spur them on to action in India, with the result
that on May 4 Seringapatam was stormed and
Tippoo Sahib slain. And thus on all sides the
hopes of attacking England in India were wrecked.

The march back to Egypt was a terrible affair.
Plague attacked the army, and many faithful
soldiers had to be left to die upon the roads. At
Jaffa, Bonaparte was so averse to leaving his
wounded—some 600 in number—to the mercy of

the Arabs, that he discussed with the doctors the desirability of poisoning them all; and there is considerable reason to suppose that he actually issued orders to this effect, and that some 580 were poisoned. Seven who survived were rescued by Sir Sidney Smith two days after the French had departed. Reaching Egypt, Bonaparte entered Cairo with flags flying, pretending that he had returned as a conqueror to his headquarters; but a month later, on July 14, an enormous Turkish army landed at Aboukir in pursuit of him. Bonaparte attacked them on the 25th, and although they were assisted by a few English ships, he thoroughly defeated them, driving them into the sea, where thousands who had escaped fire and sword were miserably drowned. The victory meant a great deal to Bonaparte, for it covered in its glory the miserable failure of his Syrian campaign. He had now digested the fact that his hopes of conquering the Orient were vain, and that it was not his destiny any longer to become a Prophet in the East; and his one idea was to slip back to France as quickly as possible. If this battle had not been fought he would have been obliged to return as a defeated commander; but now he could sail for France, bringing with him the news of the destruction of the Turkish army. Sir Sidney Smith, who was cruising off the coast, sent him after the battle a bundle of French newspapers, in which the situation in France was painted in very gloomy colours. Bonaparte sat up all night reading the news, and by morning he had definitely decided to leave at once. Two frigates were prepared with the utmost secrecy, and on the night of August 22 he set sail. He and his staff had ridden down to the vessel on horseback, for the mooring-place lay off a desolate stretch of beach several miles from his camp; and when the abandoned horses galloped riderless back to the lines at dead of night, the secret was out. The army was aghast, and imprecations were heaped upon the flying commander-in-chief, who was considered to have forsaken his faithful soldiers when most they needed him. General Kléber was left in command, but though he was popular with the soldiers he did not inspire confidence on every occasion, and the situation of the army was thus by no means pleasant.

Bonaparte slunk along the African coast, and by the exercise of the utmost care the vessels managed to elude the English ships which had gone back to Cyprus for supplies, never thinking that Bonaparte would desert in this manner. Early in October, after playing the part of a hunted hare for six weeks, he landed in France once more, and was soon thrilling the members of the Directoire with the tales of his real and imaginary victories.

The story need not here be told in detail of how the French army, abandoned in Egypt, was harried by Turks, Mamelukes, and Egyptians, how General Kléber was assassinated, and how at last they had to face a British expeditionary force which was landed near Alexandria in March 1801.   It is only necessary to state that not long after the desperate battle named after that city, the whole army of 24,000 French troops with 312 guns surrendered to the 15,000 English troops which had been sent for their chastisement.

When Bonaparte heard the news of the capitulation of his army, his anguish is said to have been really genuine.   "We have lost Egypt!" he cried. "My projects and my dreams have alike been destroyed by England."

Thus ended the French campaign in the Orient, and thus "the great adventure," as it is so often called, came to a conclusion.   Historians are much inclined to forget the details of this amazing phase in the life of Bonaparte, and to gloss it over by laying stress on its inherent romance.   The hero-worshipper does not enjoy a description of the wonderful Corsican in his *rôle* as an Eastern potentate, attributing divine powers to himself, rejecting Christianity, and incidentally cutting off people's heads.   Yet it must always be remembered that it was England who hammered sense into Napoleon, and her guns that shattered his fantastic dreams of Oriental omnipotence.   It was England who sent the would-be prophet back to Europe to begin his adventures anew; and when, instead of Sultan in the East, he had become Emperor in the West, it was England who terminated his second phase as she had his first.   He left his marks, however, on Europe; but Egypt already in 1802 is said to have shown practically no sign of his treatment. His Oriental campaign was a failure through and through, and the impression made upon the quiet Egyptians by "the Great Sultan" was absolutely nil.

In the year 1907 a detachment of English troops was route-marching in the Delta, and, being somewhat short of provisions, halted near a small village in order to purchase a few chickens and pigeons. The *Omdeh*, or headman, hearing the news and thinking that the supplies were to be commandeered without payment, hurriedly sought amongst his papers until he had found a certain document preserved with care in a sealed envelope. With this in hand he made his way to the officer in command, and told him that the village was exempt from supplying food to the troops, this document being proof of his statement. The officer opened the envelope and found therein an order signed by one of Bonaparte's generals, stating that in return for services rendered to the French army the village was to be free from interference in future.

The Englishman smiled, and laid the document aside.

"This was made out by the French over a hundred years ago," he said to the *Omdeh*. "It is no longer valid."

The Egyptian shrugged his shoulders. "French or English," he replied, "now or then: it is all the same to us. *We* are the same people."

CHAPTER II.

MOHAMMED ALI.

THE story of the life and activities of Mohammed Ali, the founder of the Khedivial dynasty of Egypt, so clearly reveals the foundations upon which the Turco-Egyptian arrangements of later years have been based, that it should be studied with care by all those who would understand the affairs of the Near East. Mohammed Ali was the first to bring Egypt into the forefront of international politics, and at one time he was the cause of such grave misunderstandings between England, Prussia, Russia, Austria, and France that a European war seemed inevitable. His rugged personality dominated the Near Eastern situation in the 'thirties and early 'forties; and for some years it was generally believed that he would overthrow the Sultan of Turkey and would establish himself upon the Ottoman throne. With extraordinary energy, courage, and ruthlessness he fought his way to power, and earned for himself the splendid nickname of "The Lion of the Levant"; and, had it not been for the intervention of England and Russia, he would have restored to Egypt a dominion as extensive as any ever governed by the proudest of the Pharaohs. Instead of this, however, he was forced to content himself with ruling Egypt as a vassal of the Sultan; and he died a disappointed man, leaving to posterity the recurrent Egyptian question and the anomalous Egypto-Turkish relationship which has been such a thorough nuisance to the Great Powers ever since.

Mohammed Ali was by nationality an Albanian, being a native of the small seaport town of Cavalla, near the frontier of Thrace and Macedonia, where his father was both a fisherman and a small land-owner, and held also the position of captain of the local watchmen of the roads. He was born in 1769, the same year in which Napoleon Bonaparte and the Duke of Wellington first saw the light. While yet a child he was left an almost penniless orphan, and was taken into the household of the Chief Magistrate of the town, to whom he was related. Here he was allowed to grow up amongst the serving-men, hangers-on, dogs, cats, cattle, and poor relations, who are always to be found in the back premises of the house of an Eastern notable; and it is said that he soon found favour in this motley throng by his good-humour and his courage in settling the constant brawls and fights which occurred alike amongst the company and the animals. It was not to be expected that in

such surroundings he would receive much education. He never learnt to read or write with any
fluency, and throughout his life he regarded books
as unnecessary lumber. "The only books I ever
read," he was wont to remark in after years, "are
men's faces, and I seldom read them amiss."

While still a youth he began to earn a little
money by trading in tobacco, a business much
practised in Cavalla; and during the course of
his small operations he formed a close friendship
with a wandering Frenchman, named Leon, who
picked up a precarious livelihood as a general
merchant in this part of the world. From Monsieur Leon he received the main portion of those
scraps of general knowledge which composed his
entire education; and from him he first learnt
of that great European world in which he was
destined to play so leading a part. The Frenchman was considerably older than himself, and the
young Albanian soon came to look up to him as
a kind of hero and monitor. Though entirely
obscure, this roving merchant must have been a
man of character, for Mohammed Ali in after
years neither forgot him nor ceased to be influenced by those friendly sentiments towards France
which Monsieur Leon had instilled into him at
Cavalla; and it may be said that when, in 1840,
France nearly took up arms against the whole of
Europe in defence of the great position which
Mohammed Ali had won for himself, she was

merely carrying to its romantic conclusion the attitude which, years previously, Monsieur Leon had adopted towards the uneducated Albanian boy. It is pleasant to find that when Mohammed Ali had become virtual Sovereign of Egypt he did not rest until he had discovered the whereabouts of his old friend, to whom he sent an invitation to come to Egypt, where, he said, a fortune awaited him. Monsieur Leon, who had fallen on evil days, hastened to accept the invitation; but poverty and hardship had undermined his health, and he died on the day of his departure. Mohammed Ali, on hearing the news, was much affected, and promptly sent a present of £400 to the merchant's sister as a memento of his youthful days at Cavalla.

At an early age the young man showed his courage and resourcefulness. The inhabitants of a village not far from Cavalla refused to pay a tax which had to be collected by the Chief Magistrate, and Mohammed Ali volunteered to go and get the money by force. With three or four men he rode over to the rebellious village, and, entering the mosque at the time of prayer, quietly performed his devotions there, until suddenly he found an opportunity to pinion the four principal inhabitants as they knelt unsuspectingly in prayer. He then announced to the astonished congregation that if there was the slightest show of hostility on their part, his prisoners would instantly be knifed; and by this hazardous device he was able to march the four men to Cavalla, where they were forced to produce the tax-money, and much more besides, ere they were suffered to return to their homes. As a reward for his services Mohammed Ali was made an officer in the town-guard; but nevertheless he continued to carry on his trade in tobacco, by which means he had been able to amass a small amount of money. It will be best, perhaps, to note without comment that the commander of the guard died suddenly shortly afterwards, whereupon Mohammed Ali stepped into his shoes and married his beautiful widow. His feet were now upon the first rung of the ladder, and Fortune smiled upon him. It is said that shortly before he was born a fortune-teller had informed his mother that her child would become a ruler of men; and this prophecy now had some influence upon him, whetting his ambitions and urging him to further activities. Already his appearance indicated to those who knew him that much was to be expected of him. He was short, thick-set, and extremely active. He had a very fine head and forehead, shaggy eyebrows, and deep-set grey eyes, in which, so it is said, a strange wild fire sometimes gleamed. He had a straight nose, a large but not coarse mouth, and a heavy beard and moustache. When angry, his countenance was very terrible; but when, as was more often the case, he was in high

and dashing humour, his eyes and mouth assumed
an expression of droll, rather malicious fun. His
mind, as well as his body, was restless and highly
strung; and there seems to have been some distinct strain of eccentricity in his blood.

In 1798, when the young man was twenty-nine
years of age, the Sultan decided to send an army
to Egypt to oust the French from that province
of his empire, where, under the command of Bonaparte, they had established themselves, ostensibly
with the purpose of protecting foreigners against
the outrages of the Mameluke chieftains who held
authority in Cairo and Alexandria. A troop of
three hundred men was beaten up in the district
of Cavalla for service in the war, the command
being given to the Chief Magistrate's son; and
Mohammed Ali managed to persuade his relative
to appoint him as his lieutenant. This force joined
the main Turkish army a few months later, and
on July 14, 1799, was landed at Aboukir, on the
Egyptian coast. Here, by a process of events
which can but be guessed at, it was arranged that
the Chief Magistrate's son should return home to
Cavalla; and as soon as he had departed Mohammed Ali promoted himself to the vacant command.
A few days later, on July 25, Bonaparte utterly
routed the Turkish army, driving it into the sea;
and Mohammed Ali was saved from drowning by
the gig of the British Admiral, Sir Sidney Smith,
who had anchored in Aboukir Bay in order to give

a helping hand to the Turks. Thereafter he disappears from the pages of history for a couple of years ; and the student's attention is turned to the confused bedlam in Egypt, out of which the Albanian adventurer is presently to emerge, sword in hand.

Bonaparte's invasion had been directed against the Mamelukes, the more or less independent rulers of this province of the Turkish empire ; but England, on the other hand, being at war with France, had naturally taken the side of these picturesque ruffians. The Turks and the English had fought side by side against the French ; but, in spite of this, the Porte was not friendly to the Mamelukes, who were regarded as insubordinate vassals. When Bonaparte deserted Egypt in August 1799, the French troops left behind fell upon troubled days. An Ottoman army (in which Mohammed Ali may have been serving) captured the frontier fortress of El Arish and marched on Cairo, but was defeated by General Kléber at Matarieh, outside the city. An insurrection in Cairo ensued, and large numbers of French and other Christians were massacred; but finally Kléber regained possession of his headquarters after a sanguinary battle on April 14, 1800. He was assassinated, however, two months later, and was succeeded in the command by General Menon, ∨ an eccentric personage, who, after having distinguished himself by causing Kléber's murderer to be put to a lingering death by torture (although he had been promised a free pardon), became a Mohammedan and deprived the Egyptian Christians of many of their privileges. His inglorious and capricious rule was brought to a close by the arrival of a British army in March 1801, which defeated the French, and caused them to capitulate in the following June. The British forces were assisted by the Turks, amongst whom Mohammed Ali once more appears, now as the officer commanding a force of Albanian cavalry. On May 9 he headed a bold charge of his horsemen at the battle of Rahmanieh, and also showed great ingenuity and pluck in carrying out a night attack upon a fort held by the French. So conspicuous was his bravery on these occasions that Khosrov Pasha, the nominal Turkish Governor of Egypt, promoted him to the command of an entire Albanian contingent, consisting of some 4000 men; and in this capacity he was attached to the British army, being particularly noticed and commended by the Commander-in-Chief

As soon as the French army had been forced to leave the country in September 1801, the British officers began to find that their association with the Turks was by no means an unqualified success. The interests of the two nations had been identical in driving Bonaparte out of Egypt, but that being accomplished, the divergence of their points of view became daily more apparent.

The Turks very naturally wished to regain control in their province, which meant that they desired to crush the independent spirit of the Mameluke chieftains whose authority was recognised by the Egyptians. These Mamelukes were mostly of Circassian origin, and were the descendants of the slaves who had been settled in the country during the Middle Ages. In some ways they were to the Egyptians what the Normans had been to the English a century or two after the Conquest; and though they acknowledged in a general way the suzerainty of the Sultan, they ruled the various districts of the Nile Valley without any appreciable interference on the part of their over-lord. They were a brave, cruel, dashing, barbaric, and picturesque company, famous for their horse-manship and for the reckless extravagance of their apparel and entourage. They clothed them-selves in splendid silks, stuck all over with gold ornaments and bejewelled daggers and pistols. Their horses were selected from the purest blood of Syria; their women slaves were purchased from amongst the most beautiful Georgian and Circas-sian stock to be found in the markets of Con-stantinople and Smyrna; and their trains of musicians, dancers, serving - men, and warriors were renowned alike for their splendour and their licentiousness. In their isolation from intimate comment, they made a very romantic appeal to the British mind, and the French attack upon them caused them to be regarded as meriting all assistance, which, in actual fact, was an absurdly generous estimate of their worth.

The British Government now made representations to the Porte, urging a tolerant treatment of the Mamelukes; but in spite of this the Turkish admiral, having invited a number of these chieftains to a *fête* upon his flagship, treacherously fired upon them while they were coming to him in open boats, and killed or captured them all. General Hely Hutchinson, the British commander, was furious at this outrage, which had taken place almost under his eyes; and as a result of his protest the prisoners were handed over to his care. At the same time, the Turkish general in Cairo arrested as many of the remaining chieftains as he could lay hands on; but the British forced him to give them up. Not long after this Khosrov Pasha, with 7000 Turks, attacked a Mameluke force of 800 men commanded by two famous chieftains, Osman el Bardisi and Mohammed el Alfi; but his large force was utterly routed, and the Ottoman hold on Egypt was thereby greatly endangered.

Mohammed Ali now began to realise that he was fighting upon the losing side, for the Mamelukes had every reason to be confident both in their own strength and in the support of the British; and he therefore showed an inclination to abandon the Turkish cause. In March 1803, however, the British army evacuated the country, taking with them to England the Mameluke chieftain El Alfi, who was to consult the Home Government as to the best method of establishing an independent Egypt under Mameluke rule. Mohammed Ali, therefore, was left to decide his attitude upon its own merits; and it was not long before he showed in which direction he believed his best interests to lie. About six weeks after the departure of the British army, the entire Albanian force in Egypt, commanded by Tahir Pasha, to whom Mohammed Ali was lieutenant, came to blows with the Turkish Governor, Khosrov Pasha, in regard to their pay. They seized the Citadel at Cairo, and from this eminence bombarded the Governor in his palace in the Esbekieh, a low-lying district at that time near the western outskirts of the city. Khosrov managed to escape by river to Damietta; and Tahir was proclaimed Governor in his stead. Less than a month later he, in his turn, found himself unable to pay his troops; and by one of those remarkable manœuvres, of which we have already noticed two instances, Mohammed Ali managed to obtain the chief command, Tahir meeting his death in the process.

Now having all the Albanians at his back, he attacked the remainder of the Turkish army, and soon afterwards made an alliance with the Mamelukes under El Bardisi. The Porte then

appointed a new Governor of Egypt, a certain
Ahmed Pasha; but Mohammed Ali of course
refused to recognise him. No sooner had the
unfortunate Turk arrived at his official residence
in the middle of Cairo, than the Albanians from
the Citadel and the Mamelukes from the west
bank of the Nile attacked him and made him
prisoner. They then marched on Damietta, and
received the surrender also of the fugitive Khosrov
Pasha. Mohammed Ali, on his return to Cairo,
made El Bardisi mayor of the city, or Shêkh-el-
Beled, and approved the appointment of a nominal
Turkish Governor whose authority was negligible.
The appointment of this representative of the
Porte was regarded by Mohammed Ali simply
as a means of holding the post open for himself, as soon as he should have opportunity to
bring his authority before the notice of the
Porte; for he now aimed at nothing less than
the complete control of Egypt. He had no intention of remaining in alliance with the Mamelukes
when once his own position was secure; and he
felt that his policy should be directed towards a
rapprochement with Turkey.

In the spring an open rupture occurred between
him and the Mameluke chieftains, owing, as usual,
to a question of the payment of the troops; and
on March 12, 1804, Mohammed Ali attacked El
Bardisi in his palace and drove him out of
Cairo. The Cairenes and Albanians then invited

Khurshîd Pasha, the Turkish Governor of Alexandria, to assume the governorship of their city ; but this personage, wishing to be secure against the domination of Mohammed Ali's troops, introduced a regiment of Moors into the city, stationing them in the Citadel, and thereby incurred the Albanian's furious displeasure. About a year later, therefore, Mohammed Ali persuaded the Cairenes to depose Khurshîd and to nominate himself as Governor of Cairo. Khurshîd very naturally refused to recognise any nomination not confirmed by the Sultan, and promptly turned the guns of the Citadel upon Mohammed Ali's forces in the town below. The energetic Albanian replied by dragging his cannon up to the summit of the Mokattam hills, which dominated the Citadel, and meanwhile he sent an embassy post-haste to Constantinople asking for the official deposition of his enemy. The document arrived in Cairo on July 9, 1805, and a Turkish force was sent to restore order. Khurshîd then surrendered, and Mohammed Ali assumed the governorship, having attained to this exalted position at the early age of thirty-six.

No sooner was he secured in his new office than he set himself to destroy the power of the Mamelukes. In August 1805 his agents led a large number of them into a prepared ambush, where they were all shot down or taken prisoners and executed. The news of this treachery was

conveyed to England ; and since the French were
still as hostile to the Mamelukes as they had been
during Bonaparte's invasion, the English all the
more heartily espoused their cause. Mohammed
Ali, calling to mind the wonderful tales of France
told to him by Monsieur Leon at Cavalla, now
began seriously to enter into that close friendship
with the French people which lasted, with some
lapses, throughout his life ; but as he was at
this time once more the dutiful servant of the
Sultan, it followed that France now supported
Turkey, while England, in defence of the Mamelukes, was estranged from the Porte.

Two years later, in 1807, a British force landed
in Egypt with the object of taking possession of
the country, and thereby frustrating any possible
alliance between Mohammed Ali and the French,
which might have been dangerous to us. The
young Albanian soldier, however, was not thus
to be crushed. He quickly out-manœuvred our
forces, who were under the command of Generals
Wauchope and Meade, utterly defeated them at
Rosetta, and took most of them prisoners. A few
days later he rode in triumph through Cairo
between avenues of British heads, which were
stuck upon stakes at regular intervals along either
side of the main streets, while at certain points
groups of British soldiers were exhibited in chains
to be reviled and spat upon by all the scum of
the city.

Mohammed Ali at once sent news of his triumph to France, at the same time inviting a number of French soldiers, sailors, and engineers to come to Egypt to help him to organise his forces. The invitation was readily accepted, and by the beginning of 1809 a formidable fleet had been built or purchased, while sailors and soldiers had been drilled according to European methods. His activities, however, were much hampered by the continuous hostility of the Mamelukes; and at length he obtained definite evidence that attempts were to be made upon his life. He therefore decided to rid himself once and for all of this menace, and in the early spring of 1811 he laid a trap for his enemies as audacious as it was pitiless. He sent an invitation to every available Mameluke notable to attend at a reception in the Citadel on March 1, in order to bid farewell to the officers of an expedition which was about to set out for Arabia with the object of bringing the holy cities under Egyptian protection. The invitations were readily accepted, and on the fatal day 460 Mamelukes rode in state into the Citadel, clad in their richest robes, wearing their finest jewels, and riding their superb horses. Mohammed Ali received them graciously, serving them with coffee, sweetmeats, and pipes; and when the ceremonies of the day were over he arranged that they should be formed up into a martial procession, the position of each chieftain being assigned with punctilious correctness according to his rank.

The glittering cavalcade then rode down the hill towards the gate of El Azab, the road here passing through a cutting in the rock; above which the sheer walls of houses towered up on either side; but on their arrival at the gateway the doors were closed in their face, and immediately a fusilade was directed upon them from the windows of the houses. A horrible scene ensued. The procession was instantly converted into a confused mass of plunging horses and staggering men, and these were presently transformed into silent heaps of sprawling slain, from which the streams of blood trickled down the hill and under the barred doors of the gateway. Two or three of the chieftains, wounded and gasping, managed to regain the higher ground, but here they were cut down with the cold steel. A prince of the highest rank, Suliman el Baoub, staggered, bleeding, into the *harîm* of Mohammed Ali's house, and claimed the right of sanctuary which, according to ancient custom, the women's quarters afforded; but the Albanian had no respect for tradition, and the head of the fugitive was struck from his body on the spot. Only one man escaped from the massacre, a certain chieftain named Emin, who galloped up the hill to a point at which the road overlooked the precipitous wall of the Citadel and here leapt into space, landing upon the rocks some thirty feet below, his fall being broken by his horse, which no doubt was killed under him.

During the massacre Mohammed Ali is said to have shown the utmost emotion. He became very pale, and moved restlessly to and fro, muttering to himself.   When no more of his recent guests remained to be murdered, his Genoese physician, Mendrici, came to convey the news to him, and to congratulate him upon what he was pleased to describe as a most happy affair; but Mohammed Ali, grey with anxiety, uttered no word except a peremptory demand for a cup of cold water. Many years afterwards he declared that his sleep at nights was made horrible by the faces of the men whom he had done to death on this occasion and on others; but it is a question whether his conscience need have troubled him unduly, for it has been truly said that the prosperity of Egypt was rooted in the shambles of the Citadel. Mohammed Ali, in after years, proved himself to be Egypt's true benefactor, and though we are appalled at the savage barbarity with which he rid the country of this crowd of undisciplined ruffians, we must remember that he thereby released the Egyptians from a tyranny which nobody in the world, except the very misinformed British Government, ever attempted to condone.

Not satisfied with the massacre at the Citadel,

Mohammed Ali issued orders that the remaining Mamelukes were to be exterminated throughout Egypt. In Cairo the slaughter continued for two days, at the end of which a general amnesty was proclaimed in behalf of the few terrified survivors; but in the provinces the hunt dragged on for many years, the Mameluke bands being gradually driven far into the Sudan.

Mohammed Ali was now free to turn his full attention to the welfare of Egypt and to the enlarging of its territories; and in all directions he instituted reforms and improvements. He possessed an absolute genius for creating and maintaining order; and although entirely un-scrupulous in regard to the methods employed to attain his ends, he soon showed that he acted at all times in the best interests of Egypt. During his reign crimes of violence were almost unknown throughout the land; and never has the country been safer for travellers. There can be no question that his ideals were, in a rough sort of way, noble, and his actions inspired by a high ambition for justice, law, and order; but he knew little of probity, considerateness, or the tenets of fair-play. The number of bad characters whom he hanged without pretence of trial was enormous, but it was far surpassed by the host of poor men whose wrongs he righted. He hated oppression, and would not tolerate it amongst his officials; and yet his methods of dealing with offenders was cruel and savage in the extreme. It is related that once, when passing through a provincial town, a baker complained to him of the ill-usage he had suffered at the hands of the local governor. Mohammed Ali, having verified the man's story, sent for the governor, and caused him to be pitched head first into the baker's oven, where he was slowly roasted to death. He set his face against all religious intolerance, and, though a good Mussulman, he disliked fanaticism. On one occasion he hanged on the spot a Dervish who, in a frenzy of religious zeal, had stabbed a Christian girl; and he always showed his partiality to intelligent Christians. At times he must have seemed to be an incarnation of ferocious righteousness, very terrible, and yet very willingly to be obeyed and honoured. Occasionally he was generous and lenient, as when he pardoned and even rewarded a miserable man who had made a showy attempt to assassinate him owing to an eccentric misanthropy due to hunger and distress.

His grizzly beard was now prematurely turning white; his eyes had sunk deeper into his head, but had lost none of their fire; and his movements were still those of a muscular soldier, though, from lack of manual work, his hands, which had always been small and feminine, were grown white and delicate. He dressed simply and without any great display. On his head he wore a red fez, around which a fine Cashmere shawl was wound. His pelisse, in the winter season, was lined with excellent furs; his baggy Turkish trousers were supported around the waist by a Cashmere shawl, from which protruded the hilt of a dagger and the butt of a pistol; and on his feet he wore red leather slippers, with upturned toes. A large diamond ring upon the little finger of his right hand was his only ornament. In his habits, also, he practised a certain simplicity. At this period he ate very plain food, and drank nothing but water. He did not waste much of his time with the women of his *harîm*, but preferred to pass his leisure hours in athletic sports or in the practice of horsemanship, in which he excelled. He slept little and was usually up before sunrise. His restless mind was always scheming for the aggrandisement both of his adopted country and of his own position; and with almost childish credulity he listened to every proposal of industrial or administrative reform which seemed to bear the cachet of European approval. Although outwardly loyal to the Porte, he shunned the thought that any man on earth was his master. Once, when he was reading a communication from the Sultan, he turned excitedly to an Englishman who happened to be present, and complained with bitterness of his vassalage. "My father had ten children," he declared, "but not one of them ever contradicted me. Later, the principal people in my native town took no step without my consent. I came to Egypt an obscure adventurer, yet I advanced step by step; and now here I am. Yes, here I am, and," he added, savagely tapping the document, "I never had a master!"

In this manner he governed Egypt with astonishing ability and progress for eleven quiet, though strenuous, years. In 1818 he brought the war in Arabia to a successful close, restoring the holy cities of Islâm to the suzerainty of the Sultan, from which they had seceded, and establishing an Egyptian protective influence over them, which, unfortunately, has now been allowed to lapse. In 1820 he conquered the Oasis of Siwa, nowadays famous as a seat of the Senoussi sect; and in 1823 he laid the foundations of Khartoum. His rising power, however, began to trouble the Sultan, Mahmoud II., who saw in it a menace to his own authority in Egypt; and England, meanwhile, looked on with equal dissatisfaction, for it was not easy to forget that Mohammed Ali had brought disgrace upon British arms, and had treacherously destroyed the Mamelukes, whom we had supported.

In 1822 the Sultan ordered his vassal to aid him against the Greeks, who were then fighting for their independence; but Mohammed Ali, instead of complying quietly with the order as was his duty, informed his sovereign that he would expect, as a reward for his services, the governorships of Crete, Syria, and Damascus, as well as that of Egypt. To this the Sultan agreed, and in the following year the Egyptian fleet and expeditionary force were despatched across the Mediterranean under the command of Mohammed Ali's son, Ibrahîm. The war dragged on for some years, but in 1827 the Egyptian forces met with an unexpected disaster. On October 20 of that year, their ships were anchored in the harbour of Navarino, and Mohammed Ali's son, Ibrahîm, was merrily burning Greek villages ashore, when a fleet of English, French, and Russian men-o'-war sailed into the harbour and anchored amongst them. The officers of these three nationalities now being united by their common interest in the Greek revolutionaries, sent a joint demand to the Egyptians that they should cease their pillaging. The Egyptians made an evasive reply; but shortly afterwards a scrimmage between the crews of an English and an Egyptian ship led to a general action at close quarters. The combined Egyptian and Turkish fleet consisted of 3 large battleships, 15 frigates, and some 70 smaller craft; and these were all speedily sunk or captured by the vastly superior European force, whose entire loss was only about 700 killed and wounded. Shortly afterwards Ibrahîm returned to Egypt, bringing the sad tidings to Mohammed Ali, who was naturally filled with bitterness against his old enemy, England, and against

France, who had assisted him to build the very ships which now she had helped to destroy. With great courage, however, he at once set to work to construct a new fleet; and meanwhile he demanded of the Sultan the promised governorates. This demand was ignored, and with eager haste Mohammed Ali prepared to enforce his rights. In four years' time his preparations were complete, and on November 1, 1831, 9000 Egyptian infantry and 2000 cavalry crossed the frontier into Syria, where they effected a junction at Jaffa with the new fleet.

The Sultan was immensely startled by this bold move. He believed that Mohammed Ali, in collusion with the Sherîf of Mecca, intended to seize not only his throne but also his office of Caliph of Islam, which his ancestor, the Sultan Selim I., had wrested from Egypt in 1517. Mohammed Ali, on his part, stated that he was merely about to take possession of the provinces which had been promised to him. By the early summer of 1833, Ìbrahîm, who was again in command of his father's forces, had captured Gaza, Jerusalem, Damascus, Acre, and Aleppo; and in August he crossed the mountains into Asia Minor. The Sultan, thoroughly frightened, now appealed to the Powers for aid, and expressed a wish for an alliance with England. Sir Stratford Canning, who was at that time in Constantinople, urged the home Government to make this alliance, but

Lord Palmerston emphatically showed his conviction that the Turk was neither desirable as a friend in his present state of civilisation, nor capable of regeneration.

On December 21 of the same year, a new Turkish force was utterly defeated by the Egyptians at Konia, and therefore the distracted Sultan, failing to enlist the aid of England, invited Russian co-operation. The Tsar was not slow to seize his opportunity. On February 20, 1834, a Russian squadron entered the Bosphorus, and Russian soldiers, sailors, diplomats, engineers, and craftsmen were poured into Constantinople. Very soon the British ambassador had to report that Turkey appeared to stand as a kind of vassal of Russia. Only Russians were admitted to the Sultan's presence; only Russian engineers were employed in the new fortifications which were being erected in the straits; and only Russian officers directed the Turkish troops.

Meanwhile Mohammed Ali again protested that he was perfectly loyal to the Sultan, but merely wished to take possession of the gifts which his sovereign had made to him. Ibrahîm, at the head of the Egyptian armies, adopted the same tone, and when next he advanced against the Turkish forces he wrote to the Sultan, politely asking his permission to do so. As he had at that time some 100,000 victorious Egyptians behind him, and as the Ottoman army had practically ceased to exist, it is not to be supposed that he awaited the answer with any anxiety.

England and France were naturally very disturbed at the Russian incursion into Constantinople; and they informed the Sultan that if he would invite the Tsar to withdraw his forces they would themselves guarantee that Mohammed Ali should be kept at a safe distance. This move was, on England's part, quite in keeping with our open dislike of the great Albanian; but in regard to France, it is clear that the fear of Russia had obscured the friendly sentiments so often expressed to the ruler of Egypt. The Sultan did not take much notice of the new proposals; but French and English diplomatic pressure having been brought to bear both on him and on Mohammed Ali, a convention was signed between the belligerents on April 8, 1834, by which it was agreed that Mohammed Ali should retain the provinces of Syria, Aleppo, and Damascus, while Ibrahîm should govern that of Adana, all, of course, under the Sultan's suzerainty. On July 8 the famous Turco-Russian treaty was signed, by which Russia came practically into control of the entrance to the Black Sea.

Shortly after this the inhabitants of Syria revolted against Mohammed Ali's stern and capable rule, and the Sultan immediately gave the revolutionaries his moral support. Thereupon he declared himself independent of the Porte and ceased to pay the annual tribute, although he realised well enough that the Powers would not support his action. "If I am crushed by the Powers of Europe," he declared, "I shall fall gloriously. I rose from nothing: to nothing I shall return; and as I rose by the sword, so shall I fall by the sword." England and France continned to do their best to preserve peace, so that Russia should no longer have an excuse for remaining in Constantinople; and at the same time they encouraged Prussia and Austria to show interest in Turkish affairs. The result was that Russian prestige declined, and soon the Prussians had become the Sultan's teachers in all military matters. A large number of German officers under von Moltke were commissioned to train the Turkish troops; but Mohammed Ali, with the aid of French officers under Colonel Sève, worked ceaselessly upon the drilling of his Egyptian army, and was all the more determined to break the Sultan's power.

During all these years of warfare and diplomatic struggles Mohammed Ali had been regarded in Europe as the rising star of the Orient. It was expected that he would reorganise the entire Near East, and would bring law and order into the most backward districts of the Turkish Empire. His reforms in Egypt were watched with the keenest interest; and many sentimentalists in England, unconscious of his terrible greatness, sent him patronising little letters of approval. Political philosophers, such as Jeremy Bentham, posted reams of good advice to him; and one may imagine the sardonic expression on the face of the splendid old Lion as these were read to him. For, let it be understood, Mohammed Ali was actually very far removed from the polite ideal of greatness.   He was a born intriguer, who as heartily enjoyed the great diplomatic and political struggles of his reign as he did his military campaigns and his administrative activities.   He had no regard whatsoever for human life; and all that may be said in his favour in this respect is, that he generally slaughtered his enemies in public and not by secret methods.   The sudden death of his son Tusûn is said to have been due to poison administered by Mohammed Ali; but there is no proof of the crime.   On more than one occasion he threatened to kill his son Ibrahîm for insubordination, and he was only prevented from dealing in a like manner with his daughter, Nazli Hanûm, whose profligacy had offended him, by the intervention of his nephew Abbas.   On one occasion it was reported to him that there had been some mutinous talk in the bazaars, and, desiring to check this as speedily as possible, he sent orders to the head of the police to hang forty of the worst criminals in the city, whether or not they were in this case the guilty persons.   " I have no doubt," he said, " that the victims have spoken, or might have spoken, seditiously; and anyhow they are a good riddance, and their death will put an end to the sedition of the real offenders." Any form of laziness was abhorrent to him, and during these years he kept his officials working at high pressure. Once, when he was arranging for the cutting of a new canal in Lower Egypt, he asked the local engineer what was the shortest time in which that section of the channel could be cut. The man, having made some rapid calculations, stated that the work could be done in one year. Mohammed Ali calmly turned to his servants, and ordered them to administer two hundred blows with a stick on the soles of the engineer's feet. This being done, he told the fainting wretch that he would return in four months' time, and that, if the canal were not then finished, another two hundred blows would be administered. Needless to say the work was completed long before the four months had passed.

Even after he had attained to a ripe old age Mohammed Ali did not lose the habit of walking to and fro when in thought or while conversing, his small hands clasped nervously behind his back, and his brows knitted together. He generally talked to himself when alone, and sometimes would break into violent tirades against the Sultan or his other particular enemies. His sleep was always brief and disturbed, and he could not ever lie comfortably abed. Although his sleeping apartment was furnished with a magnificent four-poster in the European style, he liked not a soft mattress, and invariably stretched himself on the hard floor beside it, upon a small strip of carpet.

The industrial experiments which were carried out in Egypt at this time were not entirely successful. Mohammed Ali's ideas were always very grand and imposing, but often they were entirely impracticable. His attempts to grow cotton and sugar, now the main products of the country, were a complete failure; and the elaborate silk looms which he set up were soon abandoned. He purchased every new mechanical device which was brought to his notice, and after his death an English engineer, who visited his workshops at Boulak, estimated that a million and a quarter pounds worth of machinery there lay rusting and unused. He was the ready victim of all cranks and unscrupulous inventors; and when any new industrial concern which had had his approval came to inevitable bankruptcy, he paid its debts out of the public funds. On one occasion he asked an Englishman to purchase him a steamer which was to ply on the Nile above the cataracts. The Englishman answered that such a scheme was absurd, for in those regions no fuel could be obtained, nor were there any passengers or cargoes to be carried; and moreover, the initial cost would be £5000 at least. Mohammed Ali turned furiously

upon him, and exclaimed, "Pray, sir, what the
devil is it to *you* if it costs me a million?" Yet
with all these faults there was a rugged magnificence and strength in his character, which,
combined with the charm of his manners to his
friends and to foreigners, caused him to be much
reverenced and beloved. His conversation is said
to have been gay and animated, and his politeness
exquisite. Thus, on one occasion when a chair
had not been provided for one of the foreign
diplomats to whom he was giving audience, he
refused to be seated himself until this had been
supplied.

The five years between 1834 and 1839 passed in
superficial quietude, while urgent preparations
were being made both in Egypt and in Turkey for
a decisive trial of strength. The Sultan, with his
German officers, was the first to consider himself
ready for the fray; and in April 1839 his army
crossed the frontier into Syria, with the uncon-
cealed purpose of chastising Mohammed Ali for his
insubordination, and regaining control of Syria
and Egypt. The Egyptian army, with its French
officers, again under the command of Ibrahîm, met
the Turks at Nezib on June 23, and annihilated
them. A week later the Sultan died, and was
succeeded by Abdul-Mejid, a boy of sixteen.
Ahmed Pasha, the Turkish admiral, now went
over to the Egyptians with his entire fleet, and
the Ottoman Grand Vizir wrote to Mohammed

Ali, offering him the hereditary governorship of Egypt, and his son Ibrahîm the governorship of Syria, and all manner of honours, if he would but make peace. Mohammed Ali, however, now felt that he had fairly beaten the Porte, and he knew that, if the Powers but allowed him, he could become supreme master of the Turkish Empire. He therefore sent an evasive answer to the Grand Vizir, and anxiously awaited to see what Europe would do.

The Powers, however, were in a hopeless muddle. France wanted Russia to leave Constantinople, but, on the other hand, wished Mohammed Ali to retain the provinces which he and his son had conquered with such military skill and perseverance. Austria and Prussia both favoured the Turkish point of view in regard to Mohammed Ali, but mistrusted Russia, and were determined to oppose her in all Near Eastern affairs. England was, as always, hostile to Mohammed Ali, and believed that there would be no peace until he was forced back into Egypt; and in this attitude we came into serious conflict with France. Russia then made a most praiseworthy and generous move. The Tsar informed the Powers that if only they would hold a conference and assume a united front, as it were for the honour of Christendom, he would be prepared to give up his rights according to the Turko-Russian Treaty mentioned above, to close the Dardanelles to warships of all

nations, and to retire from Constantinople. Lord
Palmerston stated in reply that he had received
the proposal "with surprise and admiration," and
steps were at once taken with a view to joint
action. France, however, was the stumbling-block.
Nothing would induce her to agree to any measure depriving Mohammed Ali of the fruits of his
conquests; and at last, abandoning the other
Powers, she opened private negotiations with
Egypt with a view to an alliance. As a result
of this, the European concert deliberately left
France out of its consultations; and when, on
July 15, 1840, a convention was signed with
Turkey, French opinion was not invited. This
convention took the form of an ultimatum to
Mohammed Ali. It stated that if he would make
peace within ten days he should be made hereditary Pasha of Egypt and life-governor of Syria.
If he had not accepted these terms within the
time-limit, the offer of the governorship of Syria
would be withdrawn; and at the end of another
ten days the offer in regard to Egypt would also
be withdrawn. When these terms became known
in Paris a wave of fury swept over the French
people. The brave Mohammed Ali, who had
raised Egypt from the depths of misery, and had
conquered the Turks in fair fight, was now to
be peremptorily ordered about by the European
Powers, whose only wish was to maintain the
status quo lest they should fall out amongst them-

selves.   Was this fair-play, they asked?—was this chivalry?   The attitude of the Powers, however, was based on the recognition of the fact that Mohammed Ali was, in spite of his splendid qualities, simply a rebellious provincial governor in revolt against his sovereign.   France, however, reasoned in more romantic fashion, and the nation clamoured for war.

Meanwhile the British, Austrian, and Russian fleets appeared off Beirout, on the Syrian coast, to enforce the terms of the ultimatum upon the Egyptian garrisons; and their arrival was a signal for a second Syrian revolt.   Ibrahîm could not withstand the combined attacks of the three Powers, the "rebels," and the Turks; and, when Beirout and Acre had fallen to the guns of the fleet, he was obliged to retire to Egypt, and Syria was lost to Mohammed Ali.   On September 15, 1840, the old man was deposed by the Sultan; but when this decree was read to him he replied with a sad smile that it signified little, since this was the fourth occasion on which he had been deposed, and he hoped to get over it as he had over the others.   What confidence he had was due to his belief in the support of France; but in this he was soon to be disappointed.

On October 8, France presented a note to England demanding the reinstatement of Mohammed Ali; and to this the British Government replied in as conciliatory a manner as possible.   But while the diplomatic negotiations were still in progress the British Fleet arrived at Alexandria, and Sir Charles Napier, pointing out that France was not in a position to go to war, managed to persuade the tired and disappointed Mohammed Ali to come to terms with the Sultan. On January 30, 1841, a treaty was signed, by the terms of which Mohammed Ali became hereditary Pasha of Egypt and Governor of the Sudan, undertaking to reduce his army to 18,000 and to pay an annual tribute to Turkey of £412,000; and when this settlement was reported in Paris the French Government abandoned its chivalrous championship of Egypt, and a European war was averted. The arrangement, however, broke the aged man's heart, and a few years later a stroke affected his brain. The government was taken over by Ibrahîm, who, however, died in November 1848, thus completing the sorrows of his stern but affectionate father. A profound gloom fell upon the old Lion of the Levant, now nearly eighty years of age. For hours he would sit staring in front of him, until suddenly the sound of the midday gun, or the neighing of a horse, would arouse him and set him pacing to and fro. At other times, with eyes ablaze, he would tell those around him that his agents had discovered mines where gold and precious stones lay as thick as the gravel, or that his armies had conquered the world and his ships had scoured the uttermost seas. His thoughts

were all of the greatness of Egypt and the
supremacy of his throne, for a kindly providence
had obliterated from his mind the disappointments of his life; and when, on August 2, 1849,
he breathed his last, he no longer remembered
that he was leaving Egypt as he had found it, a
vassal of the Porte, only infinitely richer, happier,
and more to be coveted by the rapacious Turks.

CHAPTER III.

ISMAIL PASHA.

THE name of Ismail Pasha, the prodigal Khedive of Egypt, whose most praiseworthy son is now Sultan of that country, is still so well remembered by the reading public that little introduction is necessary. It was he who brought Egypt into close touch with Europe, and attempted to make of his capital city of Cairo a little Paris of the East; it was he who as host so lavishly entertained the Emperor of Austria and the Empress of France, together with several other important royal personages, at the historic opening of the Suez Canal; and it was he who, having run into debt at the rate of some seven million pounds a year, was forced to place the finances of Egypt in the hands of European controllers, and at length was deposed from his throne. His reign marks an epoch in the history of Egypt which, in view of the present situation, it is very desirable to recall to mind. The technical relationship of Egypt to the Porte was formulated by Ismail; and though the British advent in 1882 introduced superficially a new state of affairs, the diplomatic arrangements made by him still held good at the beginning of the great European war in 1914. Indeed, had it not been for Ismail's peculiar financial methods and their consequences, England would never have occupied the Nile Valley, and the British Protectorate over Egypt would not have been dreamed of.

The grandson of that fine old warrior, Mohammed Ali, Ismail inherited from his forebears much of the fire, and not a little of the untamable spirit, of his Albanian family; and the reckless use which he made of his power, the wholesale squandering of public money in which he indulged, assumes, by reason of his inspiring and charming personality, a romantic quality which cannot fail to be stimulating to the imagination on first thoughts. It is indisputable that this extraordinary potentate makes his appeal to the student as one of the great histrionic figures of the past, whose personality seems to demand a sympathetic and favourable interpretation; and yet there can be no doubt that, viewed from a moral or ethical standpoint, his character is highly reprehensible and his actions generally culpable. So great is the public affection for brilliantly staged drama that the ordinary student of Egyptian affairs is almost invariably impressed in the first instance by the imposing glamour of Ismail's reign and the romantic qualities of his character; but it ought not to be forgotten that the enchantment of the scenes in which he played was created by the sullen labour and the bitter agony of the majority of his people, and that the splendid illumination of the court at Cairo was paid for, and still is being paid for, by those who daily have fretted in the darkness outside.

Ismail's appearance was not an asset in his favour, nor was there any suggestion of the unsubstantial pageant in his figure and bearing. He was short, fat, and ungainly; and his walk suggested that of a performing bear. While giving audiences he was wont to roam about the room, rolling from side to side like a sailor at sea; or, when tired of such ambulations, he would waddle to a divan and there sit nursing his legs, which were crossed in Turkish fashion, and playing with his toes. There appeared to be no dignity in his carriage, but rather a comicality; and although friends who knew him well observed, after a while, a certain stateliness of demeanour which it was not easy to define, those who saw him for the first time could with difficulty refrain from smiling. His face was peculiarly ugly. His ears were large and thick, and of a form different from those of ordinary men. His tangled red eyebrows screened two eyes which had no resemblance one to the other, nor acted in unison. The left eyelid drooped, and while his mind was engaged in thought the eye became almost closed, but at the same time his right orbit wandered or shifted without cessation; and thus it came to be said of him that he heard with one eye and spoke with the other. His red beard grew in an unkempt condition, while his hair protruded around the ears from below a crimson fez, which was worn low on one side of his head, as though some sizes too large for him. His hands were clumsy and ill-shaped, and had the twisted stiff-ness of those of a Guy Fawkes; and when he was about to speak his head was jerked to one side in the manner of an automaton. He wore usually a frock-coat cut out in the clerical style, made of some shiny black material; and his feet were hidden by large elastic-sided black boots.

He made up by the charm of his manner, how-ever, all that he lost by the grotesqueness of his appearance. His personality was fascinating in an extraordinary degree; and, by reason of his adaptability, he was able to couch his remarks in the manner most suited to his hearers. To an Englishman he spoke shortly, concisely, and frankly; to a Frenchman his words were well chosen and his thoughts delicately and diplo-matically expressed; to a German he showed his mastery of detail. He was gifted with the keenest insight; and his impressions being always rapidly formed, he was able to decide on the instant the tone which he should adopt. His

ISMAIL PASHA.

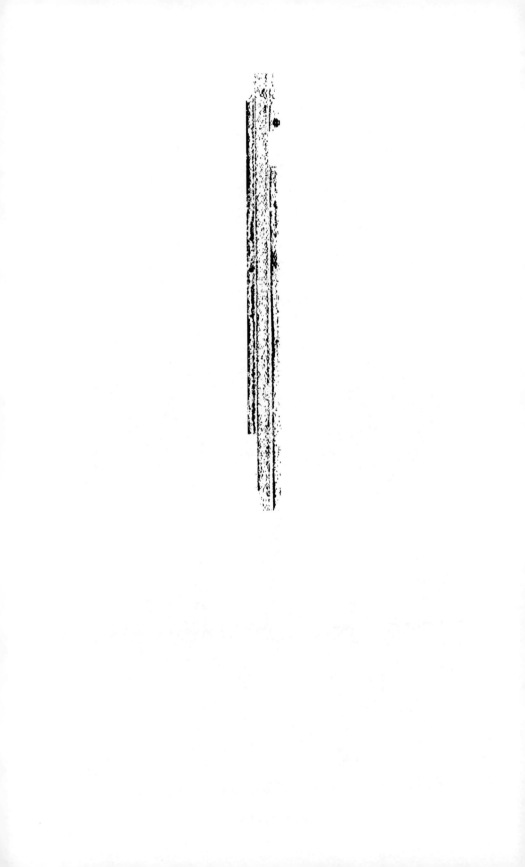

savoir faire was the wonder of all those who
came into contact with him, and his superficiality
was seldom detected. He persuaded even his most
angered opponents that his intentions were sincere, and those who entered his palace with black
murder in their hearts left it cooing and purring
like contented animals. His personal magnetism
was such that not even experienced diplomatists
could resist the appeal of his words; and although
they might, in the seclusion of their offices, write
disparaging reports of him to their Governments,
they seldom held to their adverse opinions while
in his presence. His powers of flattery were also
highly developed, and he was able to make the
person to whom he was speaking feel that he was
his Highness's particular confidant. His memory
was extraordinary, and he seldom failed to delight
his auditor by calling to mind the details of past
conversations. The expression of his face was
alluringly happy, and his manner was almost
invariably good-humoured. He enjoyed cracking
a joke with his intimates or telling a comic story;
and there was seldom any spite to be detected in
the anecdotes which he delighted to relate at the
expense of the members of his entourage. He
presided at his daily meals with great geniality,
charming his European guests, and even succeeding in the difficult task of setting his Egyptian
associates at their ease as they smacked their lips
around his lavish table. He had spent some time

in France, and spoke French fluently—that, indeed, being his favourite tongue; and his manners were to be distinguished as French rather than as Turkish or Egyptian. Although a Mohammedan, he did not observe the Moslem fasts nor limit his diet according to the dictates of the Koran. He ate ham with relish, and enjoyed without disguise his bottle of *Sauterne* or *Veuve Clicquot*; and if by such indulgences he caused misgivings amongst the stricter members of his court, he strengthened thereby the ties of good-fellowship which existed between him and his European friends and officials. His prodigal hospitality, and his open and courteous manner, won the hearts of those around him; and very rapidly his extraordinary appearance and awkward movements were forgotten under the spell of his captivating personality.

Mohammed Ali was succeeded at his death by his nephew Abbas, who died five years later, leaving the Viceregal throne to Said, who occupied it for nine somewhat uneventful years. Ismail Pasha was born in 1830, and was educated for a time in Paris. On the death of Said he came to the throne in 1863, under somewhat suspicious circumstances. Until a few years before his accession his elder half-brother, Ahmed, had been the heir-apparent; but this prince was removed from Ismail's path by an accident, which some have declared, without any real proof, to have been designed by the younger claimant. Ahmed and

Ismail had both been invited to a *fête*, which was held at Alexandria, and to which they were to proceed by train from Cairo. Ismail declined to attend the function, and Ahmed therefore travelled down alone with his suite. On the return journey the royal train, while crossing the Nile, was precipitated into the water under very surprising circumstances, and Ahmed and some twenty members of his entourage were drowned. Ismail, being thus left heir to the throne, was given some share of the Government, and acted as Regent in 1861 during the absence of the reigning prince. During the same year he was placed in command of an expedition to Nubia, which successfully accomplished its task of subduing the rebellious tribes of those regions. At another time he was sent on diplomatic missions to Rome and Paris; and thus he had already gathered considerable experience in public affairs when he succeeded at the age of thirty-three. High hopes were entertained of his abilities; for as a young man he had shown some promise of developing into a conscientious and statesmanlike ruler. He, who afterwards proved to be the wildest spendthrift of his age, was at that time noted for his economy in the management of his estates; and many were the stories told of his thrift and his habit of counting the piastres. At his accession his first public speech dealt feelingly with the need of sound economy in the finances of the country, and he then declared that he would teach a practical lesson on this subject to all by at once cutting down his Civil List to a minimum sum, which he promised never to exceed. In the face of these declarations, therefore, it is startling to find that already, in 1864, a year after his accession, he had spent every penny in his treasury and was obliged to borrow nearly six million pounds at a ruinous rate of interest. The loan was floated by Messrs Fruhling and Goschen, and was nominally for £5,704,000, but Ismail only realised £4,864,000 after the fees had been paid.

The first cause of his financial difficulties was his inordinate ambition, which led him to pay a visit to Constantinople in order to obtain from his overlord, the Sultan, a greater recognition of his dignity. At that time the rulers of Egypt were simple Viceroys for the Porte, and Ismail's rank was actually no higher than that of the *Vali* of Smyrna, Baghdad, or any other Turkish Province. He was keenly anxious to be recognised as a powerful vassal sovereign, and it was this desire that took him post-haste to the Bosphorus as soon as he had succeeded to the Viceregal Throne. But by the Porte his visit was regarded as purely ceremonial and deferential, and the Sultan, Abd'el Aziz, was duly patronising to him. This attitude gave considerable annoyance to Ismail, who endeavoured at once to prove to the Porte by lavish expenditure how wealthy and puissant a vassal he was. He had journeyed across the Mediterranean to Constantinople in his private yacht, which had been built at a cost of £150,000; and now, in his anxiety to create the desired impression, he casually made a gift of the vessel to the Sultan, adding thereto a large sum in gold. He gave huge sums of money also to the court officials, the Chamberlain alone receiving a present of £15,000, which, as a gratuity for the attentions of a few days, may be regarded as somewhat excessive! The Sultan, as a man of business, was delighted with Ismail's free and liberal manners; and, desiring that so profitable a communion should not terminate, he made arrangements for a return visit to Cairo, which was accomplished six weeks later. This was Ismail's chance to create a lasting impression, and he threw himself into the task with enthusiasm. Abd'el Aziz had never in his life before enjoyed so lavish an entertainment. For ten days he was fêted in the most splendid manner, and banquets which outshone those of Lucullus were held each night in his honour. Moreover, he received from his vassal a personal present of £100,000; his suite received £20,000; and a further £15,000 was distributed amongst the officers and crews of the imperial squadron. It does not seem to have occurred to the Sultan, however, that the Prince desired some return for this expenditure, in the form of an increase of power; and when he went back, replete, to Constantinople he left his Egyptian host still in the comparatively humble position of Viceroy of his Province of Egypt.

Ismail, however, held a very different estimate of his own importance; and after such a gay series of royal festivities in the company of the Turkish monarch, he felt that he himself was virtually a sovereign ruler, and the cousin of the kings of the world. From the day of his accession he worked untiringly to make himself the most mighty ruler outside of Europe, and it was his constant hope to extend his power northwards, ultimately succeeding the Sultan, whose fall he anticipated, as ruler of the Faithful and lord of the Eastern Mediterranean. Already he saw himself master of a new Egypto-Turkish Empire, and his powerful imagination led him to picture himself one day the absolute equal of the greatest European sovereigns. This attitude of mind was strengthened by the deference paid to him by France and England, and the manner in which both countries sought to establish intimate relations with him. With the Emperor Napoleon he was on excellent terms, and he even went so far as to send—like a patronising ally—1200 Nubian troops to help the French in their ill-fated Mexican campaign in 1863, of which number, it may be mentioned, only 300, sick and wounded, ever returned to Egpyt; nor was it long before he received at the hands of a deferential embassy of English noblemen the Grand Cross of the Bath and the Grand Cross of the Star of India, presented to him by Queen Victoria and her Government as a mark of respect.

When, therefore, Ismail paid his next visit to Constantinople, he went in even greater pomp than on the previous occasion. He took with him his *harîm*, a large personal suite, a menagerie of Sudanese animals, a number of Arab horses, and a huge amount of furniture and baggage. He gave splendid presents to all the court officials, and to the Sultan he is said to have given the sum of £300,000 as a slight token of his affection and regard. He bought the interest of almost every newspaper in Constantinople, and by means of these lavish bribes he obtained from the Sultan a decree which arranged that the Viceregal throne of Egypt should pass from father to son in his family for ever. Previous to this the descent had followed the usual Mohammedan order, passing always to the eldest member of the entire reigning family—a system, by the way, which has been accidentally reverted to in the appointment of Hussein Kamel, the present Sultan, who is the eldest surviving descendant of Mohammed Ali. At the same time Ismail undertook to pay £300,000 more tribute each year to the Porte.

Returning to Cairo, he felt it incumbent upon him to reign nominally as a constitutional ruler; and he therefore established a Grand Council, which was intended to act as a kind of parliament.   It was inaugurated in the most solemn and approved manner, the name of the Almighty being most reverently invoked; but the experiment was a signal failure, owing to the fact that no delegate would oppose the Government or argue with Ismail's Ministers.   "God forbid," said each Councillor, "that I should think of questioning the fitness of any measure proposed by his Highness," and not one of them would pass over to the Opposition benches.   Nevertheless, the establishment of this Council, whether or no it did any work, greatly increased Ismail's prestige in Europe, and everywhere he was hailed as the most enlightened and the most powerful prince of the East.   On the strength of this renewed confidence in his abilities, he borrowed through the Anglo-Egyptian Bank the nominal sum of £3,387,000, and set himself with a will to the pleasant task of spending the £2,750,000 which it realised.

He now demanded from the Sultan a further recognition of his dignity.   He asked the right to make treaties with foreign Powers, to establish diplomatic agencies throughout Europe, to raise a large navy and army, and so forth.   He further requested his overlord to allow him to be called *Aziz el Misr* instead of Viceroy.   The word Aziz means "Almighty," and is one of the Mohammedan names of God.   Now, the Sultan's own name, Abd'el Aziz, meant "The slave of the Almighty," and it was obvious that if Ismail were to be called Aziz, it might have been suggested by the frivolous that the Sultan was his servant. This, and all the other requests, therefore, were flatly refused; and the only concession which was made to him was the granting of the hereditary appellation of *Khedive*, an obscure title of Persian origin, which seemed to the Sultan to be less pretentious than that proposed by Ismail. The Prince was deeply mortified at this snub, and determined to seek consolation in a visit to Europe, where, he knew, he would be accorded the deference he so much desired.

He was prepared to pay for the honours which he hoped to receive, and to pose as the fabulously wealthy potentate of his European friends' belief. He had replenished his empty purse with two large loans, and for the moment he felt himself to be in very comfortable circumstances. The first of these two loans was raised by Messrs Fruhling and Goschen, and represented a nominal £3,000,000 and a net £2,640,000; and the second was engineered by the Imperial Ottoman Bank, being nominally for £2,080,000 and actually producing £1,700,000.

In Paris he was received with royal honours; and, having crossed to England, he was met at Dover by a brilliant company of court and military officers, who, amidst the cheers of the crowd and the firing of salutes from the guns in the Castle,

set out with him for London.   Here the Prince of
Wales met him and conducted him to the Queen
at Windsor, by whom he was royally entertained
for two days.   A breathless round of festivities in
his honour followed; and at length he returned to
Paris, where again he was everywhere treated *en
roi.*   All men were anxious to pay their respects
to this charming-mannered ruler of historic Egypt,
whose wealth, moreover, appeared to be so bound-
less, and whose personal expenses at that time
probably exceeded those of any European monarch;
and it was thus, with a very enlarged opinion
of himself, that he returned once more to Constantinople for a further visit to the Sultan.
On this occasion, during his stay in that city,
he paid out, in one way and another, over
£1,000,000; but he does not appear to have
obtained any further concession in return for his
vast expenditure.

On his arrival in Egypt he was received both at
Alexandria and at Cairo by a royal salute of 101
guns, and for several days fêtes in honour of his
return were celebrated throughout the country at
a general cost of about £6000 per hour.   Large
numbers of tourists were now wont to flock to
Egypt during the winter seasons, and many of
Ismail's European friends paid him visits in his
own country.   Egypt was no longer a barbaric
land cut off from the civilised world; and its
ruler's great ambition was to give to his city of

Cairo a European aspect which should excite the favourable comment of all visitors. He therefore modernised many of the streets of the capital, erected several fine buildings, built himself numerous palaces, and even constructed a large Opera House. He also laid down railways through the Delta, and made large docks at Suez.

The advance of civilisation in Egypt under his enlightened rule was watched with intense interest by the European Powers. It was believed that he was about to found a great Egyptian Empire as mighty as that created by the ancient Pharaohs; and, indeed, there can be no doubt that such was Ismail's aim throughout his reign. It was stated on all sides that Cairo and Alexandria would soon vie in magnificence with the first cities of Europe, and that from their gates the newly-trained armies of the Khedive would march out to subdue the neighbouring nations. Sir Samuel Baker was to be sent to Central Africa to bring those regions under his sway, and the British public noted with especial pleasure that this expedition had for one of its objects the suppression of the slave trade. In a few years it was expected that the Turkish Empire would collapse, and that the Khedive would find himself master of the entire east end of the Mediterranean at the same time that he was lord of the Sudan and suzeraine of Arabia. There was no limit to European expectations or to Ismail's dreams; and it was with deep satisfaction that the Khedive now found himself the object of all men's interest.

The cost of these undertakings, and his own enormous expenditure, led him once more into serious debt; and in 1867 he was obliged to borrow the sum of £11,890,000 at a high rate of interest. The loan was obtained through Messrs Oppenheim, and so great were the charges and fees that only £7,193,000 ever reached Ismail's hands. At the same time the peasantry were taxed in the most cruel manner, and the distress in the provinces was acute. Ismail had at his disposal the entire revenues of the country, and he retained in his possession both the private ledgers of his personal estate and also the public books of the Ministry of Finance. Being a keen business man in regard to the development of his own fortune, he entered into all manner of remunerative schemes, and his private income must have been enormous. He was a partner in a bank which lent money to the peasants at high rates of interest, and as the enforced taxes generally obliged the farmers to borrow, there was never any lack of business. He owned extensive sugar plantations and factories, and his hand was heavy upon those persons who purchased their sugar elsewhere. He was half shareholder in a Nile transport company, which brought large profits to himself, owing to his privileged trading rights. He was the largest cotton-grower and merchant in the country. He owned vast herds of sheep and cattle, which, by sovereign privilege, he was able to import free of all quarantine duties. He dealt also in coal, bringing it into Egypt free of duty and on Government vessels. He owned at least a quarter of the best lands in the country, having himself obtained in one way or another some 970,000 acres of good ground; and, being Khedive, he was exempt from the land tax, and could employ forced and unpaid labour. Thus he was able to amass a very considerable private fortune at the same time that the treasury of the country was being depleted in so startling a manner.

The year 1869 may be regarded as that in which the revelries and extravagances of Ismail's reign reached their height. One of the first events of the year was a ball given at the palace of Ghezireh; and, as an example of the Khedive's excesses, a single fact may be mentioned in regard to this fête. To reach the palace the broad Nile had to be crossed, and his Highness felt that the obtaining of launches and boats would be a nuisance both to himself and to his guests. He therefore gave instructions that a temporary bridge should be constructed across the river, here nearly half a mile broad, and this was done with infinite pains at a huge cost. The refreshments, illuminations, fireworks, and so forth, which formed an indispensable part of both this and of other functions, cost the country thousands of pounds; and so prodigal was Ismail's hospitality that all manner of Europeans and Americans who had met his Highness in various parts of the world, or who had obtained letters of introduction to him, were catered for and entertained in the most lavish manner at the expense of the nation, whenever and for whatever length of time they chose to stay in Egypt. Moreover, at the palace of Abdin it is said on the highest authority that something like 10,000 natives were daily fed, as being in some way employed by the Khedive. In February of this year the Prince and Princess of Wales paid a visit to Egypt, and marvellous were the festivities organised in their honour. Two vast palaces were placed at their disposal while they remained in Cairo, and when they went up the Nile a fine fleet of vessels accompanied the sumptuous Khedivial steamer upon which they travelled. Meanwhile practically all Government work was suspended, owing to the fact that Ismail had engaged the services of almost every clerk who could speak French, in order that he might obtain some sort of translation into Arabic of the ' Œil Grevé,' the ' Belle Hélène,' the ' Mariée de Mardi Gras,' and other works of Offenbach which he desired his court and *harîm* to appreciate, although, of course, he had never read them himself.

Ismail always held strong views in regard to the education of his womenkind. He liked them to be able to converse freely with the European ladies who visited them, and he desired them to imitate to the best of their ability the manners and accomplishments of the ladies he met in Paris and London. He insisted, too, that they should be well and fashionably dressed; and in the pursuit of this object he permitted, in one case, a bill of £150,000 to accumulate at a French dressmaker's for clothes supplied to a lady of his *harîm*.

Very naturally, the Egyptian people began to murmur at the tyrannical manner in which money was forced from them. The peasants throughout the country were starving, and the importunate tax-gatherers were obliged to wring from them the uttermost piastre by means of torture or by the forcible sale of their miserable effects. Thousands emigrated into Syria, and vast tracts of land passed into barren disuse. Many were obliged to raise money from usurers at the rate of 30 per cent per month, and by no means an inconsiderable number of once wealthy landowners preferred to live the life of unattached mendicants rather than cultivate the crops upon which they would be forced to pay such outrageous taxes. It was not surprising, therefore, that rumours of plots to assassinate the Khedive now began to circulate. The most serious of these emanated from the ranks of the military, and it was freely stated that a mutiny or revolution was about to take place. The troops were badly fed, and their pay had fallen into arrears; and, moreover, the constant news which came to them of the distress in their homes and villages irritated them into acts of flagrant disloyalty, which eventually came to the ears of Ismail.   His Highness acted promptly. Eleven wretched soldiers were court-martialled and shot ; and a few weeks later four others who were found trespassing in the palace grounds were by his orders slaughtered on the spot, their bodies being thrown into the Nile.

Ismail was in character purely Oriental, and the careful veneer of Parisian polish did not obliterate the crude tendencies due to his upbringing.   The courteous and fascinating Prince who so successfully graced the drawing-rooms of London and Paris, and so completely charmed the Kings and Queens of Europe, was hardly to be recognised in the grotesque despot who roamed uneasily about his palace when his English and French friends were not nigh, ordering the instant execution of those who had incurred his wrath, or devising means of robbing his subjects of their hard-earned money. It is said on good authority that his dealings with the very numerous ladies of his *harîm* were of a truly Oriental character ; and on one occasion, having discovered that certain of these unfortunate women were carrying on small intrigues with the officers of the guard, he is related to have flogged them to death and to have thrown their bodies, tied up in sacks, into the river.

" The people he liked best to talk to," said his

English coachman in after years, "were his servants, the lads who brought him his pipes, and stood before him with their arms crossed. He sometimes sat on his sofa and smoked, and talked to them for hours, all about women and such things. I have known him sometimes try to read a French novel, but he would be two hours getting through a page. Once or twice I saw him attempt to write. His letters were half an inch high, like those of a child's copybook. I don't think that he ever finished a sentence."

He was, of course, a consummate actor, and he managed to play the *rôle* of a civilised, and even constitutional, monarch with almost invariable success. Europeans considered him to be not only enlightened, but by nature humane and benevolent; and great would have been the consternation in many a scrupulous home had the true character of the honoured guest at that time become known. Ismail enjoyed acting a part, and he loved to surround himself with the stage-like attributes which he considered best able to set off his own royal dignity. On one occasion he organised a grand review of his troops for the benefit of his European visitors, and he took particular pride in the parade of what he was pleased to call his camel corps; but it was discovered at a later date that the fierce, white-clad Bedouîns who rode past the grand-stand in their martial hundreds were in reality loafers and beggars who had been whipped in for this one performance, and had been mounted on baggage camels commandeered from the neighbouring farms. Ismail had observed in Europe that on state occasions the halls of the palaces were guarded by bearded and magnificently-apparelled men-at-arms, such as the Yeomen of the Guard in London or the Swiss Guard in Paris; and he decided to adopt this pleasing custom at his fêtes in Cairo. But Egyptians are not often bearded, and Ismail therefore bought a number of false beards, issued them to the tallest men in his bodyguard, together with a set of comic-opera uniforms, and thus formed a company of state sentinels who were the pride of his eye. When the rooms in which the fêtes were being held grew hot, it is said that these men were wont to push up their beards and mop their necks in a manner most startling to the assembled guests. Instances of this theatrical love of display are too numerous to mention; but this one illustration will give a fair idea of the turn of Ismail's mind in this regard.

In the summer of 1869 his Highness again visited Europe for the ostensible purpose of drinking the waters at Vichy. He sailed from Egypt in his magnificent yacht, accompanied by three men-o'-war, a salute of 101 guns being fired from the Alexandria forts as he steamed out of the harbour. At Corfu he paid a call on the King of

Greece, and personally invited him to attend the ceremony of opening the Suez Canal, which was then nearing completion. To Queen Olga be presented the sum of 100,000 francs for the relief of the Cretan refugees, an action which very naturally gave great offence to his overlord, the Sultan. He then travelled on to Florence, whither King Victor Emanuel hastened to meet him; and there he was lodged in royal state in the Pitti Palace. Having also invited the Italian King to attend the coming fêtes in Egypt, he made his way to Vienna, where he was lavishly entertained, and where he gave a similar invitation to the Emperor of Austria. Thence he travelled to Berlin, being received there with sovereign honours, and in return inviting the King and the Crown Prince of Prussia to attend the Suez celebrations. At Paris he issued a similar invitation to the Emperor and Empress of France, and so at length he reached London. Here Buckingham Palace itself was assigned to him for his use; and the Queen, the Prince of Wales, and, in fact, the entire assemblage of British celebrities, did him every possible honour, to all of whom he sent formal invitations to the inauguration of the great Canal. The Czar of Russia and other royal personages requested him to do them the honour of visiting their capitals; but Ismail, being surfeited with glory and renown, did not accede to their requests.

Before he returned to his native land he placed

with a well-known firm of shipbuilders an order for
two powerful ironclads, and elsewhere he purchased 200,000 chassepots and several needle-guns.
This was for the Sultan the last straw. Abd'el
Aziz had heard with fury of his vassal's magnificent reception in Europe, and, through the
Ottoman agencies, he had informed the various
royalties that the invitations issued to them by
Ismail were invalid and spurious. He, the Sultan,
was alone Ruler of Egypt, and his Viceroy had no
right, he declared, to act in any way without his
knowledge and sanction. To Ismail he then sent
a letter demanding that he should come to Constantinople immediately to tender his apologies,
that he should hand over at once the battleships
which he had ordered, and that he should promise
in future to act strictly as the Viceroy of the
Porte.

Ismail prevaricated and hedged until the late
autumn, when, for a time, a truce was called in
order that the opening of the Suez Canal might be
celebrated without any untoward incident. In the
second week of November, 1869, the Khedive's
guests began to pour into Egypt. Of the royalties
invited, only the Empress Eugénie, the Emperor
of Austria, the Crown Prince of Prussia, Prince
Henry of the Netherlands, and Prince Louis of
Hesse presented themselves; but large numbers
of minor celebrities, and some three thousand
guests of no particular importance, availed them-

selves of his Highness's invitation to spend a week
or more in Egypt at his expense.

The preparations for the reception of the royal
personages were prodigious. Ismail was told by
his French friends that the Empress Eugénie
would be sure to visit the Pyramids and Sphinx,
which stand some seven miles outside Cairo; and
he therefore gave immediate orders that a fine
embanked road should be constructed in a straight
line from the Nile to these monuments, and that a
large house should be built on the spot, in order
that her Majesty might have a place wherein to
take her luncheon. Realising that it would be
correct to give a state ball at Ismailia during
the fêtes, he caused a magnificent palace to be
built there solely for that purpose. The most
costly suites of furniture were procured from Paris
to furnish the rooms in which the royalties should
reside during their brief visit to Egypt; and expensive pictures from the Paris Salon were
purchased to hang upon the walls.

On November 17, amidst salvoes from the Egyptian and European men-o'-war and batteries, and
the music of massed naval and military bands,
the Canal was declared open. A procession of
forty-eight ships, headed by the Empress's yacht,
sailed through the Canal to Ismailia, where a
vast banquet was given in a city of tents and
temporary kiosks. Watched by the Egyptian
stars, and in the light of ten thousand lanterns,

Ismail sat that night with the Empress of France on his right hand and the Emperor of Austria on his left, drinking toasts to the future of Egypt and to the progress of civilisation; while around his splendid pavilion his thousands of guests jested, revelled, and stuffed themselves with good things, the bands playing and the richly-robed servants hurrying to and fro with inexhaustible supplies of wine and food. There was not a thought in the mind of any man present of the impending storm; yet on all sides events were working towards a crisis. The Sultan sat at Constantinople moodily promising to humiliate his vassal; the Egyptian peasants, groaning under their cruel taxation, were murmuring against their rulers; and in Europe the financiers who had loaned money to the Khedive were becoming anxious and restless. The Canal celebrations cost the country about £1,300,000; and another £10,000 was spent in publishing the official history of the proceedings in elephant folio.

No sooner had the guests departed to their homes across the sea than the Sultan sent the Khedive an ultimatum demanding complete surrender on all points. Ismail, however, having said farewell to his friends, had gone up the Nile with an American lady; and he did not trouble to reply to the Porte until his return to Cairo. Meanwhile, considerable preparations for war were made; and it seemed at one time as though his Highness intended to try his strength with Turkey and to attempt to obtain his independence by force of arms. Great fortifications were constructed at Alexandria, and there was a continuous movement of troops throughout the Delta. A large number of American free-lances were enrolled as Egyptian officers, and a certain degree of efficiency was obtained. A heated exchange of letters now took place between Cairo and Constantinople, and at length a compromise was arrived at. Ismail agreed to hand over the two men-o'-war which he had purchased in Europe, on condition that the money paid for them was returned to him by the Porte. He made certain apologies and certain worthless promises to his overlord, and a few minor concessions were granted to him by the Sultan. Honour being thus satisfied, Ismail obtained through the firm of Bischoffsheim a loan of £7,142,860, which had a net value of £5,000,000, and settled down quietly to the spending of this sum. In all directions he Europeanised Cairo, Alexandria, and other parts of the country. During his reign, it is to be recorded to his credit, nearly 5000 schools were built, 8000 miles of canals were dug, 1000 miles of railway laid down, and about 5500 miles of telegraph wires set up. Great public buildings were erected; a fine harbour was built at Alexandria at a cost of £2,500,000; and all manner of industrial works were put in hand. These expenses and his own amazing extravagances again involved him in huge debts, and in 1872 he was obliged to raise a further loan of £4,000,000.

He now arranged to pay a visit once more to Constantinople in order to renew friendly relations with the Sultan, who had undertaken to let bygones be bygones. On his arrival he was received with great cordiality, it having come to the ears of Abd'el Aziz that his vassal possessed at the moment a full purse. Ismail did not disappoint him in this regard. He presented his overlord with 50,000 Martini-Henry rifles of the latest pattern, and gave him for himself the sum of £900,000. To the Grand-Vizier he gave £25,000, to the Minister of War £15,000, and to other officials £20,000. Furthermore, he invited the Sultan to a superb fête, and at the end of the banquet with which it opened he presented to him a gorgeous Parisian dinner-service made of pure gold studded with large diamonds and other precious stones. In return for these gifts he received a *firmân* granting him practical sovereignty over Egypt, liberty to contract loans without the interference which lately had been threatened, and power to make certain commercial, but not political, treaties with foreign countries. At the same time, however, Egypt's tribute to the Porte was raised to £682,000; and at that figure it remained till present times. In view of recent events, it is interesting to note also some of the

other points in the arrangement then made
between Turkey and Egypt. It was agreed that
Egypt should remain an integral part of the
Turkish Empire, and that taxes should be collected, and coinage issued, in the name of the
Sultan. The Egyptian Army should be at the
service of the Porte in the event of that Power
being at war; and in order to demonstrate the
fact that Egyptian troops were actually under the
authority of the Sultan, it was agreed that all
orders should be given in Turkish and all ranks
should be described in that language. It was
understood also that Turkish troops might cross
Egyptian territory on their way to Tripoli, or
might use Egyptian harbours for their transports.

On his return to Egypt, Ismail found himself in
very great financial straits; and together with his
Minister of Finance, by name Ismail Sadyk, he
was obliged to devise all manner of means for
relieving his embarrassment. Sadyk was a cruel
and cunning little man, at this time much given
to taking small doses of neat brandy at all hours
of the day and night. He was on terms of the
greatest intimacy with his master; and when they
were not poring together over their disreputable
cash-books and ledgers, they were usually eating,
drinking, or making merry with one another in the
palace. Sadyk now devised a wonderful scheme
for raising the urgently needed funds: it was

known as the *Moukabaleh*, or "Act of Compensa-
tion." The plan was that the peasants should pay
in advance six years' land tax, and, in return, half
of the tax should be for ever redeemed. It was
hoped that by this means some £28,000,000 would
be raised at once; but although pamphlets were
issued pointing out that the money was required
to free Egypt from the clutches of wicked European
usurers, and that all patriots should make this
heroic effort for the saving of their country, only
the wealthy landowners responded to the appeal,
the small holders being already too fleeced to be
able to find the money, and not more than
£8,000,000 was raised. Ismail was obliged, therefore, to turn once more to Europe; and, after
considerable difficulty, he borrowed, in 1873,
from Messrs Oppenheim the nominal sum of
£32,000,000, the net value of which was not more
than £17,000,000. In the following year he
borrowed a further £3,000,000, and also raised
a native loan of £3,420,000.

Having some reason to be annoyed with the
Sultan of Darfur, a country situated beyond his
southern frontiers, Ismail now thought that it
might be profitable to annex his dominions; and
he therefore despatched an expedition to those
regions. The enemy was easily conquered, and
the Sultan and his family were brought in chains
to Cairo, where, so it is said, Ismail caused them
to be quietly murdered. Similar tactics were

applied to Abyssinia both in 1873 and 1875, but the campaigns were not altogether successful, and the Treasury gained nothing by them.

Ismail and Sadyk were now at their wits' end, for already in 1875 all the money which had been borrowed or raised in taxes was exhausted, and not another piastre could be flogged out of the peasants. In despair, Treasury bonds were issued to the extent of as much as £400,000 in return for cash advances of £100,000 at 20 per cent. Egyptian credit had fallen to its lowest level, and nowhere could financiers be found who would take the risk of lending the princely spendthrift another pound. During this time Ismail retained his cheerful demeanour in a most remarkable manner. He never appeared to be ruffled, and his behaviour to those around him was invariably considerate and gracious. Even those most opposed to him were obliged to admit that he made a gallant struggle against the crushing consequences of his extravagance; and it would even seem that the fighting instincts in his nature found a desired vent in the battles which he daily fought against his creditors and against the controllers of his finances. It was at this period of gloom and despair that England came to the rescue, through Disraeli's astute purchase of the Suez Canal shares for £4,000,000, a move which has proved most hugely profitable to England, and which at the time saved Egypt from immediate ruin. No sooner did it become known that the British Government had made this investment, and was going, moreover, to send out a great financial expert—Mr Cave—to make a thorough examination of Egyptian finances, than Egyptian credit went up once more with a bound, and Ismail could have borrowed at that moment any sum he cared to ask for.   His hand was stayed, however, by the consideration of a scheme proposed by Messrs Goschen and Joubert, by which the whole of the Khedive's debts were to be consolidated into a preference 5 per cent stock of £17,000,000 and a general unified debt of £59,000,000.

Sadyk was strongly opposed to this scheme, but Ismail, on the other hand, was in favour of it; and thus it came about that the friendship of these two experts in abnormal finance was brought to a sudden end.   The Khedive felt that his Minister stood in the way of a successful termination of his difficulties, and, without further to-do, he determined to rid himself of the encumbrance.   On November 9, 1876, therefore, he behaved himself towards his old friend in such a manner that Sadyk was obliged to tender his resignation.   The letter in which he did so, however, was worded in a somewhat insulting manner, and Ismail's placid temper was considerably ruffled.   On the following day his Highness sent a message to the fallen Minister inviting him to drive with him, as was their wont in the past; and Sadyk, believing that

Ismail desired to patch up the quarrel, accepted the invitation with alacrity. At the palace he was received by the Khedive most cordially, and together the two men took their seats in the carriage, laughing and chatting in the most friendly manner. Thus they drove to the Ghezireh Palace outside the city,[1] but as the carriage pulled up at the door, the unsuspecting Sadyk was seized by waiting soldiers and was speedily locked in a room at the back of the building. If the story current both in native and European circles may be believed, he was then stripped of his clothes, and for the space of about an hour sat shivering in the corner, his eyes bleared by hard drinking and his face grey with fear. At length a powerful Arab was admitted into the room and was told by an officer who was present to make an end of the miserable little man, either by strangling him with his hands or by employing some other method which would leave few tell-tale marks upon the body.[2] The Arab chose one of the latter alternatives. For a few moments he chased the naked financier, leaping and screaming, around the room, and then, having caught him, silenced his shrieks by placing a hand over his mouth. Sadyk, in his agony, fastened his teeth into his murderer's thumb and bit it off; but he was soon overpowered

---

[1] Now the Ghezireh Palace Hotel.

[2] Lord Cromer, in his 'Modern Egypt,' records his belief that the murder took place a few days later on board a Nile steamer.

and done to death. His body was then carried
down to the Nile and thrown into the water.

Ismail, meanwhile, drove back to Cairo and
announced that Sadyk had been arrested for
treason, having incited the natives to revolt and
having stirred up religious animosity both against
Europeans and against the Khedive.   On the next
day it was announced that the late Minister had
been banished to Dongola, where it was to be
supposed that he would die of drink.   His estates,
valued at some £3,000,000, were confiscated and
sold, the profits going for the most part to Ismail ;
and thus terminated a partnership, the twin
members of which had been responsible for the
wasting of more millions of money than had any
other two persons in the world.

The Khedive was now so pressed for cash, and
so pestered by the bondholders, whose money had
been advanced to him for so many years, that in
March 1877 he was obliged. to sign a decree
appointing commissioners to inquire into the
general state of Egyptian finances.   With extraordinary astuteness, he proposed to the English
and French Governments that the task should be
entrusted to General Gordon and M. de Lesseps.
Now Gordon was a peculiar idealist, whose views
on finance were palpably absurd, and whose knowledge of human nature was that of a child.   He
had a profound admiration for Ismail, and had
expressed the amazing hope that, on his death-

bed, he himself might feel that he had been as good and honest a man as the Khedive. Ismail realised that Gordon was at that time the idol of the British public, and he was aware that de Lesseps, in like manner, was a popular favourite in France, as being the adventurous engineer who had carried out the great work of cutting the Suez Canal. In Gordon he saw a man who would look into the state of the country's finances in the belief that they were above suspicion; and in de Lesseps he hoped to find a friend who was closely bound to him by the ties of mutual understanding and common interests. The proposal, however, was not accepted; and indeed General Gordon, in what has been described as "one of his rare flashes of common-sense," declined to undertake the task. A commission of six persons was appointed, of whom the three most noteworthy members were Mr Rivers Wilson, Major Baring (afterwards Lord Cromer), and Monsieur de Blignières. They sat from April 13 to August 19, 1878, and to the Khedive's horror and dismay they came to the conclusion that he himself was mainly responsible for the excessive expenditure, and that practically the whole of his private estate must be included in the list of assets which was to be drawn up. For some time he refused to consent to their demands; but at length, being urged by the threat of deposition, he gave way. At the same time, awed by his responsibilities, he agreed to rule in future through the medium of a responsible Ministry; and he therefore appointed one of his most tried statesmen, Nubar Pasha, as Premier, Mr Wilson as Minister of Finance, and M. de Blignières as Minister of Public Works. For a short time he took considerable delight in foisting all difficulties on to this Ministry; and to all those who asked him awkward questions he replied: "You must speak to my Ministers. It is they who govern, not I." But after a while he tired of this diversion, and began to feel the need for action. He found it impossible to tolerate the dominance of Nubar, who was both an Armenian Christian and an honest man, and he felt it extremely distasteful to submit to the scrutiny of his Ministry. For the first time in his life he experienced the touch of the cold hand of restraint; and so vital had a sense of power become to him that the very thought of impotence caused him the keenest distress. He therefore began now to scheme for the overthrow of the Ministry, and it was not long before an opportunity presented itself. A large number of Egyptian officers had been retrenched from the army by order of Mr Wilson, whose laudable desire was to cut down expenses in all directions; but by some oversight these unfortunate men had not received the full amount of pay due to them. They made representations to the Khedive, and it would seem that Ismail played upon them his favourite joke of shifting all responsibility to his Ministers. How far he actually took these disaffected officers into his confidence is not known; but it is certain from their subsequent conduct that they regarded him as their friend. One morning, while Nubar and Wilson were driving towards the Ministry, they openly attacked the two Ministers, and with cries of " Death to the Christians !" surrounded their carriages and severely hustled them. No blows were struck, however, and the two men were at last able to force their way into their offices, where they remained besieged by the mob for about two hours. At the end of this time Ismail, fat and omnipotent, appeared upon the scene in the guise of a deliverer. The crowd dispersed at once, as if by arrangement ; and the Khedive returned to his palace with the pleasant knowledge that he had fairly demonstrated his power as real Sovereign of Egypt.

A day or two later, as though in response to a public demand, he dismissed Nubar from office ; and on April 7, 1879, he issued a statement to the effect that, in view of the public dislike of the two foreign Ministers, he could not be responsible for their safety should they remain in office, and that, therefore, he considered it prudent to dispense with their services. A few days later the Commission, which had once more met to inquire further into the state of the finances, finding the Khedive still sufficiently powerful to obstruct their work and to refuse to fall in with their recommendations, registered their protest against the existing conditions by resigning ; and thus once more Ismail found himself monarch of all he surveyed.

During the whole of this troubled period the revels and fêtes at the palace had proceeded with undiminished splendour. Night after night magnificent dinner - parties were given, and the strangest companies of European, American, and Egyptian guests sat down upon the priceless Sèvres chairs to discuss the dainty French dishes, which were served to them upon jewel-studded plates of solid gold.   At these functions the corpulent Khedive presided with his accustomed good-humour, rolling his divergent eyes from one to another of his friends, and raising his glass in his awkward hand to their very good health. During the daytime he was busy forming a plan for the payment of his debts, and so great was his confidence in his own sagacity that he believed the scheme would be accepted by the bondholders. He did not think that either France or England would be able to persuade the Sultan to depose him, for he had proved too constant a source of financial help to his overlord thus to be discarded. He therefore banished care from his mind, and gave himself freely to the enjoyment of his still enormous fortune.

The crash came unexpectedly. Those who will consider the erratic methods of German diplomacy will recall to mind with no surprise the sudden action of Prince Bismarck in this year 1879, when, without any reason other than a desire to assert its authority, and to frustrate Franco-British policy in North Africa, the Berlin Government threatened immediate and active interference in Egyptian affairs, unless the Khedive were deposed and the financial questions settled. After a short period of astonished consternation, England and France joined with Germany in requiring the Sultan to depose Ismail; and on June 25, 1879, his Highness received a telegram from Abd'el Aziz, addressed to "Ismail Pasha, *late* Khedive of Egypt," informing him that henceforth his son Tewfik was to reign in his stead.

The blow was sudden and overwhelming, but Ismail, with fine courage, met it in a calm and most dignified manner. To his Ministers he said: "Send for *his Highness*, Tewfik Pasha, at once"; and when they had brought the agitated young man to his father, the deposed potentate bowed himself before him and kissed his hand, saluting him as Khedive. Ismail had often declared—rather unjustly it would seem—that Tewfik was a fool, unworthy to sit upon the throne of Egypt; and it must have been with feelings of the utmost bitterness that he did homage to his despised and unloved son, who now stood trembling before him. Retiring to the *harîm*, the ex-Khedive at once busied himself with preparations for his departure. He selected from amongst his numerous wives those who most pleased him; but no sooner was the choice made than the rejected ladies, breaking into a frenzy of anger, smashed every article of furniture upon which they could lay their fair hands, the damage being estimated afterwards at nearly £10,000. Ismail then collected from them all the jewellery which from time to time he had given them; and for several days he employed a number of jewellers in removing all precious stones from their settings in order that they might be more easily portable. He next caused most of the valuables in the palace to be packed, twenty-two superb services of gold plate which he selected to take with him being alone worth £800,000. It is declared by some that he also laid hands on some £300,000 which was then lying in cash in the palace treasury. On June 30 the packing-cases containing this wonderful collection of treasures were sent down by goods train to the Khedivial yacht *Mahroussa*, which was lying in readiness at Alexandria; and in the afternoon of the same day Ismail followed in a special train, accompanied by his selected *harîm*, his sons, Hussein (the present Sultan) and Hassan, and a small suite. On his arrival on board the yacht towards evening, many European and Egyptian notables of Alexandria came to

wish him *bon voyage;* and it was while bidding
these persons farewell that the ex-Khedive, for
the first and last time, showed any signs of
emotion. Turning from them with tears in his
eyes, he retired to his cabin; the cables were
almost immediately slipped; and amidst the
saluting thunders of the guns in the forts and
on the English battleships in the harbour, the
yacht passed out into the Mediterranean as the
summer sun went down.

A few days later Ismail arrived at Naples, and
took up his residence at the Favorita Palace, near
Portici, where he lived for some years; but in the
early 'eighties he abandoned Italy, and for a long
time lived an itinerant existence, passing from one
European city to another in restless dissatisfaction.
He was still received with deference at many noble
houses; and in London or Paris he was constantly
the guest of honour at large society functions. But
the kings and queens who had once been proud to
call themselves his friends now no longer received
him as their equal; and not for one moment did
he cease to be tormented by the thought of his
fallen glory. Day after day throughout these
years he plotted and schemed for his restoration
to power; and enormous were the bribes he offered
to any person who showed signs of a desire to assist
him in the attainment of his object. In spite, however, of the constant failure of his plans and the
protracted disappointments which he suffered, his

genial demeanour never deserted him, and on all occasions he did his best to make himself pleasant and agreeable to those around him.   At last, in 1887, he was invited by the Sultan to take up his residence at Constantinople, and, weary of his wandering life, he at length agreed to do this. No sooner had he set foot in Turkey, however, than he became a political prisoner; and never again was he permitted to leave that country. For eight years he lived the miserable existence of a man shadowed by the police.   He was suffering from a serious liver complaint, but in vain he implored the Sultan to permit him to go to Carlsbad for its treatment.   His petitions were ignored; and, in almost constant pain, the last years of his life were dragged out in the hopeless seclusion of his guarded palace.   The whole pleasure of his life had lain in the possession of power, and in the ability to display himself to all men as the mighty ruler of an ancient land; and when he found himself cast out from his kingdom and trapped in that country whose homage he had hoped one day to receive, the condition of his mind was such that death must have come to him as a most happy release from the miseries of his life.

CHAPTER IV.

AHMED PASHA ARÂBI.

ON September 21, 1911, there died at Helouan, near Cairo, a venerable but apparently quite un-distinguished old Egyptian of the peasant class, who, some thirty odd years ago, from a precarious situation as doorkeeper to a small Levantine warehouseman in Alexandria, pushed his way, as it were by the aid of an ironical Fortune, into the office of Commander-in-Chief of the Egyptian army and Dictator of the country's destinies, only to be bundled back into obscurity once more after an ecstatic month or two, like a discarded doll into the cupboard. It is sometimes difficult to decide whether rather simple men have a special liability to become the tools of Destiny by reason of some potent quality only comprehended by men in their more sheep-like moments, or whether Fate, being very very young, selects her instruments with the most noteworthy gullibility. For Ahmed Arabi was unquestionably a man of no great intelligence and of no brilliance at all; and yet at one time he

found himself—somewhat bewildered, it is true—
in a position to measure swords with the armies
of Britain, and to set the entire civilised world to
discussing his personality.   How he came to reach
that elevated position is a matter of wonder to all
those who do not bear in mind the seeming ab-
surdities practised so often by Fortune, nor call a
kind of brutal simplicity one of Nature's particular
passes to eminence.   No one who saw the white-
bearded Arabi sitting half asleep in his little house
in Ceylon, or afterwards at Helouan, would have
dreamed that it had been his lot once to make all
the Powers thoroughly excited, and finally to go
to war with England; yet, so strangely do things
happen, this rough old man, whose death caused
not the slightest stir either in Egypt or in Europe,
was at one time the most important figure in the
Near East, and acted as a kind of burly monarch
of the Nile.

Ahmed Arabi was born in 1839, so far as he
knew, at a small village of the province of Char-
kieh, in Lower Egypt.   His father was a *fellah*,
or peasant, who owned two or three acres of
ground which he cultivated with his own hands,
bringing up his four sons to follow the same means
of livelihood.   The young Arabi thus passed his
youth without education and without any knowledge of the outside world; but, being of a restless
disposition, he made his way, while still in his
'teens, to Alexandria, where after some vicissitudes

he obtained a situation as *bowab*, or doorkeeper,
at a small warehouse. His large imposing figure
and strong massive features, however, soon caused
him to fall under the notice of the army recruiting
officers; and he was speedily conscribed, probably
at about the age of eighteen.

As a soldier he was a considerable success, and
it was not long before he received promotion. At
that time the Egyptian army was a mere rabble,
officered by men of all social grades. Any tinker
or tailor who had come into the good graces of an
important personage might be given a commission
in the army; or again, any private soldier or corporal who showed the slightest ascendancy over
his colleagues might suddenly find himself raised
to the rank of captain,—a position which carried
with it little more than the right to shout and
gesticulate on parade with freedom. At the death
of the Viceroy Said, in 1863, Arabi was already
a captain in the regiment which was permanently
on duty at the palace in Cairo; and, although still
under twenty-five years of age, he seems to have
been a somewhat conspicuous figure, not only by
reason of his hulking size and of his noisy, good-
natured boisterousness, but because of his rather
pushing and assertive manners.

One day, early in the reign of Ismail, a sad
misfortune befell the young man. He was be-
having in his usual hearty manner in front of
the palace, jesting, laughing, and indulging in

some form of horse-play, when the Khedive looked out of the window in a very black temper. "Upon my word," said his Highness, "you are more noisy than the big drum, and much less useful"; and therewith he gave orders for Arabi's immediate punishment. The punishment does not seem to have been severe, but it was sufficient to engender in his heart the most bitter resentment towards the Khedive, who was already much disliked by Egyptian military men owing to his favouritism towards the Turkish and Circassian officers, of whom there was a large number in the army. In this state of mind he attached himself to a secret society, whose aim was the deposition of the Khedive, thus relieving his distraught feelings by plotting all manner of calamities for his sovereign lord. Nothing, of course, resulted from these proceedings, and many years had passed before Arabi came into any prominence outside his small circle of discontented brother officers.

War broke out between Abyssinia and Egypt, and Arabi, now a man not far short of forty years of age, was placed in charge of the transports at Massowah. Being left to his own devices, he soon found that the job could be made a very profitable one to himself, and for some time he laboured wholeheartedly at the pleasurable task of amassing money at Government expense. In the end, however, a charge of corruption was brought against him, and he was disgraced and cashiered.

Stranded in Cairo with nothing to do, and with his heart full of hatred towards the Khedive Ismail, who had dismissed him, Arabi began to frequent El Azhar, the great Moslem college, where, in the open galleries, he listened to the lectures of the Mohammedan teachers, and learnt by heart a large number of passages from the Koran, which in after life he quoted on all possible occasions. This piety seems to have served him in good stead, for it was not long before he was pardoned by the Khedive and readmitted into the army—a fact, however, which did not deter him from joining once more the secret society, and resuming the intrigues against his Highness.

This society had now assumed some importance, and its power in the army was something of a menace to discipline. Arabi, by his vehement and incautious denunciations of the Khedive, came to be regarded as a moving spirit in its councils; and his rustic violence seems to have supplied just that touch of excitement to the community which made each member feel that at last he really was participating in big things. Too unwise to feel the need of restraint, Arabi ranted and cursed, and sent shivers of nervous ecstasy down the backs of his colleagues, thereby providing that very sensation for which every member of a secret society is in search. Somebody, however, betrayed them to Ismail, who at once sent for the ring-leaders. They went to the Palace with haggard faces and shaking knees, like so many naughty schoolboys, Arabi himself being in a most mortal fear. The Khedive, however, had no intention of being hard upon them. None realised better than he the delights of intrigue. He was, to use a paraphrase, always playing at Pirates and Red Indians himself; and he felt that, in this case, it would be much more amusing for them all to play together in one big game. He therefore, there and then, promoted the seventy worst offenders to be colonels in his army; and to Arabi, as being the most noisy of them all, he gave one of his concubines (in whom he had lost interest) to be his wife and helpmeet. Arabi then swore to defend Ismail's honour with his life, and to work only for his interests. Shortly after this, however, in 1879, Ismail was deposed, as we have seen in the last chapter; and, forty-eight hours after the deposition, Arabi was on his knee before the new Khedive, Tewfik, swearing to defend *his* honour till death.

With the deposition of Ismail it was agreed that the army, which now stood at some 45,000 men, should be reduced to 18,000; and this, of course, produced very considerable discontent in military circles. A great many officers had to be put on half-pay, and much annoyance was caused to the Egyptians when it was found that the majority of Turkish and Circassian officers serving in the army were retained on the active list.

Arabi, now a full colonel in command of the 4th Regiment, at once recommenced his intrigues, and soon became the not unwilling tool of a certain cunning Turkish officer named Mahmoud Sami, who had his own axe to grind. Sami induced Arabi and two other colonels, Ali Fehmy, commanding the 1st Regiment, and Abd' el 'Al, to write a petition to the Khedive, asking that the Minister of War, Osman Rifki, should be dismissed, and that an inquiry should be held into the qualifications of the foreign officers who had recently received promotion,—"for," said the petitioners, in the true Egyptian manner, "we ourselves are far superior to those who have been elevated."

The petition was insolent in tone, and it was presently decided to put the three signatories under arrest. On February 1, 1881, on the pretext that arrangements had to be made for a certain procession which was about to take place, they were ordered to appear at Kasr-el-Nil barracks, which stand on the east bank of the Nile; and the location of this building suggested to Arabi's ignorant mind that they were about to be done to death. He had reason to suppose, he declared, that a steamer was moored against the barrack-square, and upon this he and his friends were to be taken a short way down-stream. Iron chests were prepared on board, into which he and his colleagues were to be pushed, the chests being then dropped into the Nile. Their friend Sami

warned them that death in some horrible form no
doubt awaited them; and between them a plan
of action was concocted. It was decided that if
the three colonels had not returned from Kasr-el-
Nil after two hours had elapsed, their soldiers
should come to their rescue, led by Sami. Thus,
with this assurance but with heavy hearts, Arabi,
Ali Fehmy, and Abd' el 'Al were led off to their
unknown fate.

At the barracks their worst fears were realised.
They found themselves in the presence of a court-
martial, and were forthwith subjected to a cross-
examination of the most penetrating character.
Such procedure in Egypt, however, is always a
slow matter, and the two hours had elapsed before
the case for the prosecution began to form itself.
But it was never completed; for suddenly, with a
rush and a yell, the rescue party, some hundreds
strong, charged into the barracks and burst into
the court-room. Chairs and tables were upset,
the judges were pelted with their own manu-
scripts, and were good-humouredly tumbled head
first into the pools of ink which lay upon the
floor before them; the officers of the court were
pushed and bumped about by the soldiery; and
in a moment the court-martial presented a spectacle which might have suggested a scene in
' Alice in Wonderland.' Nobody, of course, was
hurt, for the Egyptians are inclined to treat these
affairs in the manner of a game, but everybody

was hot, and flushed, and splashed with ink; and in this condition the whole company, headed by the regimental band, marched over to the palace, where, in the courtyard before the windows, the three colonels demanded that Osman Rifki should resign from the Ministry of War in favour of Mahmoud Sami, that the Turkish and Circassian officers should be excluded from the service, and that the strength of the army should be increased.

It was now the height of the tourist season in Cairo, and it happened that the regimental band had an engagement to play at a hotel during the hour of tea. As the troops awaited the Khedive's decision, the bandmaster looked at his watch and reminded Arabi of the appointment, for the hour was drawing near. The officers knew quite well that if the band marched off the troops would wander away too, and the demonstration would prove a fiasco; but, on the other hand, nothing would persuade the bandsmen to neglect their remunerative engagement. The whole matter, therefore, resolved itself into the question as to whether the Khedive would hold out until the tourists' tea-time, or whether he would give in before that hour. Thus the mutinous officers spent their time in whispering and looking at their watches, or in turning anxious, pleading eyes towards the benign musicians, who did not seem to realise that they held at that moment the destinies of Egypt in their power.

The Khedive Tewfik, however, did not know of the musical arrangements for the day, and, after one last look at the formidable host outside his windows, decided to grant — for the moment—all their requests, whereupon the troops dispersed with cries of "Long live the Khedive!" and the band hurried off to play to the tourists at the hotel. On the next morning Arabi and his colleagues waited on the Khedive, and made their humble apologies to him for the disturbance of the previous day. They were extremely nervous as to their safety, and their deeds of the day before now seemed to them to have been terribly bold. They believed that the Khedive would find means of putting them to death, and, although his Highness accepted their protestations of loyalty, they looked for no mercy from him in the event of a return of his power.

For some months Arabi and his brother officers lived, thus, in a perpetual state of nervousness; but in July 1881 matters once more came to a head. The Khedive suddenly dismissed Mahmoud Sami from the Ministry of War, and the office was given to his Highness's brother-in-law, Daoud Pasha. At about the same time a story began to be circulated that Tewfik had obtained a secret *fetwa*, or decree, from the Shêkh - ul - Islam, the active head of the Mohammedan religion, authorising him to put the three colonels to death for high treason. There was no truth in this, but, on the other hand, there is no doubt that the Khedive intended to take drastic measures against them. On the night of September 8 a police agent visited the house of Arabi, but was refused admission. Being convinced that the man had been sent to murder him, Arabi hurried to the house where lived his two colleagues, who reported that they had received a similar visitor, to whom admission had likewise been refused. That night, therefore, they planned the great *coup* of the following day, by which the whole history of modern Egypt was decided. Sitting in a back room, with lights turned low, these three colonels, distracted, overwrought, and thoroughly frightened, agreed that a mutiny was their only possible means of escape, — that the time had come for them to lead their regiments to the Khedive's palace and to make their power recognised at the point of the sword.

On the next morning, September 9, the 3rd Regiment received orders to proceed at once to Alexandria, it being the obvious intention of the Government to diminish the numbers of the disaffected troops in Cairo. This order served as the signal for the mutiny; and, under the leadership of Arabi, the troops announced their intention of marching to Abdin Palace. On hearing this the Khedive was distracted; and, mistrusting in this moment of despair the advice of all his native councillors, sent for the one man upon whom he felt that he could rely, Sir Auckland Colvin, the British Controller-General of the Egyptian Debt. Sir Auckland believed that the only decent course to adopt was that of bold opposition to the mutineers, and he advised the Khedive to put himself immediately at the head of whatever loyal troops he could collect and to await the arrival of Arabi in formidable array. The Khedive seemed to agree to this, and together they drove over to the Abdin barracks, where the troops were known to be loyal. Here they were received with protestations of fidelity; and therefore with more confidence they drove on to the Citadel, where again the troops received them with approval. As it was now mid-afternoon, Sir Auckland Colvin advised the Khedive to march the loyal troops to Abdin; but his Highness, much elated by his apparent popularity, decided that it would be nice to drive on to the distant Abbassieh barracks where Arabi was lodged, in order to parley with the mutineers. This was done; but when they arrived they learnt, as everybody knew all the time, that Arabi had already marched with 2500 men and 18 guns to Abdin. The carriage was therefore turned, and, by making a long detour, the Khedive and Sir Auckland reached a back door of the palace without molestation. Hastening into one of the front rooms and looking through the windows, they saw that the court in front of the building was held by troops in open square, and that the 18 guns were trained upon the palace. The unwieldy Arabi could be seen prancing about on horseback, together with some of his brother officers, making a very brave show · in the light of the afternoon sun. Sir Auckland Colvin at once told the Khedive that without delay he must come out into the square and face his enemies. Together, therefore, they descended the great staircase and advanced towards the mutineers.

"When Arabi presents himself," whispered Sir Auckland to his Highness, "tell him to give you his sword, and to give the troops the order to disperse. Then go the round of the square and address each regiment separately." In a few moments Arabi approached, still on horseback. The Khedive, with some nervousness, told him to dismount. Arabi awkwardly obeyed, and, after disentangling himself, advanced on foot, having with him several officers and a guard with fixed bayonets.

"Now is your moment," said Sir Auckland to his Highness.

"We are between four fires," said the Khedive, adding after a while, "What can I do? We shall be killed."

A painful pause ensued, and at last the Khedive, much agitated, told Arabi to sheath his sword. Arabi, however, was himself so frightened that, though he hastily attempted to obey the order, his shaking hands would not fulfil their office, and for some moments the point of his sword rattled and blundered aimlessly around the mouth of the scabbard. The Khedive, getting control of his voice, then asked what all the trouble was about; and Arabi, wiping the cold sweat from his face, stated his demands — namely, that all the Ministers should be dismissed, that a Parliament should be convoked, and that the strength of the army should be increased. These demands in actual fact did not in any way represent the urgent wishes or needs of the people, and it would seem that they had been formulated without much consideration to serve as a *casus belli*. Arabi did not represent a patriotic movement, and at that time he was not popular outside the disaffected regiments. The proposal to increase the strength of the army, and thereby add further to the load of the tax-payer at a time when the country was painfully in debt, was neither wise nor magnanimous. However, with troops and guns facing them, the Khedive did not feel inclined to resist; and, turning to Sir Auckland, he gloomily remarked, "You hear what he says."

Sir Auckland replied somewhat sharply that it was not fitting for the Khedive to discuss such questions with his colonels, and advised him to retire to the palace. This his Highness did with great promptness, and Sir Auckland Colvin remained in the square for about an hour arguing with Arabi and his officers. Sir Charles Cookson, the acting British Consul-General, then arrived, and the negotiations were continued, the Khedive being consulted every now and then by means of messages.

At length his Highness agreed to dismiss his Ministers and to refer the other two points to the Porte. Sherif Pasha, chosen by the mutineers, was made President of the Council, the announcement being received with shouts of "Long live the Khedive!" Arabi then made his submission to his Highness, swearing once more to be a loyal servant of the throne, and the troops marched off in perfect quietness. The Khedive thereupon sat down and telegraphed to Constantinople for 10,000 Turkish troops with which to quell the mutineers (a request which was not granted), and Arabi, on his part, issued a kingly circular signed "Colonel Ahmed Arabi, representing the Egyptian army," assuring the consuls - general that he would continue to protect the interests of foreigners, and so forth.

Sherif Pasha having agreed to take office only on condition that the disaffected regiments should leave Cairo, Arabi, nervous for his own safety and horrified by his own daring, thought it would be prudent to comply. He therefore retired to Suez, and his colleagues were sent to Damietta. His departure from Cairo had the nature of a royal progress through the streets, for the deeds of September 9 had made him very popular; and at the railway station he made a speech, stating that a new era had dawned for Egypt. At Zagazig a fête was held in his honour, at which about a thousand persons were present; and here he made another speech, urging the dismissal of all Europeans in Egyptian Government employment, and stating that he had three regiments in Cairo which could be relied on to carry out his wishes. At about this time Arabi made a long statement to Sir Auckland Colvin, the tone of which was curiously naïve and ignorant. At great length, and with much labour, he explained that men came of one common stock and should have equal rights, and that it was for equal rights that the army contended. He now disclaimed his desire to get rid of foreigners, explaining that they were the necessary instructors of the people, and pointing out that they had given him the only schooling he had ever had. The impression left on the mind of Sir Auckland by this declamation was that Arabi was a sincere, but not at all a practical, man.

In the first week of January 1882 Arabi was recalled to Cairo and made Under-Secretary for War, it being felt that it was better for him to belong to the Government than to be outside it; whereupon he at once began again to plot against the Khedive. At about this time there appeared in 'The Times' a manifesto demanding Egypt for the Egyptians, and asking that all foreigners should be dismissed; and it was generally supposed that it was written or suggested by Arabi. Various letters signed "Ahmed the Egyptian" appeared in the papers, and people in England began to question whether Arabi was not, after all, a noble patriot.

On February 5 Arabi managed to get himself made Minister of War, and now, with the army at his back, he felt that he could call himself virtual ruler of Egypt. He used his power in the most extravagant manner. Fresh battalions were raised, in the main with the object of giving employment to the numerous officers who supported his cause. Pay was increased all round, in spite of the desperate financial state of the country. Hundreds of officers were promoted; and when the Khedive remarked that there should be some sort of examination before promotion, Arabi replied, firstly, that the officers were of such well-known capacity that examination was unnecessary, and secondly, that they refused to be examined. He declared openly at this time that he did not see why a hereditary Khedivate was necessary, and that if the dynasty were abolished £300,000 a year would be economised.

Arabi's quarrel with the Khedive was now made more bitter by the following occurrence. Nineteen Circassian and Egyptian officers, desiring to rid themselves of the colonels of their regiments, Abd'

el 'Al and Arabi, were said to have plotted to
disgrace the one and to murder the other. Into
this charge an official inquiry had to be made.
Abd' el 'Al was, as we have seen, one of the
three ringleaders in the mutiny, and his disgrace
was therefore a matter which closely touched
Arabi. The evidence was heard by a court of
Egyptian officers on April 2, 1882; and, considering the rivalry and enmity between the
Circassians and Egyptians, the result was, of
course, a foregone conclusion. Abd' el 'Al was
shown to be entirely innocent in the opinion of
the court, and the plot to murder Arabi was
proved. The nineteen officers, together with
twenty-one other persons, mostly Turkish or Circassian, including the late Minister of War, Osman
Rifki, were sentenced to banishment for life to
the remotest part of the Sudan, a sentence practically equivalent to that of death. This flagrant
injustice was deeply resented by the Khedive, who,
very rightly, refused to confirm the sentence. By
his orders the officers were removed temporarily
from the active list of the army, and after a short
time had elapsed were reinstated.

The fight between the Khedive and the army
led to the utmost disorder in the country, and the
position of Europeans became far from safe. The
maintenance of law and order under the circumstances was impossible, and throughout Egypt,
murder, robbery, and crime of all kinds were rife.

This being so, the English and French Consuls-General advised their respective Governments to interfere, and, on May 15, 1882, after prolonged discussion as to whether the duty of restoring order should be left to Turkey (a solution of the difficulty strongly advocated by England), the Egyptian Government was advised that an Anglo-French fleet had sailed for Alexandria. Arabi at once circulated a statement that if the English and French were allowed to interfere, it would mean the disbanding of the army, the dismissal of the Ministry, and all manner of other troubles. In reply to this the Consuls-General on May 25 demanded the forcible retirement of Arabi from Egypt for one year; but the only effect of the note was that Arabi and the entire Ministry resigned. On May 28 the chiefs of the various religions, Moslem, Coptic, Jewish, &c., waited on the Khedive and begged him to reinstate Arabi as the Minister of War, for Arabi had threatened them all with death unless they persuaded his Highness to do so. The colonel of the palace guard, meanwhile, stated that he had received orders to keep his Highness a prisoner in the palace, and to shoot him if he attempted to escape. Under these circumstances the Khedive was obliged to reinstate the rebellious colonel.

In the opinion of the masses his return to office meant the expulsion of all foreigners from Egypt, and the triumph of the Egyptian national party;

and consequently a number of outrages against Christians were perpetrated.   The ill - temper of the people was increased by the arrival of the Anglo - French fleets, which assembled at Alexandria during the first week in June.   A further complication ensued.   The Sultan, as suzerain of Egypt, sent over a Commissioner, Dervish Pasha, with orders to assert Turkish authority.   He was received royally at Alexandria on June 7, but on his arrival in Cairo he was much annoyed by the mob of Egyptians who surrounded his carriage and shouted the praises of Arabi in his ears.   Upon the next day the Ministers, all of the Arabi party, came to call upon him in a body, but the Turk received them with marked discourtesy, remaining seated upon the divan in conversation with his secretary, whilst the Egyptians stood awkwardly before him. Every now and then Dervish would smile pleasantly at them, but he made no attempt to treat them as intelligent beings.   Presently he asked his secretary to repeat to him the tale of how Mohammed Ali had rid himself of the Egyptian Mamelukes who had annoyed him.   The secretary thereupon related how they had all been beguiled into the Citadel and there set upon and massacred, only one escaping by jumping his horse from the ramparts into the street below.   "Ah," said Dervish, turning a benign face to the Ministers, "the man who escaped *was* a lucky dog"; and, with a brief remark on the weather, he dismissed them.

On June 10 Arabi, acting through the Ulema
of Cairo, sent a deputation to the Commissioner,
and a certain well-known rebel delivered a speech
in praise of Arabi.   But this was too much for the
Turk, who, briefly remarking that he had come
to give instructions and not to listen to sermons,
ordered the orator to be thrown out of the room.

Having received this snub, and believing that
the Sultan's representative intended to support the
Khedive against him, Arabi felt that the time had
come to set Egypt in a blaze, so that all men might
turn to him for protection, and thus his power
might become absolute.   What drastic step he
contemplated is not known, for on the next day,
June 11, a terrible event occurred which brought
matters at once to a definite issue.

For some days the natives resident in the low
quarters of Alexandria had been showing signs of
an intended attack upon Christians living in the
same quarter.   Several Greeks and Italians had
received warnings, and the British Consul had
taken some steps for the protection of British
subjects.   The foreign fleets lying in the harbour
were, as has been said, a further cause of irritation to the natives, for the presence of the battleships made the Europeans somewhat confident,
and, in certain cases, offensive.   The morning of
June 11 passed quietly, and, it being Sunday,
the Europeans attended their churches in the
customary manner.   Early in the afternoon, how-

ever, a Maltese Greek and an Arab had a dispute
about some money, and in the conflict which ensued
the Arab was stabbed in the stomach. Instantly
a crowd collected, and a riot followed, which was
fortunately confined to certain quarters of the
town. About sixty Europeans of the lower classes
were killed under circumstances of great brutality;
and it is said that over a hundred Arabs also met
their deaths. The British Consul escaped with his
life by a miracle. The native Governor of Alexandria communicated with Cairo and asked what
he should do, but there the utmost confusion
reigned administratively, and the only man whose
orders were listened to, Arabi, was sulking, owing
to his treatment at the hands of the Turkish
Commissioner. Arabi seems to have expressed
his opinion that he could stop the riot by telegraph at any moment, but that Dervish Pasha
must ask him to do so; and thus, at last, the
haughty Turk was obliged to come to see Arabi
and to beg him to issue the necessary orders.
Arabi, quite unmoved by the loss of life which
was momentarily occurring, and caring only for
his personal prestige, loftily consented to put an
end to the riot. He telegraphed to the Governor
to call out the troops, who had until now remained
in barracks, and immediately the mob dispersed.

Mr Farman, an American judge, at that time
resident in Alexandria, describes how he walked
down from his hotel to the Place Mohammed Ali,

after the troops had been called out, to learn what was happening; but he saw only a few persons dispersing before the military. In his published account of these events he makes light of the affair, and says that for three days afterwards no one termed it anything other than a lamentable and serious riot, commenced by a foreigner. It was the papers, he declares, which worked it up into a "massacre." Mr Charles Royle, an English judge, however, is of a very different opinion; and his description of the fighting, or rather of the murders, in the streets is gruesome in the extreme. Be this as it may, there can be no doubt that the blame is to be attributed, indirectly if not directly, to Arabi. It was he who had instigated the natives to acts of lawlessness, and who had inculcated in them those anti-foreign sentiments which found vent in the riot. He must have known the trend of events in Alexandria, and it would seem that he had almost purposely refrained from instructing the Governor and the troops as to how to act in the event of trouble. Arabi here showed himself to be a stupid, ignorant peasant, without foresight and without magnanimity; and that he did not hang for his misdeeds was due only to the forbearance of the British public.

On the night following the riot many of the European residents collected in the consulates, where they passed the long hours in painful suspense. It was agreed that it would be most inadvisable to land any force from the battle-ships, for a general massacre might ensue, and the three or four hundred available bluejackets and marines would not be able to protect more than a limited number of the Christian popu-lation. The next morning, however, tranquillity was restored, and the Europeans, who immediately began to seek refuge on the ships in the harbour, were not molested as they made their way to the docks. The exodus both from Cairo and from Alexandria soon became very general, although the peace of the former city had not been dis-turbed; and during the next three weeks or so the Alexandria sea-front is said to have presented a most lively spectacle. The men-o'-war lying in the harbour with flags flying, the steamers and sailing-ships of all nationalities surrounded by small craft, the rowing- and sailing-boats passing to and fro between the quays and this crowded fleet of vessels, presented in the brilliant June weather a most cheery and animated scene. The native boatmen haggled and bargained, jested and laughed, with the refugees, as though the events of June 11 had never occurred.

Meanwhile an attempt was made to bring the ringleaders of the riot to justice; but Arabi, choosing to believe that the fault lay as much on the one side as on the other, declared that he would not allow any Arab to be executed unless, for every one, a European was also hanged. Shortly after this the Sultan sent Arabi the grand cordon of the Order of the Medjidieh, in recognition of the services he had rendered to Islam ; and the Order had to be handed personally to him by the Khedive.

Egyptian hostility to foreigners had now reached a most dangerous pitch, and Arabi was carried along by the wave of warlike enthusiasm which he himself had done so much to arouse. He was aware that the French and English Governments, mistrusting one another, were hesitating to decide upon a course of action, and that the proposal to introduce Turkish troops into Egypt was not likely to be put into execution. He felt a profound contempt for the European fleets, under whose very guns the Alexandria riots had taken place. Moreover, there were certain Englishmen of unbalanced mind who, posing as his friends, pretended that they had great influence with the British public, always ready as it was to support a patriotic movement. They had induced Arabi to write letters to the papers full of nationalist fervour, and had done their utmost to arouse in the rustic mind of the mutinous colonel those patriotic sentiments which were so foreign to his nature. Patriotism is an intellectual pursuit, unknown to those who lack education,— for the sentiment which so often passes as patriotism both in Egypt and elsewhere is simply ignorant dislike of the foreigner. Arabi was not a patriot; he was a hater of Europeans. He did not care a brass farthing about his country as a whole, he did not work to make better the lot of the masses. He blindly plotted and schemed and intrigued and mutinied in order to place in the hands of himself and his friends the power to act as he might choose. He had no definite schemes in view: he talked vaguely of deposing the Khedive, of calling a parliament, of expelling all foreigners, and so forth; but he knew not, either by experience or by consecutive thought, what would be the result of his enterprises. Let him get *power:* that was all. Lord Cromer has recorded his belief that, during the first stages of the revolt, Arabi was impelled simply by fear for his personal safety; but now he was urged forward by sheer joy in the possession of power, a form of intoxication against which his simple mind was in no way proof.

Defying the fleets in the harbour, Arabi now prepared for war by strengthening the fortresses at Alexandria and by attempting to institute a general conscription for the army. The Sultan, acting in agreement with the British and French Governments, ordered Dervish Pasha to stay Arabi's hand; but on July 5, at a Council of Ministers, Arabi made a violent speech against the Turks, and commanded the officers of the Egyptian army to discontinue all communication

AHMED PASHA ARÂBI.

with the Sultan's representative. Thus his quarrel now was not only with the Khedive and with the European Powers who wished, for the sake of law and order, to support his Highness, but also with the Porte. He had played his cards as badly as was to be expected of him, and with the army at his back he now turned blindly to face the consequences of his folly.

When Admiral Seymour, who was in command of the British fleet, became aware that the fortifications opposite his ships were being strengthened, and that guns were being mounted, he conferred with the French Admiral, both telegraphing to their Governments for instructions. The British Government, until now most averse to meddling with Egyptian matters, advocated a bombardment, but the French Government strongly disapproved of this course, and for some days an animated discussion was kept up. At last, however, the British Government, realising the seriousness of the situation, telegraphed to Admiral Seymour instructing him to bombard the forts unless the strengthening works therein were abandoned. "Before taking any hostile step," said the telegram, "invite co-operation of French Admiral; but you are not to postpone acting on your instructions because French decline to join."

On July 10 Admiral Seymour informed the Military Commandant of Alexandria that unless the fortresses were temporarily surrendered to

him for the purpose of disarmament, he would
bombard them on the next morning. He received
an unsatisfactory reply, and consequently informed
the French of his intentions. The Gallic Admiral
thereupon ordered the ships under his command to
withdraw to Port Said, and at the same time all
the foreign vessels took their departure. As each
one steamed past the British flagship in the light
of the sunset, Admiral Seymour's band played
the national anthem of the departing vessel;
and thus, with the most pleasant international
courtesies, the foreign fleets left England to solve
the Egyptian question. When darkness fell the
British men-o'-war alone remained on the scene.

There were still a number of lower-class
Europeans left in Alexandria, and these fortified
themselves in the consulates and other buildings.
All the remaining British residents, with two or
three exceptions, betook themselves to the P. & O.
ss. *Tanjore*, and Sir Auckland Colvin and other
high officials went quietly on board a battleship
during the afternoon.

On the next morning the natives began to leave
the city in enormous numbers; and just before
7 A.M., when the watering-carts were sprinkling
the streets and the incredulous *bowabs* were yawn-
ing and smoking their early cigarettes, a warning
bell was rung and a signal shot was fired. Immediately the bombardment commenced. Arabi
had stationed himself in the Arsenal at the

Ministry of Marine, but as soon as the shells began to fall in that quarter he moved over to certain fortifications which, being behind a hill, were less exposed. The Khedive, meanwhile, remained in his summer palace at Ramleh, a few miles outside the city; and during the day he continued in constant communication with Arabi, sending through him encouraging messages to the Egyptian troops who were working the guns in the fortresses with considerable courage. The fire from the men-o'-war was murderous, and it was not long before the Egyptian response began to be silenced. By noon only two forts, Adda and Pharos, were still offering resistance. The British sailors seem to have had the time of their lives, for there were hardly any casualties on our side, and the forts made most interesting targets. Light-hearted messages were exchanged between the ships, as though the whole affair was a pleasant game. The *Sultan*, for example, signalled to the *Inflexible* about noon : "If you happen to be steaming in the direction of Adda and Pharos, one or two shells from your heavy guns would do much good, if you don't mind." At 1.30 P.M. the same vessel signalled to the *Superb*: "Can you touch up Pharos a bit?"

The firing continued all day, and, as may be imagined, the havoc wrought amongst the Egyptian troops was very terrible. The towns-people, meanwhile, amused themselves by looting the shops; and it is not to be wondered at that several Europeans were killed by the angry mob, who, however, made no serious attempts to massacre the foreigners in the consulates. The refugees in the Danish consulate were at one time in considerable danger, but a shell which burst near by, killing three natives, dispersed the mob. The German Hospital, wherein numerous Europeans were collected, was attacked by the natives, but one of the inmates having produced a revolver, the invaders discreetly retired. The famous Hôtel Abbat was saved from looting by the presence of mind of the native caretaker. As soon as the mob began to batter at the door the Egyptian uttered a string of the most frightful British oaths, which at various times he had learnt from Jack Tar. Immediately the looters stopped short, and, crying out "There are English gentlemen here," fled down the street.

At seven o'clock in the evening the Khedive sent for Arabi and had some consultation with him, and Arabi explained that the forts were all destroyed. Negotiations were therefore opened with the British Admiral, who, early next morning, declared that unless he was allowed peaceably to land his men at three points he would recommence the bombardment at 2 P.M. Arabi at once began to argue the matter, until, nothing being settled, the vessels were obliged to open fire once more. Arabi, fearing that the Khedive might communicate with the fleet, now decided to make him a prisoner, and therefore sent 400 men to surround the palace, at the same time distributing a sum of £2000 amongst the loyal Bedouîn who had appointed themselves the Khedive's protectors, and showed some signs of actually protecting him. This bribe induced them to retire, and for several hours his Highness was surrounded by troops who, for all he knew, might have had orders to murder him. It was a trying position for him, and he is said to have shown great fortitude under the strain. In the afternoon Arabi decided to retreat from Alexandria, and, leaving 250 men to keep the Khedive prisoner, he marched out of the city with all his troops, taking up his position ultimately at a point some miles inland. The 250 men at once declared their loyalty to his Highness, and communication was established between the palace and the British Admiral.

Meanwhile looting went on steadily, and when the troops began to retreat the natives indulged in the maddest orgies of plundering ere they, too, fled from the city. Men were seen staggering along the roads carrying enormous gilt - framed mirrors, or plush and gilt pieces of furniture, upon their backs ; others were burdened with heavy clocks and vases ; and yet others were half-smothered beneath enormous bundles of valuable clothes. Turkish and Egyptian women flying towards the interior were robbed of their jewellery and were outraged on the public roads. At the gates of the city the looters were met by Bedouîn marauders, who fought them for the spoil, and scenes of the wildest confusion ensued.

Either by the orders of Arabi or at the instigation of the ringleaders of the mob, the city was now set on fire. Stores of paraffin having been looted, the oil was poured in all directions and lighted, with the result that very soon the city was in flames. All night long the conflagration raged, and by the next morning it became necessary for the Europeans still confined in the consulates to break their way through to the sea. They found the streets deserted, and had no difficulty in securing boats, in which they rowed out to the fleet.

The Khedive now informed Admiral Seymour that he wished to take up his residence at the palace of Ras-el-Tin, which stands on a promontory of land near the harbour. His Highness would here be under the protection of the fleet, and could easily steam out to them in his launch should the fire or the mob attack the palace in the rear. The Admiral approved of this move, and the Khedive therefore drove into the city, avoiding by a detour the areas already in flames, and passing on his way several retreating gangs of plunderers. At the palace he was met by a force of bluejackets, who, however, were not of sufficient strength to penetrate into the city to fight the flames.

On the next day, the 14th, as many men as could be spared were landed in the city; and on the following day reinforcements arrived from Malta, these being quickly landed. Conflagrations continued, however, until the 17th; but on the 18th the work of clearing the remains of the city commenced, the post-office was reopened, several looters caught in the act were summarily dealt with, one being shot, and some semblance of order was established. On the 16th some 200 Bedouîn of the desert—those lords of romance and adventure—made a determined attempt to loot a number of buildings which still remained undamaged. They had, however, only succeeded in capturing a donkey, when a small midshipman appeared before them with five or six bluejackets, shot two of their number with his revolver, and chased the remainder headlong out of the city. Incidentally a remark of another young midshipman may here be recorded. After he had marched about the smouldering ruins of the town all day, and had tried in vain amongst the looted shops to expend some of his accumulated pocket-money in making purchases from the returning tradesmen, he was asked by his superior officer what he thought of the inferno that had once been Alexandria. " Oh," he replied, " the place is nice enough; the only thing is, *jam* is so dear."

Arabi, as has been said, had entrenched himself at a village several miles inland, and he was reported to have with him a force of over 6000 men. On the 17th Commander Maude rode up to within 300 yards of his entrenchments and had a good look at them; but the British forces had yet no reason to make an attack upon the position. Behind the entrenchments the railway in Cairo stood intact, and Arabi was able to move freely between the two points. In Cairo there was considerable excitement, and in several smaller towns Europeans were murdered. Arabi rapidly gathered a large army, his methods of recruiting being described as "unscrupulous and barbarous." On the 21st the Egyptians dammed the canals which supplied Alexandria with drinking water, and later let salt water into the channels. This led to fighting between Arabi's army and the British troops, which were now arriving in considerable numbers, and it decided the home Government to despatch a large force to Egypt, with Turkish consent, France having refused to co-operate. On the 22nd the Khedive issued a decree declaring Arabi a rebel and traitor; but the authorities in Cairo replied with a decree confirming him in his office of Commander-in-Chief and Minister of War.

Desultory fighting continued for the next fortnight, while the British expeditionary force—sent with most remarkable reluctance by the home Government — was landing at Alexandria. On

August 10 the whole Brigade of Guards arrived, and marched through the streets out to Ramleh, the Duke of Connaught riding at their head. The Egyptians, accustomed to their own somewhat slovenly troops, were filled with awe at the magnificent bearing of these picked men, and reports of their might were conveyed to Arabi's unfortunate soldiers, troubling them much as they lay behind their entrenchments. On August 15 Sir Garnet Wolseley arrived to take up his command, and after making a hasty study of the position of the enemy, he ordered the entire army to embark on the waiting transports, giving out that he intended to land at Aboukir, a short way along the coast. In the afternoon of the 19th the ships steamed out of the harbour, and the sun rose next morning revealing to the Alexandrians a deserted sea.

Opposite Aboukir a number of battleships anchored and went through the pretence of clearing for action. The Egyptian troops, entirely deceived, concentrated on the sea-shore and in the forts, awaiting anxiously the opening of a bombardment; but when night fell the ships moved off, and hurried after the transports, which in reality were steaming hard for Port Said.

Now it will be remembered that the French fleet had retired to Port Said before the bombardment of Alexandria; and the presence of these vessels at this headquarters of the French Suez

Canal Company, which was presided over by the eminent engineer but violent Anglophobe, Monsieur de Lesseps, had turned the town into a Gallic stronghold. The sympathies of de Lesseps were entirely with Arabi, and the fear that the English might occupy what he considered as *his* canal led him to make a very hearty attempt to prevent such an event. The question as to whether the Canal should remain neutral or not was argued with passion in the French newspapers; and the feeling was general that, as an international explosion of the utmost magnitude might be expected if the English appeared at Port Said, such a manœuvre was altogether out of the question. De Lesseps at one time telegraphed to Arabi: "Jamais les Anglais n'y pénétreront — jamais, jamais!" to which Arabi replied: "Sincere thanks; assurances consolatory, but not sufficient under existing circumstances," and he went on to say that he would probably be obliged to destroy the canal, which communication must have sent the excitable de Lesseps into paroxysms of rage.

But while the British fleet and the transports were steaming on through the darkness of the night of the 19th-20th, those British battleships which had already arrived at Port Said carried out a daring *coup*, which formed an essential part of Sir Garnet Wolseley's plan of campaign. At 3.30 A.M. two companies of seamen and one of marines from the *Monarch*, and a small naval force and a company of marines from the *Iris*, with two Gatling guns, were landed in the profoundest silence. So stealthily were the boats rowed ashore that the sentries on the French battleship *La Gallissonière*, moored to the same buoy as the *Monarch*, did not give the alarm, and did not know till daylight what had happened. The British force surrounded the Egyptian Government barracks, and in complete silence the native garrison was made to surrender. The seamen then so planted themselves that they divided the native town from the European, and, by the narrowness of the sandbank upon which the town is built, were able to coop up the Egyptians in their own quarter. Other troops, meanwhile, quietly took possession of the offices of the Suez Canal Company; and a midshipman, not more than fifteen years of age, was sent with a few bluejackets to occupy the Company's telegraph station. In the early morning the pompous French Telegraph Agent arrived, as usual, at his office, but was stopped at the door by the minute midshipman, who said politely in French that he was not allowed to enter. "Qui êtes-vous?" cried the official, staring in furious amazement at this boy with the enormous revolver in his hand. "Que voulez-vous ici?" The midshipman drew himself up. "Je suis ici," he said sternly, "pour empêcher le monde d'entrer"; and the infuriated Frenchman was obliged to remain outside.

During the same night another force was landed at the railway junction of Nefiché, a short distance up the canal; and thus the French officials woke up, rubbing their eyes, to find the audacious English, who really had no manners at all, in possession of the town and waterway. In the morning the fleet of transports arrived and passed into the canal, whose officials could only retaliate by refusing them the aid of the pilots. The canal dues were punctiliously paid by the British Government to the Canal Company, and the ships were successfully navigated by their own officers. Ismailia was the important station to seize, for it is from this point that the direct road to Cairo led out; and here the main part of the army was landed. M. de Lesseps, from his office at Ismailia, sullenly watched the immense fleet of transports defile before him; and when the troops began to disembark he is said to have taken up his position on the quay, crying out that no English soldier should land except over his dead body. A bluejacket, however, quietly pushed him aside, remarking, "We don't want no dead bodies about here, sir; all you've got to do is to step back a bit."

Thus with sublime indifference to French opposition, and in the teeth of an army of some 7000 to 10,000 Egyptians which had rapidly collected behind Ismailia, the British expeditionary force was landed. Three weeks later the troops had come in touch with Arabi's main army, which had entrenched itself in the desert at Tel-el-Kebir, a village on the road from Ismailia to Cairo.

The Egyptian position was a strong one, and Sir Garnet Wolseley decided that it would be best to make a night attack upon it. This was done, and just before dawn on September 13 the British forces, consisting of 11,000 infantry and 2000 cavalry, silently marched towards the Egyptian redoubts, guided by the stars. They approached to within a few hundred yards of the entrenchments without being detected, for it was Arabi's somewhat original custom to call in his sentries at sunset. At last, however, the Egyptians were aroused, and poured a heavy rifle-fire into the darkness before them. With a rousing cheer the British troops charged straight at the earthworks, and twenty minutes later the whole Egyptian army was in headlong flight. Arabi, who was in bed at the time, afterwards bitterly complained that the English had not given him time even to put his boots on, and he was obliged to fly barefooted across the desert to the nearest railway station, where he caught a train for Cairo.

Sir Garnet Wolseley at once issued orders that the fugitives were to be followed up by the cavalry, but that the chase was not to be made too sanguinary. Tommy Atkins has a kindly heart, and he had no wish to murder the wretched Egyptians who were racing madly before him. The pursuit, thus, is said to have been at times the most ludicrous spectacle. On overtaking a flying Egyptian, the troopers in most cases would give him a sounding smack on the seat of his trousers with the flat of the sabre, and thus would speed him on his way.

Two small cavalry contingents were now sent forward, one to capture the town of Zagazig and the other to take Cairo. The former contingent trotted briskly to the outskirts of the town, and then galloped forward in a straggling line, those best mounted arriving first. Two officers and six troopers were the first to enter the narrow streets, and these eight men at once clattered up to the station through crowds of natives; and there they found five train-loads of fugitive Egyptian troops about to start for Cairo. One of the officers shot the engine-driver of the foremost train, and thereupon all the soldiers either surrendered to the eight perspiring Englishmen, or else, throwing away their arms, ran for their lives. The Cairo contingent rode hard all day, and arrived at the metropolis on the afternoon of the next day, the 14th.

When Arabi reached Cairo he was in a state of complete exhaustion. "It is all finished," he muttered as he collapsed into a chair; and, with the tears pouring down his cheeks, he told those around him that they might expect the British forces to reach the capital in three or four days. Nevertheless some steps were taken for the city's

defence, and the digging of trenches was commenced.   But in the afternoon of the 14th the
above-mentioned British force appeared in sight.
The trench-digging was at once abandoned, and
10,000 Egyptian infantry surrendered to the
advance - guard of fifty exhausted Englishmen.
As soon as darkness had fallen, about 140 officers
and men under Major (afterwards Sir) Charles
Watson rode boldly up to the gates of the
Citadel and there demanded the surrender of
the garrison and the keys of the fortress. The
Egyptian commandant had gone to bed, and there
was some delay in arousing him; but at last he
appeared.   Believing the whole British army to
have arrived, he speedily surrendered, and for
the next three hours the Egyptian garrison of
about 6000 men filed through the gates and dispersed into the city below.   Major Watson then
took over the vast fortress with his handful of
men and quietly locked the gates.   Another
Egyptian force, meanwhile, was garrisoned in a
small fort on the top of the neighbouring hills;
and nobody could decide in what manner they
were to be dislodged, for no troops could be spared,
and, indeed, they were too exhausted to set out
on any further expedition.   At last, however, a
bright idea occurred to Major Watson.   Sending
for one of the Egyptian officers who had been
retained as an interpreter, he casually asked him
if he would mind just going up to the fort, turning

the garrison out, and bringing back the keys. The Egyptian scratched his head for a moment or two, and then, with a cheery "Very well, sir," went off on his errand. Two hours later he returned with the keys, and stated that he had dismissed the garrison and had safely locked up the place! Major Watson, having thanked him kindly for his trouble, told him to go home to bed, which he promptly did.

Major Watson then calmly rode into Cairo, accompanied by two Egyptian officers who had surrendered. One of these, feeling cold, asked whether a detour might be made so that he might pass his home and get his coat. Major Watson agreed, and the three men made their way through a large number of deserted streets, at last coming out into the Esbekieh in the centre of the city, where all was peaceful and silent; and having thus ridden until daybreak and shown himself to a considerable number of people, he returned to the Citadel, leaving in the streets the general impression that the city was occupied in all quarters by British troops. On his return he found that Arabi had given himself up during the night.

The rapid seizure of the Citadel prevented Arabi carrying out a scheme which he is said to have been determined to put into execution. He had decided to burn this ancient city as Alexandria had been burned, not to bring destruction on the invaders as in the case of the burning of Moscow, but to satisfy some barbarous instinct which the events of the last few weeks had so strongly roused in him. But when he was informed that the British had already arrived, he decided that the best thing to do was to bend the knee to them. He therefore published a statement explaining what nice kind people the English were, and forthwith surrendered to them. On September 25 the Khedive, accompanied by the Duke of Connaught, Sir Garnet Wolseley, and the British Consul-General, made their state entry into the city, the streets being lined with British troops.

Arabi was speedily put upon his trial; and, although Egyptian law does not permit a rebel to have counsel, a section of the English public insisted that he should be defended, and they sent out by public subscription two barristers to conduct his case. Moreover, the home Government appointed an English delegate to watch the trial and to see that the old rebel had fair-play. At first no one supposed that Arabi would escape with his life; but presently it dawned upon the bewildered court that British public opinion would never permit his execution. Some terrible charges were brought against the prisoner, but in an Oriental country it is almost impossible to arrive at the truth. In the end it was arranged that Arabi should plead guilty; sentence of death was passed; and the Khedive immediately commuted this to banishment. The prisoner's escape from death was received with cheers by the few English people in the court, and the wife of one of the barristers rushed forward and presented the startled Arabi with a large bouquet of flowers, while the Egyptian judges and officials stared blankly at each other, wondering what manner of people this was who had raised the fallen rebel to the status of patriot and hero.

On December 26, 1882, Arabi embarked upon a British vessel, and was conveyed to Ceylon, where he lived for nineteen years, a forgotten exile. As old age crept upon him he began to express the keenest desire to return to Egypt, and to Mr Clement Scott he once said : " I have done with politics, as I have done with war. I want to return to Egypt, there to live as a private man. . . . This is what I ask from your great country, which has treated me with such merciful consideration. I have been punished, and I have suffered. I have asked pardon, and still, knowing the English, I ask for mercy." In 1901 the old man was permitted to return to Egypt, which had forgotten him ; and for ten years he lived at Helouan, in a small house on the edge of the desert. He died at the age of seventy-two, and was buried in a neighbouring cemetery, the funeral being attended only by a few relatives and friends. The days of his triumphs were all forgotten, and his death was barely noticed by the people to whom his smallest word had once been law.

PART II.

EGYPT DURING THE BRITISH OCCUPATION

"In the land of Egypt we sat by the flesh pots, and we did eat bread to the full."—*Exodus* xvi. 3.

"We remember the fish which we did eat in Egypt freely; and the cucumbers, and the melons, and the leeks, and the onions, and the garlick."—*Numbers* xi. 5.

CHAPTER V.

LORD CROMER.

IN the history of the nations the great outstanding rulers of men may be divided into two general classes: those who have carried all before them by reason of their genius, and those who have attained eminence by quiet and persistent labour. In the former class the greatness of the man is more often personal, and his deeds go down to posterity stamped with his own name; in the latter class the fame of the ruler speedily becomes merged into the fame he has given to that which he has ruled. Napoleon Bonaparte was a genius, and in considering his actions we are apt to follow his individual fortunes rather than those of France. On the other hand, General Joffre affords a pertinent example of a man of sober labour, and his name will be merged into that of the French nation whose fortunes are in his hands.

Lord Cromer belongs to this latter category, and his quiet perseverance has earned for him that reward which he would most desire—namely, the privilege of being remembered in future generations, not as a personage but as a movement, not as an individual of whom a thousand anecdotes may be told, but as the essence of that regeneration of Egypt which will stand for all time to the general credit of England.

As soon as the battle of Tel-el-Kebir had been fought and Arabi Pasha brought to trial, the home Government began to consider the desirability of withdrawing the British army from Egypt; and Sir Edward Malet, the British Agent in Cairo, was asked to prepare a scheme for the administration of the country by the Khedive's Government, without any extensive British assistance, while Lord Dufferin was officially informed that " Her Majesty's Government contemplated shortly commencing the withdrawal of the British troops from Egypt." These somewhat hasty steps caused great anxiety amongst the European population, and nearly three thousand European residents of Alexandria sent petitions to the British authorities asking that a Protectorate might be declared. It was felt, however, that since the British expedition had been sent out under definite orders to maintain the *status quo* as between Egypt and Turkey, England could not honourably take any sort of possession of the conquered territory; and it was further realised that any such action on our part would involve us in trouble with France, who now gravely regretted her refusal to participate in the quelling of the Arabi revolt and her consequent loss of control on the banks of the Nile. In October 1882, only a few weeks after the surrender of the Egyptian army, Lord Dufferin was sent out to Egypt to study the general condition of affairs in that country, and in his report he stated that in his opinion " European assistance in the various departments of Egyptian administration would be absolutely necessary for some time to come," for, he wrote, "it is frightful to contemplate the misery and misfortune which would be entailed on the population were these departments to be left unorganised by a few high-minded European officials. . . . This," he added, "is especially true in regard to financial matters, for the maintenance of Egypt's financial equilibrium is the guarantee of her independence." In summing up the conclusions at which he had arrived, he stated that " before a guarantee of Egypt's independence can be said to exist, the administrative system of which it is the leading characteristic must have time to consolidate, and . . . we can hardly consider the work of reorganisation complete, or the responsibilities imposed upon us by circumstances adequately discharged, until we have seen Egypt shake herself free from the initial embarrassments which I have enumerated in this report."

Acting upon Lord Dufferin's advice, the British

Government, therefore, decided to leave an Army of Occupation in Egypt for the time being, and to appoint a diplomatic agent to supervise the government of the country, with the assistance of a number of Europeans who should work hand in hand with the native Ministers and officials in a nominally native Egyptian administration. It was arranged that the existing treaties with the Porte should be upheld—that is to say, Egypt was to be regarded as a part of the Turkish Empire, paying the established tribute of £682,000 per annum to its overlord, the Sultan, in the manner of a loyal vassal state, but having that degree of independence which had been guaranteed to it by the military successes of Mohammed Ali and the purse of Ismail Pasha. The Turco-Egyptian treaties, as we have seen on page 90, placed certain restrictions upon the Khedive's Government: no political arrangements could be made with any other state without the consent of the Porte, nor could war or peace be declared at any time or in any direction by Egypt; the Egyptian army was still limited to a maximum of 18,000 men; the coinage was to be issued and the taxes collected in the name of the Sultan, and so on. But, apart from these qualifications, the Egyptian Government, with the assistance of British advice, was to continue to be in control of the country's affairs; and very little interference was expected or offered by Turkey.

Although the different governmental departments were under the direction of native Ministers who were responsible to the Khedive, it was apparent that the country would in reality be ruled by the British Agent and Consul-General; and to this important post the home Government appointed Sir Evelyn Baring (whom it will be more convenient to speak of as Lord Cromer at once), an officer at that time engaged in civil work in India. He arrived in Cairo on September 11, 1883.

Apart from the difficulties inherent in the situation in Egypt, there was at this time one great problem which occupied the anxious attention of all concerned in the government of the country—namely, the control of the Sudan. For many years Egyptian influence in the Sudan had decayed and diminished; and though the nominal authority of the Khedive extended over an area as vast as Great Britain, France, Germany, Italy, and Scandinavia put together, the sphere of his rule was actually confined to the banks of the Nile as far as Khartoum. This portion of the country had been terribly impoverished by the exactions of Ismail Pasha, and, in the words of Sir Samuel Baker, "There was hardly a dog left to howl for a lost master." Now, to add to Egypt's difficulties, a Mahdi, or prophet, had arisen, to whose holy standard the miserable remnants of the population were flocking, in the hope of some relief from their terrible lot; and before the new British Agent had arrived in Egypt matters had come to a head. The Egyptian troops at Khartoum were in a deplorable condition, and had not received their pay for many months; and the Treasury in Cairo was too exhausted to furnish the necessary funds. Soon after the suppression of the Arabi revolt, a handful of English officers, under General Hicks, was sent to the Sudan for the purpose of establishing some order amongst the tatterdemalion native troops; but as the money supplied was so inadequate very little could be done. The rebellion spread, and at length it was decided that General Hicks should lead an expedition into Kordofan, the seat of the rebel government. The miserable condition and untrustworthy temper of the Egyptian troops, however, caused the British officers the gravest misgivings; and though General Hicks, from a mistaken sense of duty, did not care to abandon the task which had been set, he must have known the risks which he ran and his small likelihood of success. With almost incredible narrowness of view, Lord Granville, acting in the name of the British Government, now issued a statement that they were "in no way responsible for the operations in the Sudan, which had been undertaken under the authority of the Egyptian Government, or for the appointment or actions of General Hicks." Commenting on this declaration, Lord Cromer afterwards made the remark that there could hardly have been a greater error than that committed by Lord Granville in thinking he effectually threw off all responsibility by declaring that it was none of his business. The responsibility of the home Government was based on the fact that England was in military occupation of the Nile Valley, that the weakness and inefficiency of the native rulers were notorious, and that the civilised world looked to us to protect life and property in the Egyptian dominions. "Instead of recognising the facts of the situation," wrote Lord Cromer in after years, "Lord Granville took shelter behind an illusory abnegation of responsibility which was a mere phantasm of the diplomatic and parliamentary mind."

At the height of the summer of 1883 the expedition set out on the march across the desert, and to this day the traveller may see in the unfrequented valleys behind the Nubian village of Korosko the tracks of the expedition's waggons and gun-carriages deeply marked in the eternal sand, winding away into the desert until they are lost amongst the hills. In all my wanderings in Egypt I have come upon no more pathetic or dramatic spectacle than that of these silent witnesses to the folly of the British Government and the undaunted heroism of British officers, which time has seemed unwilling to obliterate. Of the ten thousand men who set out upon the expedition not one returned. Led astray by treacherous guides, the men died of thirst within a stone's-throw of hidden drinking-pools, and at last the enfeebled remnant of the army was overwhelmed by the enemy. General Hicks and the British and Egyptian officers of his staff made a brilliant charge upon the forces which had surrounded them, and thus died fighting like men; but it was not till many years afterwards that the details of the disaster filtered through native sources into common knowledge.

The new British Agent arrived in Cairo a few days after the expedition had set out; and as soon as the news of its fate was made known, Lord Cromer very wisely advised the Government to abandon the Sudan entirely for the moment, and to devote all its energies to the building up of Egypt proper. The British Government, however, now entertained the idea of reconquering the lost territory by the introduction of Turkish troops, and the Egyptian Government acquiesced in this solution of the difficulty. The aid of British troops was absolutely refused; and soon the proposal to invite the aid of the Porte in the settlement of its vassal's difficulties was also abandoned. The followers of the Mahdi did not at once march on Khartoum, and that town was therefore held for the time being.

The reorganisation of the Egyptian Government and the management of the financial resources of

LORD CROMER.

the country constituted a difficult but most interesting task, and the new British Agent set himself to his congenial labours with real enthusiasm, though the menace in the Sudan continued to cause him grave misgivings. A piece of work of this kind makes a peculiar appeal to Englishmen; and, in the case of Egypt, so adaptable and so docile a people had to be governed that the direction of affairs assumed in these first years a most satisfying character. In whatever direction he turned Lord Cromer found in Egypt the need for that kind of constructive administration which he most enjoyed, and for the exercise of that sound sense and bold judgment with which he was so eminently gifted. In no disparaging sense it may be said at once that he did not trouble himself to understand the Egyptian mind, nor to study the prejudices and temper of the people over whom he ruled. He never learnt to speak Arabic — the language of the country—and he made no effort to adapt his manners to the habit of the land. When he retired in 1907 he knew as little of Egyptian thought outside the range of his official experience as he did of Arabic grammar. His entire time was occupied in regulating the public affairs of the country, harbouring its financial resources, and contending with the diplomatic difficulties created by the vagaries of foreign interests. He stood always for British high - mindedness, justice, and integrity; and though jovial in manner to his intimates and hotly wrathful to transgressors, he appeared to reign, like a guiding star, in calm and shining imperturbability. From the outset his administration was hallowed, if I may so express myself, by a very beautiful nobility and cleanliness. His actions were essentially those of a gentleman, as we in England interpret the word. In a land where fortunes were to be made daily, and where a material reward was the recognised acknowledgment of every service, he remained throughout his career a poor man; and though his word dictated the fluctuations of all Egyptian stocks and shares, and his patronage might serve to enrich any merchant in the land, he never profited in the smallest degree by his manifold opportunities, either in regard to comforts, artistic luxuries, or indirect emoluments. Nor was he ever turned a hair's-breadth from the stern path of his duty by the overtures of foreign diplomats or by the blandishments of native rulers.

His forceful actions and bluff manners brought him speedily into collision with France. Since the days of Mohammed Ali French prestige had been paramount in Egypt, and Ismail Pasha's affection for that country had imposed a veneer of French polish upon the entire upper class life of the Egyptians. The French language was spoken by the Khedivial court, and was learnt by all Government officials; the fashions of Paris were studiously emulated by the young Egyptians; the Code

Napoleon was employed in the law courts; and French ideals were followed by all those who desired to modernise their country and its institutions. The administration of the Suez Canal, like its construction, was conducted by Frenchmen; the sugar plantations and refineries were mainly French; and both in Cairo and Alexandria the streets and public buildings bore an unmistakably Gallic character. It is not surprising, therefore, that the introduction of British customs and the sudden infusion of British ideals into the country should have caused grave irritation to Frenchmen and a somewhat anti-English tone amongst educated Egyptians, though for the moment the latter were too cowed by their recent conquest to give expression to their feelings. It is useless now to recall the many bickerings and quarrels which ensued, and which were not arrested until the establishment of the *Entente Cordiale* in 1904; but it is to be remembered that the policy of the home Government in regard to Egypt, and the actions of the British Agent on the spot, were always hampered by this undercurrent of ill-feeling now so happily removed.

Lord Cromer's relations with the Khedive were, on the whole, cordial. Tewfik Pasha was in no sense of the word a great man; but he was kindly, pleasant, and fairly reasonable. He had never visited Europe, and knew little of international politics, and therefore he was always completely bewildered by the tortuous ways of foreign diplomacy. He wished Egypt to be ruled alone by Egyptians, and he saw no reason for outside interference, save in so far as it protected his throne; but, at the same time, he offered no objection to the reforms which were being instituted in his country. His position was one of extreme difficulty; for, on the one had, he realised how unwise would be his opposition to England, and, on the other, he was aware that his advocacy of British institutions would alienate him from a large section of influential Egyptians. Under these trying conditions he carried himself with mild dignity, and in after years Lord Cromer said of him that he should be remembered with gratitude as "the Khedive who *allowed* Egypt to be reformed in spite of the Egyptians."

It is not easy to give any idea of the anomalous position of the British Agent in these early years of the occupation; and it will perhaps be best to quote at some length Lord Cromer's own amusing reference to the difficulties with which he had to contend.

"The duty of a diplomatic agent in a foreign country," he wrote many years later, "is to carry out to the best of his ability the policy of the Government which he serves. My main difficulty in Egypt was that the British Government never had any definite policy which was capable of execution; they were, indeed, at one time constantly striving to square the circle—that is to say, they were endeavouring to carry out two policies which were irreconcilable — namely, the policy of reform and the counter-policy of evacuation. The British Government are not to be blamed on this account. The circumstances were of a nature to preclude the possibility of adopting a clear-cut line of action, which would have enabled the means to be on all occasions logically adapted to the end.

" I never received any general instructions for my guidance during the time I held the post of British Consul - General in Egypt, and I never asked for any such instructions, for I knew that it was useless for me to do so. My course of action was decided according to the merits of each case with which I had to deal. Sometimes I spurred the unwilling Egyptian along the path of reform. At other times I curbed the impatience of the British reformer. Sometimes I had to explain to the old - world Mohammedan, the Mohammedan of the Sheriat, the elementary differences between the principles of government in vogue in the seventh and in the nineteenth centuries. At other times I had to explain to the young Gallicised Egyptian that the principles of an ultra - Republican Government were not applicable in their entirety to the existing phase of Egyptian society, and that, when we speak of the rights of man, some distinction has necessarily to be made in practice between a European spouting nonsense through the medium of a fifth-rate newspaper in his own country, and man in the person of a ragged Egyptian fellah, possessed of a sole garment, and who is unable to read a newspaper in any language whatsoever.   I had to support the reformer sufficiently to prevent him from being discouraged, and sufficiently also to enable him to carry into execution all that was essential in his reforming policy. I had to check the reformer when he wished to push his reforms so far as to shake the whole political fabric in his endeavour to overcome the tiresome and, to his eyes, often trumpery obstacles in his path. I had to support the supremacy of the Sultan, and, at the same time, to oppose any practical Turkish interference in the administration, which necessarily connoted a relapse into barbarism. I had at one time to do nothing inconsistent with a speedy return to Egyptian self-government, or, at all events, a return to government by the hybrid coterie of Cairo, which flaunts before the world as the personification of Egyptian autonomy ; whilst, at the same time, I was well aware that, for a long time to come, European guidance will be essential if the ad-minstration is to be conducted on sound principles. I had at times to retire into my diplomatic shell, and to pose as one amongst many representatives of foreign Powers. At other times I had to step forward as the representative of the Sovereign whose soldiers held Egypt in their grip. At one time I had to defend Egypt against European aggression, and, not unfrequently, I had in the early days of the occupation to defend the British position against foreign attack. I had to keep in touch with the well-intentioned, generally reasonable, but occasionally ill-informed public opinion of England, when I knew that the praise or blame of the British Parliament and press was a very faulty standard by which to judge the wisdom or unwisdom of my acts. I had to maintain British authority, and, at the same time, to hide as much as possible the fact that I was maintaining it. I had a military force at my disposal, which I could not use save in the face of some great emergency. I had to work through British agents over whom I possessed no control, save that based on personal authority and moral suasion. I had to avoid any step which might involve the creation of European difficulties by reason of local troubles. I had to keep the Egyptian question simmering, and to avoid any action which might tend to force on its premature consideration, and I had to do this at one time when all, and at another time when some, of the most important Powers were more or less opposed to British policy. Lastly, the most heterogeneous petty questions were continually coming before me. If a young British officer was cheated at cards, I had to get him out of his difficulties. If a slave girl wanted to marry, I had to bring moral pressure on her master or mistress to give their consent. If a Jewish sect wished for official recognition from the Egyptian Government, I was expected to obtain it, and to explain to an Egyptian Minister all I knew of the difference between Ashkenazian and Sephardic practices. If the inhabitants of some remote village in Upper Egypt were discontented with their Sheikh, they appealed to me. I have had to write telegrams and despatches about the most miscellaneous subjects,—about the dismissal of the Khedive's English coachman, about preserving the lives of Irish reformers from the Clan-na-Gael conspirators, and about the tenets of the Abyssinian Church in respect to the Procession of the Holy Ghost. I have been asked to interfere in order to get a German missionary who had been guilty of embezzlement out of prison; in order to get a place for the French and Italian Catholics to bury their dead; in order to get a dead Mohammedan of great sanctity exumed; in order to prevent a female member of the Khedivial family from striking her husband over the mouth with a slipper; and in order to arrange a marriage between two other members of the same family whom hard-hearted relatives kept apart. I have had to take one English maniac in my own carriage to a lunatic asylum; I have caused another to be turned out of the English Church ; and I have been informed that a third and remarkably muscular madman was on his way to my house, girt with a towel round his loins, and bearing a poker in his hands with the intention of using that implement on my head. I have been asked by an Egyptian fellah to find out the whereabouts of his wife who had eloped ; and by a German professor to send him at once six live electric shad-fish from the Nile. To sum up the situation in a few words, I had not, indeed, to govern Egypt, but to assist in the government of the country without the appearance of doing so, and without any legitimate authority over the agents with whom I had to deal."

Meanwhile the situation in the Sudan was growing daily more threatening, and Lord Cromer's attention was constantly called away from his work in Egypt by the menace in the south. Khartoum was now the only town held by the Egyptians, and the route from thence to the lower Nile was kept open only with great difficulty. Some 5000 native troops were here garrisoned under the command of Colonel de Coetlogon, an officer who had as little faith in his men as they had in him. In November 1883 Lord Cromer again advised the British and Egyptian Governments to evacuate the Sudan entirely, but Cherif Pasha, the Egyptian Prime Minister, opposed this measure, and in consequence was obliged to resign. England did not wish to be involved in a further campaign, and it was felt that France would regard an expedition as a somewhat provocative attempt to enlarge the British dominions. On the other hand, the despatch of a Turkish army to restore order was now thought to be very undesirable; while it was recognised that the Egyptian army was in no condition to effect the reconquest of the southern provinces unaided.

In this dilemma the home Government decided to send the popular but eccentric General Gordon to Khartoum to report on the situation, and, if necessary, to carry out the evacuation of the country. To this step Lord Cromer was at first much opposed, but at length he acquiesced, very half-heartedly, in the arrangement; and Gordon left London on 18th January 1884. When he arrived in Cairo, however, the nature of his status was altered at his request, and he was appointed Governor-General of the Sudan, his instructions to carry out the evacuation being confirmed. On January 26 he left Cairo on his ill-fated mission. "He was in excellent spirits at his departure," wrote Lord Cromer, "and hopeful of success. But my own heart was heavy within me. I knew the difficulties of the task which had to be accomplished. In spite of many fine and attractive qualities, Gordon was even more eccentric than I had originally supposed; and I was not relieved of the doubts which I had entertained as to the wisdom of employing him."

The historian of the future will have, I am sure, the utmost difficulty in giving an opinion as to the character and abilities of the heroic General Gordon. Even at the present time so many divergent interpretations of his remarkable personality are current that one cannot form a decision with any degree of certainty; and in future years there will be an ever diminishing likelihood of arriving at a true judgment. The seeming contradictions of Gordon's character appear to me to be due to the fact that in him is to be found the unusual combination of the qualities of a brave and high-minded Christian gentleman of the provincial type with those not infrequently observed in an erratic genius of the artistic world. Had Gordon's life been lived in the Latin quarter he might very possibly have left behind him the memory of a generous, eccentric, wild - living, lovable crank: had he passed his days as a country squire he might have been known as a kindly martinet, an unpractical social reformer, and a pillar of the local church or chapel. As it was, however, Fate led him into strange distant lands where the hard-and-fast rules in which he had been brought up were able to be relaxed, and where the individual characteristics of his dual nature were equally given free rein. Thus sometimes we see him acting like one of Arthur's Knights reincarnate in the body of a rather untidy British officer, and at other times his behaviour suggests that of an irresponsible artistic idealist suddenly called from the cafés of Montmartre to enact the *rôle* of a public hero. There can be no question that he was a superbly gallant and fearless soldier, whose lofty idealism and transparent frankness and simplicity won the love of all men; but at the same time a more flighty and less controlled nature than his could hardly be imagined.   He was an impatient, short-tempered, and liverish man, whose delicate frame and stooping shoulders in no way suggested the inherent largeness of his nature.   His eyes, how-ever, revealed the power of his mind.   They were peculiarly bright, and were of an extraordinary blue-grey colour, "like the sky," it was said, "on a bitter March morning."   His voice was very soft and sweet, except when he was excited; but, though a voluminous writer, he was not a great speaker, and his manner was generally abrupt. He was extremely immoderate in his habits, and smoked to excess.

If the absurd tales still current were to be believed, one would think of Gordon at Khartoum as an intemperate fanatic who, with bloodshot eyes, wandered restlessly to and fro before his lonely quarters, a sword in one hand and a Bible in the other.   Stories are related which describe him, for example, entering his tent when some decision had to be arrived at, thrusting his sword into the sand outside as the recognised signal that he was not to be disturbed, opening his Bible with his eyes tight shut, placing his finger upon some portion of the unseen page, and then hurrying out to announce his decision as formed by an inter- pretation of the words to which the unguided finger had pointed. Such tales, however, I believe to be due to a misunderstanding of his character. Gordon was perfectly capable of soliciting Divine aid by some such oracular method, but that his behaviour ever gave the impression that he was under the influence of alcohol is fully explained by the fact that in times of anxiety his erratic manner when sober was remarkably similar to that of other men when intoxicated.

As regards his religion, Gordon was a typical enthusiast, and had he been born a few centuries earlier he might have played the *rôle* of a prophet. In appointing the officials who were to serve with him, he usually relied on what he called a "mystic feeling," which controlled his judgment as though from on high; and thus it came about that he was often served by very unreliable persons. During his residence at Khartoum he believed that he had a divine mission to perform in the Sudan. He regarded himself as the person chosen by Almighty God to be the saviour of these lost Egyptian pro- vinces. In a letter to a friend, dated January 3, 1884, he pointed out the prophecy of Isaiah con-

cerning himself, which is to be found in chapter
xix., verses 19 and 20, of that Book :—

"In that day shall there be an altar to the
Lord in the midst of the land of Egypt, and a
pillar at the border thereof to the Lord.

"And it shall be for a sign and for a witness
unto the Lord of hosts in the land of Egypt : for
they shall cry unto the Lord because of the
oppressors, *and he shall send them a saviour, and
a great one, and he shall deliver them.*"

In spite, however, of this belief in a divine
mission, he never quite made up his mind what
that mission was ; and Lord Cromer has pointed
out that there were no less than five different
plans of action and interpretations of situations
propounded by Gordon during the early days of
his residence in the Sudan. "His revulsions
of opinion," wrote Lord Cromer in after years,
"were so rapid and so complete that it was
almost impossible to follow him. I had to distin-
guish between such proposals as represented his
matured opinions, and others which were mere
bubbles thrown up by his imaginative brain, and
probably forgotten as soon as made." He would
sometimes send twenty or thirty telegrams to
Lord Cromer in one day, and those despatched
in the afternoon would entirely contradict the
messages of the morning. His language in these
telegrams was generally involved and full of

invective, and it is said that in the spoken word he had a terrifying command of British oaths. In his official telegrams he would sometimes write of the enemy as "a damned lot of stinking Dervishes," or he would describe some high official as "a confounded silly ass." His open abuse of Lord Granville and other Ministers and officials was so astonishingly frank that a large number of his despatches have had to remain unpublished. " I own," he wrote in his journal, " to having been very insubordinate to Her Majesty's Government and its officials, but it is my nature and I cannot help it. I know if *I* was chief I would never employ *myself*, for I am incorrigible. To men like Dilke, who weigh every word, I must be perfect poison."

This was indeed very true; and his hatred of all officials, combined with his wish always to act independently according to the whim of the moment, caused him to be regarded with a sort of terror by those in authority. Yet so great a hero was he in the eyes of the British public, who loved his unconventionality and enjoyed the droll manner in which he attacked the Government, that nobody dared to gainsay him. In England he was regarded as the champion of British common-sense, independence, and justice, as opposed to the obscure red tape of officialdom. But by those who had to deal with him, on the contrary, he was found to be the very personification of instability, mental insobriety, and immoderation. "In Gordon," wrote one of his friends, "strength and weakness were most fantastically mingled." He had, however, the courage of his opinions; and his wild bravery in times of danger endeared him to all men. No one can doubt the loftiness of his ideals; and his splendid efforts to do his duty and to honour his country fill us with admiration. Yet, like Don Quixote, the manner in which he set about his work generally detracted from its value; and England's greatest obligation to him is to be found, perhaps, in the fact that his life has become, by some whimsical process, a sacred memory, and his death, very rightfully, an eternal stimulus to heroism.

General Gordon arrived in Khartoum on February 18, and was received by the townspeople and the garrison with indescribable enthusiasm. Men and women danced around him as he walked to his quarters, and many threw themselves at his feet, clasping his legs and kissing his boots. In the excitement of the moment the fact was overlooked that he had brought neither troops nor money; but it was not long before the precariousness of the situation was generally felt. Gordon himself was astonishingly undecided as to how he should act, and his fertile mind passed from one scheme to another with startling rapidity. Soon it became clear that he would

have great difficulty in extricating himself and
the garrison from their untenable position; and
it was now that his great bravery and high
sense of duty began to endanger his life. He
detested the thought of leaving the inhabitants
to the mercy of the Mahdi, and day after day
passed without his making any arrangements for
the evacuation. All manner of schemes for avoiding the retirement suggested themselves to him,
and his reckless desire to fight the rebels and to
hold the Sudan became firmly fixed in his mind.

At length the road of his retreat to Egypt
was interrupted, and he began to realise that
he would be cut off. "I shall be caught in
Khartoum," he wrote, "and even if I was mean
enough to escape I have not the power to do so."
A little later he addressed an appeal to the British
public, asking for £300,000 in order that a force
of 3000 Turkish troops might be sent to his aid,
since the home Government still objected to the
use of British soldiers in these domains of the
Sultan and the Khedive. "I don't see the fun
of being caught here," he wrote to Lord Cromer,
"to walk about the streets for years as a Dervish
with sandalled feet. Not that (*D.V.*) I will ever
be taken alive."

Meanwhile a British force of 4400 men was
being concentrated at Suakim, on the Red Sea
coast, and although this little army fought some
successful engagements with Osman Digna, the

Mahdi's lieutenant, no advance on Khartoum from that direction seemed practicable. On March 24 Lord Cromer stated officially that steps must be taken to extricate Gordon, but on April 19 all communication with Khartoum ceased. It was not till early in August, however, that the British Government decided to send a relief expedition, and September had arrived before the army began its march up the Nile.

Matters in Khartoum were now desperate, and in November Gordon managed to send a message in which he stated that he could hold out only for another six weeks or so. The relief expedition, however, met with the greatest difficulties, and the seriousness of the situation having been altogether misunderstood, the advance was slow. When all hope of speedy relief was at an end, Gordon wrote in his journal, "I have done my best for the honour of our country. Good-bye"; and this was afterwards brought to light, together with another brief message in which he had written: "What I have gone through I cannot describe. The Almighty God will help me."

On January 26, 1885, while the expedition was still very many miles from its destination, Khartoum fell, and General Gordon died fighting on the steps of his residence. His head was struck from his body and was sent to the Mahdi; and when the news of his death was received by the British Government the expedition was abandoned, the entire Sudan being forthwith evacuated.

Thus died one of the most eccentric, the most uncontrolled, and, withal, the most noble characters who have ever lived; and thus ended a very dark page of English history. For once our proverbial muddling did not carry us through, and the good luck usually attendant upon our arms entirely deserted us. Mr Gladstone, who was then in office, was of course most severely blamed for his indecisive actions, and the initials G.O.M. by which he was known to his admirers, and which stood for "Grand Old Man," were popularly reversed to M.O.G., or "Murderer of Gordon."

The Mahdi did not long survive his heroic enemy; he died on June 22 of the same year, and was succeeded by a pretender to the Caliphate, Abdullah el Taashi, commonly known as the Khalifa. No sooner was the evacuation of the Sudan accomplished than a very important step was taken by the British Government. Sir Henry Wolff was sent to Constantinople in order to effect an agreement with the Sultan in regard to England's position in Egypt, and he was instructed to invite the co-operation of the Porte in the settlement of the Egyptian question. In the following October it was agreed that a Turkish and a British commissioner should proceed to Egypt to "examine all the branches of the Egyptian administration, and introduce into them the modifications which they considered necessary, within the limits of the Imperial firmans "—*i.e.*, the Turco-Egyptian Treaties. The two delegates arrived in Cairo shortly afterwards, and for more than eighteen months they discussed and argued the many points which presented themselves. At last, in May 1887, an agreement was signed which provided, amongst many other matters, that the British troops should be withdrawn from Egypt at the expiration of three years unless there was any "appearance of danger in the interior or from without"; and it was further agreed that if the Khedive did not fulfil all his obligations as vassal of the Sultan, both the Ottoman and British Governments would have the right to occupy Egypt with troops. This last clause caused a storm of indignation in Europe, for it meant that the British evacuation would only be a temporary movement, and that at the slightest sign of internal trouble our army would return to the banks of the Nile. The Sultan, therefore, refused to ratify the convention, and the whole question was left unsettled and undefined, and so remained until the recent declaration of the Protectorate.

The events of the next few years may be briefly recorded. In 1889 the Egyptian army, which had now been properly trained and equipped under British officers, inflicted two serious defeats upon the Dervishes, and some of the provinces of the

Sudan were reoccupied. Egypt was now beginning once more to hold up its head, and in these years Lord. Cromer was able to report that, by his careful management of the public funds, the race against national bankruptcy was practically won. In 1892 the Khedive Tewfik died, and was succeeded by his son, Abbas Hilmi, whose recent deposition will be fresh in the reader's memory; and at his accession, the British and Egyptian troops stood at the salute while the Turkish national anthem was played and the Sultan's message read, the object of this demonstration being, as Lord Cromer put it, "to show publicly the desire of the British Government to recognise the legitimate rights of the Sultan." In the same year Sir Herbert (now Lord) Kitchener became Sirdar, or Commander-in-Chief of the Egyptian army. Six years later, in 1898, a large British and Egyptian army, under Lord Kitchener, set out to reconquer the Sudan and to wipe out the earlier stain upon our arms. The battle of the Atbara was fought and won on April 8, and on September 2 the Dervishes were finally defeated at Omdurman. Two days later the British and Egyptian flags were hoisted side by side above the ruined headquarters at Khartoum ; a most impressive religious service was held on the spot where Gordon died ; and the tomb of the Mahdi was blown to pieces by dynamite.

A very serious difficulty then arose with France.

A French expedition under Major Marchant, which had bravely penetrated from the south to Fashoda, a town in the interior of the Sudan, came face to face with the victorious British forces from the north; and each party regarded the other as an intruder. This may be described as the culminating point in the long quarrel between England and France in respect to Egypt; and actual war between the two countries was only narrowly averted by the retirement of the French expedition. Shortly afterwards Sir Reginald Wingate was appointed Sirdar and Governor-General of the Sudan, and, at the time of writing, he still holds with distinction that laborious office.

The international situation caused by the conquest of the Sudan was very curious. The expedition had been carried out jointly by British and Egyptian troops under the command of Lord Kitchener, who at that time held office in the service of the Khedive, by a mandate confirmed by the Sultan of Turkey, the Khedive's overlord. Legally the Sudan was simply a province of the Turkish Empire, reconquered for the Sultan by British aid, and the Porte would now have had the technical right to thank us for that aid and to request us to retire forthwith. Obviously, however, the stricken population of this vast country could not be left to the casual maladministration of a Turkish or Egyptian Government; and it was clearly England's duty to turn the national genius for organisation to the congenial task of bringing order and justice to these sorely-tried peoples. An agreement was therefore signed with Egypt, by the Articles of which the British Government assumed a definite status in the Sudan, quite different to its undefined position in Egypt proper. We announced that henceforth these reconquered provinces should be under the explicit joint control of England and Egypt; and the suzerain rights of Turkey were tacitly ignored. This assumption by us of joint authority was justified in the agreement simply and frankly on the grounds that it "gave effect to the claims *which have accrued to the British Government by right of conquest* to share in the present settlement and future working and development" of the Sudan.

This position, of course, was in practice quite easily to be justified and maintained; but technically it was absolutely ridiculous. "Diplomatists," Lord Cromer afterwards admitted, "were puzzled and shocked at the creation of a political status hitherto unknown to the law of Europe;" and on all sides the question was asked how England was going to square the circle, or both admit and deny the suzerain rights of the Porte. The Sultan, of course, was furious at the infringement of these rights; for in the early part of the nineteenth century England had most explicitly recognised that the Sudan was held by the sovereign of Egypt as a vassal province of the Turkish

Empire; and yet now the Sultan's name had not been so much as mentioned in the agreement. The Porte, however, was not in a position to protest very energetically, and presently it came to be generally recognised that our action, though technically wrong, was morally right. The happiness and welfare of millions of Sudanese, after all, were justification enough; and if the makeshift arrangements of international comity were upset, there could be no question that the eternal laws of humanity and righteousness were thereby nobly upheld. No man who had witnessed the degradation of utter misery in which these provinces were sunk before the intervention of the British, and who has now seen the glorious happiness and content of the inhabitants under Anglo-Egyptian rule, will doubt that Lord Cromer was morally right in making the arrangements which he did; and the nobility of his, and the nation's, intention has been amply proved by the subsequent labour of the British officials, who have sacrificed all the comforts of life, and frequently life itself, in order to toil in lonely, and often pestilential, stations, under a tropical sun, solely to make the fact of existence a blessing and not a curse to these down-trodden people.

Meanwhile in Egypt the work of regenerating the nation was moving on apace, and the debts incurred by Ismail Pasha were rapidly being paid off. Great improvements were made in the irrigation system; and under the able direction of that indefatigable engineer and administrator, Sir William Garstin, the huge works connected with the Aswan dam were undertaken. On all sides the prosperity of the people was noticeable, and the security of the situation led to the investment of a large amount of European capital in Egyptian concerns. Lord Cromer's work, however, was much hampered by the political situation. Not only had the hostility of the French to be continually reckoued with, not only had Turkish intrigue to be fought, and the rising power of the Egyptian Nationalist party combated, but also the Khedive's marked Anglophobia required constant repression. During the early years of his reign Abbas Hilmi had come more than once to an open passage-of-arms with the British Agent. On one occasion the Khedive dismissed his Prime Minister, deliberately refraining from asking Lord Cromer's consent; but the stern attitude of the British Agent compelled the young man to climb down, and the only result of his assumption of power was the increasing of the British garrison in Cairo. At a later date he took every opportunity to insult English officers, and so disparaging were his remarks, on the occasion of a review at Wady Halfa, that Lord Cromer was obliged to force him, on pain of dethronement, to make the proper reparation, and to publish in the Official Gazette an order of the day congratulating these officers on their

work.   On yet another occasion a mutiny occurred
in a native regiment which could be clearly traced
to the Khedive's instigation; and when the ringleaders had been arrested and sentenced, Lord
Cromer obliged the unfortunate prince to address
them publicly in words which were dictated to
him, thereby for ever nullifying any influence he
might have had with his troops.   For two or
three years the Khedive's attitude in this respect
caused him to be regarded as a patriot by those
Egyptians who desired the cessation of the Occu-
patiou; and deputations almost daily waited upon
him to congratulate him on his anti-English policy.
When he went to Constantinople to visit the
Sultan on one occasion, he took with him a petition
from a number of Egyptian sheikhs, in which they
implored his Majesty " to consider their position
in regard to the stranger who had established himself in their country and persisted in encumbering
their sacred soil with his abhorrent presence."   The
worthlessness of this petition, however, as an indication of the public temper, was shown by the
remarks of one of the sheikhs who had signed it,
when he was asked why he had done so.   " You
see," he said, " it is only empty words.   I often
say to my camel or to my horse, if in some trifling
way he tires my patience, ' Curses on you!   May
Allah strike you dead, O son of a pig!'   If I thought
it would really happen I should be silent; but I
know that the beast will remain unharmed.   So

also I know that the English will stay here whether I sign a petition or not. What does it matter then? I please our lord, the Khedive; the English remain all the same, and look after my interests, and every one is happy all round." Then, as now, the general population regarded the Occupation with mild tolerance, here and there slightly tinctured with gratitude; and it was only amongst the ranks of the upper classes, whose fleecing of the peasantry had been mercilessly checked by the British administration, that any rooted discontent was felt. Nevertheless this spurious nationalist movement was a source of constant worry to Lord Cromer, for under the guise of patriotism the Khedive was able to carry on a continual anti-English campaign, which in actual fact was inspired solely by his personal desire to be rid of the British ideals of justice and humane government.

In 1904 one of the greatest sources of anxiety in Egypt, the French hostility, disappeared as though by magic. The public does not now generally seem to remember that the *entente cordiale* with France was made possible only by the solution of the Egyptian question, and that Lord Cromer had a larger concern in the agreements then made than perhaps any one other man. Egypt had been for many years the chief bone of contention between France and England, but now good fortune placed before us the opportunity of coming to an agreement. The French position in Morocco

was somewhat similar to that of the British in
Egypt; and it occurred to Lord Cromer that
herein lay the nucleus of a wide adjustment of
all differences.   In the convention which was
drawn up England agreed to help France in
Morocco if France would assist England in Egypt.
It was a very simple adjustment of the long-
standing differences, but upon that understanding
the whole fabric of the *entente* was built up;
and it may be said that had Lord Cromer failed
to come to an agreement with the French Government in regard to the Nile Valley, the British
army would not now be fighting shoulder to
shoulder with the soldiers of France.

The removal of Gallic hostility to our *régime*
in Egypt simplified the task of the British Agent
very greatly; but the intrigues of the Khedive
and of the Nationalist party still continued un-
abated.   In 1906 a series of incidents occurred
which may be described as the culminating point
of the anti-English campaign.   In the early
summer of that year the Turks moved a number
of troops into the deserts of Sinai to the east of
the Suez Canal with the intention of claiming
that territory as outside the sphere of Egyptian
authority, and of pushing the frontier of the
Khedive's dominions back to the borders of Egypt
proper.   The Porte had already made an attempt
to gain unbridled possession of this territory in
the early days of the British Occupation, and this

second effort came as no great surprise to the
authorities. It was met, however, by extreme
firmness on the part of Lord Cromer; and on
May 15 an ultimatum was addressed to the Porte,
which stated that unless the Turkish troops were
withdrawn and the old frontier definitely fixed,
England would support the claims of Egypt by
the whole might of the Empire. In view of this
threat the Sultan reluctantly gave up all his
demands, and the frontier was fixed in accordance
with the Turco-Egyptian treaties of the time of
Mohammed Ali. The Anglophobe sentiments of
a certain class of Egyptians were now at their
height, and there was a very grave danger of an
anti-English rising in favour of the Sultan. British officials in the provinces were exposed to all
manner of insults; and I recall personally many
weeks of great anxiety when the massacre of all
Christians was openly advocated in one's very
presence, and the lonely days in remote districts
were shadowed by the hourly expectation of disaster. Then came the news that some British
officers in uniform had been attacked at the village of Deneshwai, in Lower Egypt, while they
were pigeon-shooting at the invitation of one of
the local sheikhs; and it was generally felt that
a rising was imminent. There can be no doubt
that these officers had irritated the villagers by
a somewhat indiscriminate acceptance of this invitation; but there could also be no question that

under normal circumstances no more than a quiet complaint would have been made. As it was, however, the Englishmen were attacked by a savage crowd, and were obliged to run for their lives back to their distant camp, leaving one of their number dead upon the roadway.

Lord Cromer took a very serious view of this incident, more especially since it showed the native disrespect for the British uniform, the prestige of which was the only real guarantee of law and order in the land. He therefore insisted that the ringleaders of the riot should be tried for murder and executed, and that a number of the other offenders should be publicly flogged. The sentences were carried out a few weeks later in the village of Deneshwai itself, in the presence of a detachment of British soldiers, and it is probable that by the severity of the action a general rising was averted. The execution was followed by a storm of protest in all sentimental circles throughout the world, and the Egyptian Nationalists were loud in their denunciation of British barbarism; but I think that mature consideration will place the blame for the whole affair very largely with the intriguers at the courts of the Khedive and the Sultan, whose object for some time past had been to inflame the minds of the inhabitants with anti-English animosity.

In the following year, while yet the country was in a ferment, Lord Cromer resigned. His health had been entirely wrecked by his long residence in Egypt, and the disturbances of the last years had worried him very considerably. In announcing his retirement to the House of Commons Sir Edward Grey was quite unable to control his emotion, and that fact is more eloquent than any words of mine could be in recording the obligation of the British nation to its great Pro-Consul. Lord Cromer found Egypt in 1883 a bankrupt, starving country, in which corruption and injustice were rife, and where, as a traveller once remarked, "everybody was bastinadoing everybody else." He left it in 1907 a prosperous, rich, and civilised land, where even the symptoms of unrest appear to have been but an indication of the renewed vitality of the people.

CHAPTER VI.

SIR ELDON GORST.

DURING the days of Sir Eldon Gorst's rule in Egypt one heard a great deal about the "muddle" in that country, and the old "Egyptian question" was constantly under discussion. On all sides the complaints of dissatisfied officials were heard, and one was told that the land had gone to the deuce. Now, actually, there was no muddle. There were numerous things which were wrong and out of order, sufficient, in fact, to give Colonel Roosevelt some justification for his famous remarks at the Guildhall, when he advised his English friends "either to govern or to get out"; there were a great many Departmental hitches and obstructions; and there were several large matters which were encumbering and frustrating the Government as a whole. But the situation was not confused, and the forward movement of the country was merely hampered by the ill-working of the machine.

At the time when Sir Eldon took up office in 1907 the situation was extremely grave. The retirement of Lord Cromer was mainly induced by the fact that he did not consider his health good enough to stand the strain of so serious a crisis as that which had to be faced. He must have felt that there was some likelihood of his grip being somewhat relaxed as his physical strength gave way. He was pressed on all sides by a hundred anxieties, and he realised that his enemies were taking courage from the belief that he was past his prime. It was the crowning merit of his great career in Egypt that he was willing to hand the command over to a younger man at the moment when he felt himself not in proper fighting condition to meet the emergencies of the time.

The tragedy of Deneshwai in 1906 was still in the forefront of men's minds. British officers in uniform had been attacked, and one of them had succumbed, within a few miles of their camp; and, apart from all other considerations, this outrage was to be interpreted as meaning that the very symbols and insignia of British authority were despised and disregarded. The misunderstanding with Turkey in connection with the Sinaitic frontier had caused a more than usually excited outburst of anti-British feeling; and, had there been war, it is possible that the Egyptian army would have mutinied. Rumours of forthcoming massacres of Christians were frequent, and more than once the date was fixed for a general slaughter.   Both in 1906 and 1907 a rising, directed against the English, was confidently expected; and there was one well-remembered night in Cairo when a total absence of British officers from the clubs and places of amusement revealed the fact that they were all under arms at their posts.   Massacre was openly preached in the villages throughout the country, and many Europeans were subjected to insult.

The Nationalists—that is to say, those Egyptians who wished to terminate the British Occupation and to introduce self-government—were at this time an extremely powerful party; and the Khedive, perhaps chagrined at the attitude of the Agency towards him, was openly inclined to be well-disposed to the movement. The Russo-Japanese war had supplied a powerful stimulus to Oriental aspirations, and the Egyptians were of opinion that they, too, could rise with easy rapidity to the level of a first-class Power.   The financial crisis, in which a large number of Europeans and Egyptians had lost enormous sums of money, had paralysed the Bourse.   The nerves of the whole country were on edge.

Sir Vincent Corbet, the Financial Adviser to the Egyptian Government, had sent in his resignation, and there was much confusion in that Ministry. Sir William Garstin, the indefatigable and much-beloved Adviser to the Ministry of Public Works, was about to resign.   Major Mitchell, the Adviser to the Ministry of the Interior, had also to be replaced; and other high officials had acquainted the Government of their intended departure. Sir Elwin Palmer, one of the leading financial authorities in Egypt, had died in the previous year; and the health of Mustafa Pasha Fehmy, the trustworthy old Egyptian Prime Minister, did not permit him to retain office. The appointment of so many new officials to the important vacancies added very considerably to the difficulties of a situation already almost desperate; and, as though purposely to increase the troubles of the new Agent, a number of ill-advised British members of Parliament preached open rebellion to the Egyptian hotheads.

No sooner was Lord Cromer's back turned than the vernacular Press attacked the Occupation with vicious energy. His strong hand being removed, the reaction set in; and the native journalists revelled in a demoniacal fantasy of abuse. Lord Cromer was accused of all the crimes in the calendar; and it was publicly recorded that he had left the country bearing with him many millions of pounds stolen from the Egyptian treasury. The Nationalists freely stated, and seemed actually to believe, that his resignation had been brought about by their triumphant policy, and that the home Government had required his removal owing to his stern treatment of the Deneshwai ruffians. British prestige suffered a very palpable fall, and it was thought that the days of self-government were imminent.

On these tempestuous scenes Sir Eldon Gorst arrived, without pomp or ceremony. He was a small, ill-dressed, spectacled man of some forty-six years, with a determined, but not distinguished, bearing. It was already known, and soon observed again, that he disliked notoriety. He walked on foot through the streets of Cairo, jostled by the natives; or, bareheaded and sometimes collarless, he rode his pony amidst the noisy traffic. At times he drove his own small motor-car; and, in the absence of a chauffeur, shouted to the pedestrians in the vernacular to warn them from his path. He expressed the greatest irritability when, on his official tours, the native notables presented him with the customary bouquets of flowers; and the usual mounted policemen who were despatched by the local governors to ride behind him were sent about their business with a sharpness that was absolutely inexplicable to them. Before he left Egypt for the last time he had schooled himself to bear with these distressing attributes of Oriential power in a much more liberal manner; but on his arrival in 1907 he either bewildered or offended both natives and Europeans by his apparent imitation of the manners and customs of that most democratic and most despised frequenter of the Nile—the British tourist.

This is the more remarkable because in his public

Photo by ELLIOT & FRY.]

SIR ELDON GORST.

utterances he had declared himself desirous of seeing more intimacy between the native point of view and that of the resident Englishman. It was his wish, to some extent, to do in Egypt as the Egyptians do, to sympathise with their prejudices and to give no unnecessary offence to their susceptibilities. Yet, ignoring the very essential need of discreet ostentation in the East, he held doggedly to an almost pretentious modesty and self-effacement which was as little understood in Cairo as it would have been little noticed or questioned in London. He knew Egypt very well, having spent many years in the service of the Egyptian Government; and his manners in this respect are to be attributed rather to a want of consideration for public opinion with reference to himself than to ignorance of native custom.

Sir Eldon Gorst came to Egypt in 1886, at the age of twenty-five, as Secretary at the British Agency. In 1890 he was made Controller of Direct Revenue; in 1892 he was appointed Under Secretary of State for Finance; and in 1894 he became Adviser to the Ministry of the Interior at the early age of thirty-three. In 1898 he was made Financial Adviser, this being the most important position in the Egyptian Government open to Englishmen. In all these offices Sir Eldon had shown remarkable abilities, and he was considered by Lord Cromer to be "endowed with a singular degree of tact and intelligence." It was therefore no surprise when, after his sudden and mysterious departure from Egypt in 1903, and the subsequent announcement of the *entente cordiale* with France, it leaked out that Sir Eldon had been entrusted with a large part of the diplomatic negotiations between France and England in regard to Egypt, and that the amazing success of the arbitration had been largely due to his dexterous handling of the matters in dispute.   In 1904 Sir Eldon received an appointment at the Foreign Office, but resigned this to become Lord Cromer's successor at Cairo on May 7, 1907.

Such was the rapid and eminent career of the man who now sat in the great house at Kasr el Doubâra, staring enigmatically through his large spectacles, while the political storms gathered and broke around him.   All eyes were turned upon him for some sign of his policy, and it was not long before indications were given of the direction in which he intended to move.   For some time the relations between the Khedive and the British Agent had been strained, and Sir Eldon Gorst made it his first concern to institute more friendly feelings.   This he did with such marked success that his Highness was soon completely won over by the careful deference paid to his rank, and by the cordial attitude adopted towards his person. "Whatever good work may have been done in the past year," Sir Eldon was able to say in his first annual report, "is due to the hearty co-

operation of the Khedive and his Ministers, working harmoniously and loyally with the British officials in the service of the Egyptian Government."

It is difficult to decide whether Sir Eldon fully
realised at the time what the result of this *entente*
would be; but, since the effect was so immediate,
it would seem that he was not acting solely from
a sense of duty to his Highness, though, no doubt,
his actions to some extent were the outcome of
a genuine sympathy for the awkwardly situated
Prince.   No sooner had the Khedive laid aside
his differences with the Agency than the Nationalists turned upon him, accusing him of disloyalty
to his country, and threatening to dethrone him.
It must have been with profound satisfaction that
Sir Eldon watched this break between the Khedive and the Nationalists.   The latter party had
suffered a severe blow by the death of their
leader, Mustafa Kamel Pasha, and now many
internal quarrels occurred which hastened their
fall.   With the Khedive and all Egyptians who
were loyal either to him or to the Occupation
against them, their power could not be retained,
and very soon their political redoubtability was
reduced to an irritating but not very dangerous
agitation.

In his first year of office Sir Eldon Gorst took
another important step towards the overthrow
of militant Nationalism.   The vast majority of
Egyptians are Mohammedans; and as the Occu-

patiou, against which the so - called "patriotic" movement is directed, is Christian, it became a political necessity for the Nationalists to use this religious difference as one of the main planks of their platform. While the leaders wished to convey to Europe the impression that they were too highly educated to be fanatical, they were constantly using the inherent Mohammedan enthusiasm as a means of arousing the nation. Now, a large number of educated Egyptians are Copts —i.e., Christians—and the Nationalist party had therefore to decide whether, on the one hand, they would eliminate the religious aspect of their movement and incorporate the Coptic "patriots" with themselves, or whether, on the other hand, they should retain the important asset of religious fervour and should dispense with the services of this not inconsiderable minority of native Christians. They were still undecided, and there was a chance that the two religious factions would unite, when the new British Agent suddenly appointed Boutros Pasha Ghali, a venerable Copt, to the office of Prime Minister, made vacant by the retirement of Mustafa Pasha Fehmy.

Again, it is not easy to say whether the probable results of this action had been carefully considered, or whether Boutros Pasha was appointed simply because he happened to be one of the most capable men available. The effect was immediate. The Mohammedan Nationalists, insulted at the exaltation of the Copts, turned against their Christian colleagues, and a breach was effected which it will take years to close. Soon the two factions were at one another's throats, and at last Boutros Pasha paid for his elevation with his life, being assassinated by a Mohammedan Nationalist named Wardani in February 1910. Sir Eldon Gorst, who had been watching the fight with a somewhat sardonic smile, is said to have been profoundly moved by the tragedy; and he certainly saw to it that the murderer suffered the death penalty, in spite of the most carefully organised propaganda in his favour. Sir Eldon was at his best when, as on this occasion, he fought the enemies of law and order by means of the ordinary legal procedure of the country, imposing his will on magistrates and judges who, by reasons of the methods employed, were empowered to resist him with impunity. The Nationalist leaders had sworn that Wardani should not hang, and when the black flag went up over the prison it marked the turning-point in their attitude to the Agency, for an Egyptian always knows when he is beaten.

The Copts, abandoning the Nationalist movement, now turned to the Occupation for support; and, deeming that this moment of British indignation against the assassin and his party was favourable for the redressing of certain wrongs under which they believed themselves to be labouring, they looked to Sir Eldon Gorst for encouragement.　They received none.　Sir Eldon, quite correctly, considered that their complaints were groundless, and he took the opportunity to tell them so with some sharpness, thereby estranging them from the Occupation as effectively as they were already estranged from the Nationalists.

Thus Egypt, which had presented a fairly united front in 1907, was now divided into four distinct factions: the Occupation and its supporters; the Khedive and his loyal adherents, whose fraternising with the British was rather superficial; the Copts; and the Nationalists, who themselves were much divided.　For the first time for many years the task of governing the country was made simple, and these internal dissensions caused a set-back to Egyptian aspirations from which it will take many years for the nation to recover.　In 1907 Sir Eldon Gorst found the British Agency besieged by an earnest crowd, all shouting for autonomy; in 1911 he left the Agency disencumbered and calmly watching that crowd fighting with itself.　But whether we have to see in these events the intervention of an unscrupulous Fortune, or whether we must ascribe each movement to the Machiavellian cunning of the British Agent, is a question which will now never be answered.　Even the diplomatic Secretaries in Cairo were totally undecided upon this matter, for Sir Eldon kept his policy to himself.　One prefers to think that he was not entirely responsible for these dissensions and squabbles, for it is a form of cock-fighting which does not commend itself to British sentiments. Sir Eldon Gorst was not, like Lord Cromer, a born ruler in every sense of the word, but he was amazingly clever. He was extremely anxious to benefit Egypt, and in certain minor matters he was almost ruthless in clearing obstructions from the path of what he considered his duty.

Meanwhile, his policy in regard to the larger aspect of the Egyptian question was straightforward and logical. "British intervention in the affairs of this country," he wrote in one of his reports, "is directed to the sole end of introducing and maintaining good administration and gradually educating and accustoming the Egyptians to carry this on for themselves." England entered Egypt in 1882 for the purpose of supporting the Khedive, who nominally represented law and order, against his rebellious subjects; and she took this step almost solely in the interest of the Europeans resident in the country, or those who had financial interests in it. The Army of Occupation remained in Egypt after the suppression of the rebellion, in order to maintain the peace and thereby bring prosperity to all classes; and it may be said that the healthy financial condition of the country is due primarily to the confidence and sense of security inspired by the presence of the British troops. But when the English had arrived it was found that the entire administration of the Government was corrupt and rotten, and it was not many years before Lord Cromer decided to call in a large number of English officials thoroughly to overhaul and reorganise different departments. England, being on the spot, could not sit idle and watch the mismanagement; and it was certainly her only moral course to set to work in this manner. Nevertheless, in order to quiet the agitation of those who felt that annexation was now very near, it was officially stated that it was the intention of England to educate and train the Egyptians to govern themselves. Having declared so much, Lord Cromer was able to settle down to his labours with a will, and very soon the whole machinery of government was running like clockwork, to the great comfort of the masses, but to the annoyance of those classes who no longer found fat billets awaiting them, and who had now been spoiled of the opportunities of making money by illicit means. "This is all very well," said intelligent natives, "but we are not learning how to govern ourselves in the least; we are not being taught, we are being ousted." The more hot-headed Egyptians went further than this. "We are already as fit to govern ourselves as we ever shall be," they declared, with some truth, "and we demand that the English shall now withdraw." Lord Cromer was not the man to be hustled; but gradually, and in his own time, he took certain steps to increase the participation of Egyptians in their own government. The concessions thus made were attributed by the now powerful Nationalist party to British weakness, and the demands for autonomy became louder and more violent in consequence.

Matters were in this ferment when Sir Eldon Gorst arrived; and it was deemed advisable, both by him and by the Foreign Office, that England's policy should be stated in clear terms, and should be backed by deeds. The world was therefore once more reminded that the Egyptians were being trained to rule themselves, and certain offices previously held by Englishmen, on becoming vacant, were handed over to natives. This caused a storm of indignation amongst the English officials, who had come to feel that Egypt was a British possession under the sole management of British officials. Sir Eldon Gorst, therefore, addressed himself in his 1910 report to the Englishmen in the service of the Egyptian Government, and pointed out to them that, by the terms of the unchanged policy laid down by the British Government in the early days of the Occupation, Egyptians had of necessity to be given offices; but that his countrymen need not on that account fear that their positions were endangered, for self-government was not yet in sight. As long as the standard of the Englishmen employed was retained at a high level they could not fail to be of use to Egypt. But, he added, "the only justification for the employment of non-Egyptian officials is found in their possession of qualities which do not exist among the natives of the country."

This, as a matter of fact, was not putting the case as strongly as might be supposed. A first-rate official must possess honesty, brains, and activity; and, while these qualities are often to be found in combination in an Englishman, they are very seldom united in an Egyptian. Nobody can shut his eyes to the fact that native officials are given to taking bribes, and it is common knowledge that positions which have yielded to their English holders no more than the small salary attached to them, have, on being given to natives, produced thousands of pounds a year for their enrichment. A wealthy landowner is always willing to pay the irrigation-inspector a few hundreds in order to get a larger supply of water than that to which he is entitled. Contractors will offer the engineers of the Ministry of Public Works thousands as a bribe to secure them some good contract. Judges are peculiarly exposed to temptation, and police-officers are offered money every day of their lives. Englishmen, on the other hand, are absolutely free from this taint, and they therefore do "possess qualities which do not exist amongst the natives" as a rule, and Sir Eldon was well aware of this.

Nevertheless, the English officials were considerably disturbed, and the slightly increased powers of the Egyptians were deeply resented. That type of Englishman who was inclined to pursue his capable way without regard for the fact that he was supposed to be teaching rather than ignoring his Egyptian colleagues did not attempt to understand Sir Eldon's very correct attitude. He regarded the British Agent with unmixed feelings of bitter mistrust; and Sir Eldon, on his part, did not always hide the irritation which was caused him by this lack of appreciation. The feud developed, and the un-compromising tone of the Agent, the hard, un-relenting, fearless abruptness which characterised his actions, was misinterpreted as vindictiveness —a kind of inherent nastiness. His policy was entirely misunderstood, and he was called a weak man, though nobody who came into direct contact with him laboured for long under that delusion.

It is necessary now to state the three policies which it was then possible for a British Agent in Egypt to pursue. Firstly, there was the policy of the iron-grip; secondly, there was that of the velvet-hand; and thirdly, there was the policy of the guiding-pressure. Let us first consider the policy of the iron-grip.

The population of Egypt consists of about eleven million peasants, or fellahîn, and a few thousand educated persons, or effendiât. The peasants dress in native costume; and, though a certain per-centage of them can read and write, the majority are illiterate. They are, however, an intelligent people, clever with their fingers, industrious, imitative, and inquiring. They are sober, patient, not unfaithful, not revengeful, and, on the whole, law-abiding. The educated classes wear European dress, ape the manners of the French or sometimes of the English, and have their heads turned with extraordinary ease. They are often noisy, officious, and bullying. Their object is to live in Cairo or Alexandria, where they degenerate, in many cases, into café-loafers and wastrels. Their morals are usually of the lowest, and they have little regard for those injunctions of the Koran which effect complete teetotalism amongst the peasants. A minority are good workers and are popular with Englishmen, but their almost unanimous contempt for muscle and backbone leads them to participate as little as possible in the more active labours of administration, and thereby estranges them from their more strenuous white colleagues. They despise the peasantry, who are the strength of the nation, and treat them like dogs.

Thus it comes about that the sympathies of the English official in Egypt are very largely with the peasant; and the comfort of the small farmer upon his acre or two of ground is a matter far nearer the heart of the British inspector than is the ease of the effendi in his office. This attitude is strengthened and justified by the knowledge that the effendi deems it permissible to fleece the fellah on every possible occasion, or to assist him only on payment of an exorbitant bakshish. In 1882 the effendiât were waxing fat on the tribute extorted from the fellahîn; and it has been the task of the English to check this tendency and to protect the peasant against the upper classes.

The policy of the iron-grip stated that the interests of the fellahîn had thus to be safe-guarded, and that this could only be accomplished by the very thorough sitting upon the upper ten thousand. The native official, being corrupt and prone to bribery, was to be kept out of administrative positions as much as possible, such offices being given to Englishmen, who might always be trusted to do justice and to deal fairly without hope of reward. The Government, in fact, was to be largely taken out of the hands of the Egyptians; and the little group of rather objectionable educated natives might go hang in order that the huge body of very agreeable peasants might be at peace.

Thus, by an amazing paradox, the autocratic rule of the iron-grip became a democratic and popular movement, which acted as though it were designed solely for the comfort of the masses at the expense of what may be called the aristocracy. Incidentally, it may be pointed out that when certain English Labour Members of Parliament came to Egypt to assist the Egyptians to obtain self-government, they were actually taking the part of the aristocracy against the peasantry, and were enthusiastically giving countenance to a movement which aimed at empowering the effendiât to tyrannise the fellahîn, and which might well have called for their wildest denunciation had the case been applied to English people. These misguided politicians acted as though the cry for autonomy arose from the throats of the whole Egyptian nation. The thought did not seem to occur to them that only about two per cent of the Egyptians were asking for it. The remaining ninety-eight per cent, being more or less inarticulate, though none the less thoughtful for that, were not considered. As well might Mr Keir Hardie and his friends have accepted the voice of Mayfair as the sole expression of English opinion.

The policy of the iron-grip pointed out, of course, that the ultimate granting of a constitution to Egypt and the evacuation of the country by the Army of Occupation were not in the region of practical politics. It felt that a new situation had arisen since the days when the talk of educating the Egyptians to govern themselves was current, and that the happiest solution to the difficulty was now the declaration of a British Protectorate in Egypt, or the actual annexation of the country by purchase from Turkey. It believed that the encouragement and development of certain Egyptian industries would provide work for the majority of the educated Egyptians, while the numerous minor positions in the Government would give employment to the remainder of that class. The vast lower classes, meanwhile, obviously would be only too delighted at an indefinite continuation of the security and justice which they enjoyed under British rule. Being unhampered by the need of experimenting in individual Egyptian capacity for administrative work, the Government would be free to tune things up and to make a model job of it.

We have now to consider the policy of the velvet-hand. This policy regarded the partial or complete evacuation of Egypt in the near future as an axiom. It declared that the honour of England compelled us to abide by our original promise to retire as soon as the Egyptians appeared to be able to govern themselves, and it wished to hasten that day by giving the natives every possible opportunity of trying their hand at the task of administration, whether their attempts involved the tyrannising of the lower classes or not. English officials, it said, ought to understand that they hold only watching briefs. The Egyptians should carry on the work of the Government, and the Englishmen should keep a fatherly eye upon them from a discreet distance. All natives should be treated with courtesy, sympathy, and even deference, as being lords in their own country, and their mis-demeanours should be reproved with gentleness and should not lead to discouragement.

We will take two cases at random which will show how this policy would work. It sometimes happens in the Egyptian provinces that a single rest-house provides accommodation for native and English inspectors of any one department. Now, an Englishman may be on excellent terms with his Egyptian colleague as they ride side by side through their district (and, in fact, it generally happens that they do get on very well indeed together), but he may not appreciate him so easily when they inhabit the same house. The manners of the two nations are so different; and the Englishman is notoriously narrow in his belief in the correctness of the habits practised by him-self—bathing daily, airing the room, changing his clothes sometimes, refraining from expectorating on the dining-room carpet, not hiccoughing loudly in public, and so forth. He is therefore inclined to resent this cohabitation, and to demand a rest-house exclusively for his own countrymen and for those Egyptians who have become Europeanised. But the policy of the velvet-hand denied his right to complain : he was serving the Egyptian Govern-ment, and he must put up with the proximity of his Egyptian colleagues.

When an English inspector sits in the ante-room of the office of his chief, waiting, with native officials, for an interview, the policy of the velvet-hand declared that those native officials should be invited to enter the sanctum before him, as not being foreigners; and if it was argued that this precedence was detrimental to British standing, the answer was given that it was the dignity of Egypt and not the already assured prestige of Britain for which we were striving.

The policy of the velvet-hand attempted in every possible way to increase the self-confidence and dignity of the Egyptians, and to introduce them into the councils of the nations. It considered that the small upper class was the mouthpiece of the nation, and it was willing to confide the interests of the eleven inarticulate millions to the care of that class, believing that the possible sufferings caused to the peasantry would not be so considerable as the pains endured by the Egyptian patriot who saw his country ruled by the foreigner.

Thirdly, there was the policy of the guiding-pressure—the policy, that is to say, which directed the Egyptians along the path upon which they ought to tread, but brought pressure to bear upon them at all times. This was the policy which was pursued by Sir Eldon Gorst with the sanction of the home Government and of Lord Cromer, and it is the policy in which all serious students of Egyptian affairs should have acquiesced, so long as Egypt was a part of the Turkish Empire and its incorporation in our own Empire was not forced upon us by powerful circumstances. The policy gave the Egyptians a certain control over their own affairs, but it held the power of veto unquestionably with England. It felt that we had no right to take Egypt's freedom from her, so long as that freedom was not abused. On the other hand, it believed that England had a certain right to be in Egypt, and it deemed it correct to ensure the acknowledgment of that right were the country threatened with interference from Turkey or any Western Power. The English officials were urged to deal sympathetically with their native colleagues, but to keep an eye upon them, and to exert to the full their powers in suppressing evil practices. The policy stated that Egypt was not ripe for self-government, or for the preservation of order without the aid of the Army of Occupation; but it endeavoured, nevertheless, to give the native every chance, and to place him in any post which could be safely given to him. It felt that the most simple definition of its conduct was that which explained that, owing to England's high sense of the rights of subordinate nations, Egypt was being submitted to a series of small, thoroughly supervised experiments in self-government, preparatory to possible larger ones; but that, though the trials would be continued as circumstances permit, the results were not yet sufficiently encouraging to allow of any alteration in the *status quo* during the present generation. Meanwhile it endeavoured to do all in its power to make British control as palatable as possible to the Egyptians; but, believing that the effendiât did not in any way represent the nation, it felt that as yet there had been no real or unanimous expression of disapproval of the Occupation as such.

It must be repeated that this policy involved the making of experiments, the giving and withdrawing of certain liberties, and the constant changes of portfolios; and it must be understood that the Egyptians are such a docile race that government under these conditions was a possibility, provided that the guiding-pressure was firm and the controlling hand sufficiently known to be recognised.

Sir Eldon Gorst, in carrying out this policy, made the experiment of giving the native General Assembly and Legislative Council greater powers, a step which was very severely criticised by a section of the British residents, who did not realise that it was a tentative move forced upon the Agent by a sense of fair-play. The experiment was a failure, and Sir Eldon Gorst did not hesitate to admit it. In his last report he turned upon the erring native politicians, and gave them as straight a lecturing as any national body has ever received; and it was with evident relief that, voicing the opinion of the home Government, he felt himself able to put an end to the experiment. The attempts to increase the scope of the Provincial Councils met with greater success, and no retrogression was necessary. Both Lord Cromer and Sir Eldon made experiments in allowing native Ministers a certain freedom of action in their Ministries, not always controlled by the English Advisers; and this caused a certain amount of mischief, though the policy was by no means a failure.

But while measures such as these were giving the Egyptians the opportunity of showing their powers and failings, there were two matters which called for some show of the iron-grip on the part of the British Agent. Owing to a number of causes, not the least of which was the retirement of Lord Cromer, crime in the provinces had increased to an alarming extent, and there were many cases of pure brigandage with which the police seemed to be powerless to cope. In 1909, therefore, Sir Eldon Gorst introduced the much-discussed exile laws, by which a certain class of undesirable was liable to be transported to a criminal colony in an oasis amidst the wastes of the western desert. The effect of this law was instantaneous, and the crime returns at once began to go down. In the same year the Press Law was revived, and was applied on a few occasions against journals which had published extremely inflammatory matter. This also had a good effect, and the native papers became, for a time, considerably less prone to frenzied and often obscene ravings.

The fact that Sir Eldon gently pressed laws such as these into existence through the regular channels of native legislation, and applied them with very considerable caution, led the public to give him little credit for these measures; but he did not on any occasion invite recognition, and for some time he seemed to be willing to be misunderstood on all subjects. It was only during the last months of his life, when illness had affected his equanimity, that he showed resentment in this regard. It is true that he always disliked that class of men who, not always without reason, sneered at him from the recesses of the Turf Club, and that he was pretty "short" with them; but except by an obvious irritation of manner, his annoyance was not marked. His last report, however, written during the agonies of his terrible illness, showed that the continuous misrepresentation of his actions was beginning to affect him. He was aware of his unpopularity with the majority of the English, who did not trouble to acquaint themselves with the difficulties of his position, and whose one idea and desire was to act as though Egypt were a British possession (which, it cannot be too emphatically stated, it was *not*). In his report he pointed out that nothing would be easier than to rule Egypt by a kind of martial law, but that such a policy was undesirable under the existing circumstances.

The English officials, for the most part, failed to realise this undesirability, and accused Sir Eldon of weakly pandering to Democracy, while the carelessness of his personal manners was cited as an indication of his lack of political dignity. It became the fashion to scoff at him, and Sir Eldon's keen eyes could not fail to observe this attitude of hostility towards himself and his policy. "The task of one race controlling the destinies of another race of entirely different qualities," he wrote bitterly in his last report, "is one of extreme delicacy and complexity, and cannot, unfortunately, be solved by copy-book maxims and high-sounding platitudes."

His four years as British Agent in Egypt were so occupied with the larger problems of administration and with the breaking-up of the united opposition to the Occupation that most of the Departmental work was left outside the range of his personal supervision. The Ministry of Interior was placed in the hands of Sir Arthur Chitty, who interpreted the pro-Egyptian policy of the Government in such a manner that the English inspectors under his command felt that they were made to take a very back seat. He was, however, succeeded by Mr Ronald Graham, whose policy was admitted on all sides to be excellent, upholding, as he did, the dignity of the English officials on the one hand, and showing cordiality to, and sympathy with, the Egyptians on the other. The Ministry of Finance was placed in the charge of Sir Paul Harvey, but in some of the Ministries the English Advisers were perhaps not able to be as alert as they could have been, and a number of evil practices crept in without attracting their notice—such, for example, as the delay in settling minor points of business, the receiving of bribes by native officials, and so forth. These matters, indeed, were beginning to receive Sir Eldon's attention towards the end of his life. Having cleared up the political situation, his grip was tightening at all points; but, nevertheless, there was some reason for the misconception which led to the following criticism made in a native paper : "The difference between Sir Eldon Gorst and Lord Cromer," wrote Al-Ahram, "is that the latter interested himself in every detail and did not compromise with the officials in their internecine feuds, the interests of England all the while being carefully guarded. In Sir Eldon Gorst's days these interests were as jealously guarded, but everything outside them met with little attention. It was as if he had said, 'This does not concern me.' . . . The opening of a new canal was Lord Cromer's greatest pride; the killing of the Nationalist movement was Sir Eldon Gorst's great aim."

Looking back to the days of his tenure of office

in Egypt, one may now see that he successfully
carried the rule of England on the banks of the
Nile through a period of great danger and difficulty. His policy may have been distasteful to
the British official, but it was fitted to the temper
of the times; and there can be few now who do
not realise at last that this peculiarly perilous
phase of Egyptian history was most correctly diag-
nosed and treated by Sir Eldon. His early death
from cancer removed him. at the moment when
his real power was beginning to be felt; and had
he lived a little while longer his many calumni-
ators and detractors would most assuredly have
been silenced. He would always have been open
to a certain amount of criticism on account of his
manners, which were never gracious nor engaging;
but those who had termed him weak or vacillating
would have speedily realised their mistake.

I should like to quote here some words written
soon after Sir Eldon's death by Mr Ronald Storrs,
the able Oriental Secretary at the British Agency.
"In the midst of his life," he wrote in reference
to his chief's death, " a life crowded to overflowing
with cares, duties, and occupations, a life inspired
by rapid and accurate work, perfect knowledge,
brilliant talents, and noble intentions, the courage
and the intelligence that had survived the storm
and stress of abuse, calumny, misunderstanding,
and sedition, were laid low by the most dreadful

of visitations. What Sir Eldon Gorst suffered from the beginning of the year of his death will never be realised by the public, who imagined that because he held to his work (though he had abandoned every pleasure in life) his state of health could not be really serious. That masterly, yet now pathetic, document, his last annual report, was written at a stage of his disease when the patient is usually kept, as a matter of course, under the stupefying influence of some merciful anodyne. The proofs not yet read, his pain increased to an extent which rendered the performance of his duties quite out of the question. He hurried to Italy for a cure, but there was no cure in Italy nor England nor in all the world for him.

"After the operation he bore the despairing truth with perfect calmness, begging only to be allowed to die in his father's home. And then, surrounded by those he loved, he was allowed to lie in ever-increasing weakness under the elms of Castle Combe. There he .could ponder on the reality, known now to a few only, but destined surely to live in history, that he had fought the fight and, where the world saw failure, had *succeeded*."

When the fatal nature of his illness was announced to him he expressed a desire to die as soon as possible; but when, after lingering for some time, his death was at last imminent, he told

those around him that, in spite of all the pain
endured, he was glad to have lived long enough
to discover, after all, how much he was beloved
by his colleagues.   At the same moment the news
of the close of his rule in Egypt was being received
in Cairo with an almost general sigh of relief.

CHAPTER VII.

LORD KITCHENER.

THE death of Sir Eldon Gorst led to the appointment of Britain's third Pro-Consul in Egypt, and
a new epoch began on the banks of the Nile. Its
advent was marked by the greatest optimism, for
it was patent to all who knew the country that, in
spite of the uneasiness which had been felt as to
the Government's general policy, the situation was
peculiarly undisturbed. The task of the new
Agent was not beset with profound difficulties:
the work lay to his hand uncomplicated and un-
confused, as judged by the habitual Egyptian
standards. There was every prospect that the
Anglo-Egyptian administration, like a machine
that is somewhat out of order, would be rapidly
overhauled, cleaned, and set to work once more
at an accelerated pace; and the adjusting of the
mechanism was a task which was expected to be
interesting and pleasant. The political position,
always fraught with anxiety, was, for the moment,
remarkably disembroiled, and there seemed to be
nothing which would interrupt the work.

The good sense of the home Government in appointing Lord Kitchener to the vacant office was highly to be commended. His prestige in Egypt was, and is, enormous. In the opinion of the natives, he is an embodiment of stern justice and kindly sympathy. He represents the military power of England; and he was held by the natives as the creator of the Egyptian army, the conqueror of the Dervishes and of the Boers, and as the Commander-in-Chief of all the British forces. Many of the Arabic papers rejoiced at the appointment. Al-Ahram, for example, wrote: "If we are to be ruled, let us be ruled by a manly man. Lord Kitchener's appointment should be welcome, since he is so well known to us. His justice in the army is proverbial, and Egypt is hungry for justice."

Lord Kitchener's reputation alone was expected to overcome the majority of the difficulties which beset the diplomatic path in Egypt. It was felt that he would not be subjected to the insults of the native Press so freely as was Sir Eldon Gorst; for, whereas a diplomat with what sometimes appeared to be democratic tendencies could not be expected to retaliate, a mighty soldier whose word seemed to be law to Britain's world-encircling armies was not a person to be trifled with. Every one realised that his appearance at any Government office would set the knees of every dishonest clerk knocking together, whereas Sir Eldon Gorst's presence merely aroused a gaping interest. And the General Assembly or Council of Ministers was likely to pay the respect to Lord Kitchener which they were only beginning to show to Sir Eldon Gorst after four hard years. Thanks to those years, the task of governing Egypt now seemed simple to any strong man, and the merest child's-play to a born ruler such as Lord Kitchener.

The situation, however, was more complicated than it appeared to be. The 29th of September 1911 was Lord Kitchener's first day as British Agent in Cairo. On the very next day Italy sent her ultimatum to Turkey, and on October 1, 1911, declared war upon the Ottoman Empire, of which Egypt formed an integral part. For many years the Italians had coveted that portion of the North African coast which lies opposite to their native shores; and both in speeches and in books their statesmen had advocated with the greatest vehemence the seizure of Tripoli. Italy's only rival in this proposed game of "grab" was Germany; and when events in Morocco were beginning to point to Germany's failure to obtain any footing in that country, there was some reason to suppose that the Kaiser would turn his attention to Tripoli. The Italians, therefore, felt that if the desired territory was not to slip from their grasp, they must seize upon it without delay. Preparations for war were hurriedly made, and already in the early summer of 1911 the plans were formulated.

Now it must be remembered that Italy was a nation with whom we were at that time already on the most friendly terms, but with whom Austria and Germany, in spite of the Triple Alliance, had many bones to pick. The events of July 1911 showed the Italian statesmen very clearly that the strong policy of England and France would require all the attention of Austria and Germany for the next few months, and that the moment was thus opportune for an attack upon Tripoli which would not be impeded by European interference. Austria would not interfere, lest in so doing she should fail to be ready to help Germany in her war with England and France, which at that time seemed imminent; and, in view of that coming war, neither France nor Germany were likely to worry her. England, however, had to be reckoned with; for, though our attention was fully occupied in Europe, it lay in our power to make the Tripoli expedition a most hazardous affair, simply by permitting the Turks to march through Egypt to the seat of hostilities. Before the projected expedition could be launched, therefore, it was necessary for Italy to ascertain the attitude of England, and to obtain her promise to hold Egypt neutral. This promise, however, could not be lightly given, for it might lead to grave complications with the Porte.

In England the fact was not generally appreciated that Egypt, which is next-door neighbour

to Tripoli, did not belong to Britain, but was a
Turkish province, merely policed and controlled
by us on behalf of the Sultan and his vassal, the
Khedive. In 1882, as we have seen in the foregoing pages, the English entered Egypt to quell
an insurrection which had jeopardised the Khedivial
throne; and our Army of Occupation remained on
the banks of the Nile simply for the purpose of
preventing further risings, and upholding the
authority of the Khedive as being conducive to
the maintenance of law and order. Egypt paid
a large tribute to Turkey yearly; and the Sultan
did not raise any serious objection to English rule
in this province of his, because our presence there
insured the most punctilious payment of this
tribute and maintained a state of profound peace
in an otherwise rather turbulent portion of his
empire. So great a change for the better has been
wrought in the condition of Egypt by the Occupation, however, that it was, and still is, felt by the
British Government that an evacuation of the
country would be little short of a crime against
humanity. Not only does our control of Egyptian
affairs prevent the oppression of the peasants by
the upper classes, not only does it insure all the
comforts of peace and justice both for the native
and the European population, but it also procures
that sense of general security which enables the
commerce of the country to expand and prosper.
At the time with which we are dealing, hundreds

of first-rate Englishmen were employed in the service of the Egyptian Government side by side with Egyptians; and although all governors of provinces, all heads of the ministries, and the majority of inspectors were native Egyptians, the English officials were able to exert a guiding control of the administration. These English officials were in no way connected with the British Government, let it be understood. They became, for the period of their service, Egyptians; they had to wear the Egyptian *tarboush*, or fez, during office hours; they had to work on Sundays, Friday being the Mohammedan Sabbath and day of rest; they received their appointment and their dismissal from the Khedive's Government, which acted in the name of the Sultan; and in every way they were servants, not of the British Government, but of the Khedive and his master, the Sultan. The British control was exerted through the medium of the British Consul-General, who was supposed merely to direct from the outside the general welfare of the country. Of course, the British Consul-General actually governed Egypt, and regulated its administration; but it must be clearly understood that nominally Egypt was under the absolute control of the Khedive and the Sultan. Egypt paid a tribute of nearly £700,000 per annum to Turkey; the coinage of the country was issued in the name of the Sultan; all taxes were levied in his name; the Turkish flag was used by Egypt; all military ranks were described in the Turkish language; the whole Egyptian Army, with its English or native officers, was at the absolute disposal of the Sultan in time of war; and Egyptian territory might be occupied by Turkish troops in war time. These Turkish rights were recognised as late as 1892 in an official *firmân*, or decree, and they had never been repudiated by England, who, indeed, was pledged to maintain them.

When, therefore, Italy declared war on the Porte, and seized the neighbouring province of Tripoli, the Turkish Government had an absolute right to march its armies across Egypt to fight the Italians in the next province; it was entitled to order the Egyptian Army to assist in the defence of the Empire; and it had every written authority for demanding the Khedive's assistance in money, materials, and men. Egypt was the natural base for Turkish operations in Tripoli; for the sea being held by the Italians, the Turkish armies could only reach the seat of hostilities by way of the highroad through Asia Minor, Syria, and Egypt. Thus, there can be no shadow of doubt that Italy had first to ascertain England's attitude on the Nile before the project of the invasion of Tripoli could enter the field of practical affairs. If England had stated its intention of acting according to the spirit of the *firmân* of 1892, and of allowing Turkish troops to pass through Egypt, let alone the question of allowing Egyptian soldiers to fight for the defence of their sovereign, Italy would never have risked an invasion of Tripoli. That invasion could only have been made possible by our definite assurance that Egypt would remain neutral, and would prevent the passage of the Turkish armies through its territory. Moreover, before the declaration of war, Italy had to be satisfied that the British control of Egypt was sufficiently powerful to prevent a revolution in that country, which, if successful, would have given Turkey the opportunity of marching a large force through the Delta to Tripoli.

At that time, it must be remembered, a European war was imminent; and it was generally understood that Italy was about to join with Austria and Germany in the coming attack upon the Triple Entente. Is it therefore conceivable that we should have allowed Italy to occupy the territory on the immediate west of Egypt, and should have risked giving the gravest offence to Turkey by helping the Italians to do this, if we had supposed that, in a few months' time, they would be fighting against us and menacing our position on the Nile?

No public statement was ever made which would indicate that the British Government contracted any agreement with Italy at that time; but there can be no doubt whatsoever that some sort of understanding was arrived at. England, it would seem probable, consented to prevent Turkish troops from entering Tripoli *viâ* Egypt, and so far as possible to put a stop to all gun-running or other belligerent enterprise. We appear to have undertaken to keep Egypt absolutely neutral, which, fortunately, we could do without breaking our pledge to maintain the existing Turco-Egyptian Treaties, wherein there is no actual forbidding of neutrality; and we also seem to have promised to use diplomatic persuasion to prevent the Sultan exerting his undoubted right to demand Egyptian military aid. The giving of these concessions to Italy are clearly enough indicated by our subsequent actions in Egypt, which, as will be related below, were of a very deliberate nature ; while the despatch to Cairo of Lord Kitchener, the one man who was capable of keeping Egypt quiet at such a critical time, and the outbreak of hostilities instantly on his arrival in his new abode, can hardly be attributed to mere coincidence. It seems quite evident that our attitude to Italy was as follows: "Since it appears to be inevitable," said we, "that some European Power will pounce upon Tripoli, we in Egypt much prefer you as our neighbours to, say, the Germans; and though we do not wish to offend Turkey by actively taking your part, we will show our friendliness to you by holding Egypt neutral, which we can do without breaking the *letter* of the Turco-Egyptian Treaty, though obviously we infringe the *spirit* of it. To act thus, however, we shall require to send a very strong man to Cairo, and you must promise not to declare war until he has arrived there. In return for our kindness to you we shall expect you to play a friendly part towards us in the event of a European conflagration."

Lord Kitchener thus found himself, on arriving in Egypt, in a situation which required very delicate handling; and when the expected Italian ultimatum was despatched and the expedition to Tripoli at last became a reality, he was called upon to face a possible crisis of the most violent nature. It is commonly said in Egypt that had he not been in that country during the early stages of the war, the situation would have been most dangerous. Thanks, however, to his great reputation, and to the awe and reverence in which he is held, the country remained tranquil. The Egyptians were delighted with his politeness and cordiality, and felt that in him they had a friend who would show them how to act in this difficult situation. Their sympathies were entirely with the Turks, their brother Mussulmans, and, curiously enough, they believed that Lord Kitchener's prejudices were upon the same side.

Early in the war he is said to have been approached by a number of Egyptian officers who asked permission to volunteer for active service in Tripoli. Lord Kitchener replied that he would gladly give them permission to do so, but that

their vacant posts would have to be filled by
junior officers, and they themselves would probably find on their return that they had been
placed on the retired list, not by his wishes but
by reason of the upward pressure due to the
congestion in the junior ranks. He advised them,
therefore, to curb their heroic ambitions, so natural
to Egyptians, and to stay at home : which they
did. At another time certain notables proposed
that Egypt should send several regiments to the
aid of the Turks, in accordance with the Turco-
Egyptian Treaty, which England was known to
uphold. Lord Kitchener said that he would have
no objection, should the Sultan make the request,
but that, in order to preserve internal quiet, he
would be obliged to replace the absent troops by
an equal number of British regiments ; at which
the proposal was hastily withdrawn. A few weeks
later a deputation of Bedouîn chieftains waited on
Lord Kitchener to ask him to permit them to
gather their tribes and to travel into Tripoli to
fight the Italians. His lordship congratulated
them most heartily on their warlike qualities,
which, he admitted, he had overlooked. He reminded them that up till now they, as nomads,
had been exempt from service in the Egyptian
army ; but that since they were thirsting in this
manner for military glory, he felt that Egypt
could ill afford to lose them, and he would see
that they were conscribed for the army like the

fellahîn. To these remarks he is said to have added that slight suggestion of a wink, which is so well understood by the native to mean that it is best to keep quiet. Needless to say, they did not go to the war.

Thus, with the greatest tact he kept the country quiet, and even managed to enlist the sympathies of the native Press. It is true that he was prepared instantly to suppress any paper which published inflammatory articles, and actually did so in more than one case; but, at the same time, there is no doubt that the tone of the editors was, on the whole, very friendly. Even the violent Shêkh Shawish told his readers that, after all, the English were not so bad, and that an amicable understanding with them was possible. British prestige rose to a level to which it had not attained since the first ten years of the Occupation; and the various English inspectors in the provinces found that the attitude of the natives towards them was unusually deferential.

When one remembers that at this time Christian Italy was attacking Moslem Turkey, Christian France and Spain were taking possession of Moslem Morocco, and Christian Russia was preparing to advance into Moslem Persia, an outbreak of anti-Christian feeling in Egypt was naturally to be expected; and it came as no surprise, therefore, when a riot occurred in Alexandria which, for a short time, had a very ugly appearance. One

day towards the end of October news reached
Egypt that the Turks had driven the Italians
out of Tripoli, and that the war was at an end.
This was received with the utmost joy by the
low-class inhabitants of Alexandria, who are
seldom on good terms with the Italians living
in their midst; and they began to act in much
the same manner as that in which Londoners
behaved after the relief of Mafeking. They
paraded the streets, shouting and singing, and
in many cases they playfully insulted the Italians
with whom they met, knocking their hats off and
hustling them. The victims at once took fright,
and, the news being spread, the mob was met at
a certain street corner by a compact body of
Italians, who opened fire upon them with their
revolvers, with the result that two or three natives
were killed and several wounded. The police managed to disperse the crowd, and on the next day
when the demonstration was renewed the hoses of
the municipal fire-engines were turned upon the
mob, and order was quickly restored. A detachment of British marines and bluejackets, which
was landed from one of the battleships in the
harbour for the ostensible purpose of carrying out
certain ordinary manœuvres, was received with
wild enthusiasm by the European population, as
though it had come to save them from dire peril.
In Cairo on the same day there was a small disturbance in the native quarter; and an old man

was arrested in the bazaars for preaching the Holy War. A much-exaggerated account of the riot was cabled to certain London newspapers, and caused a flutter of nervousness which was entirely unjustified by the facts.

When the date of King George's passage through the Suez Canal on his return from the Coronation Durbar in India drew near, the Egyptian Nationalists evinced a keen desire that a Turkish prince of the Imperial House should be present at Port Said to greet His Majesty, it being felt by them that in this manner they might demonstrate to the world that Egypt really was a part of the Turkish Empire. Lord Kitchener, wishing to show friendliness to the Porte in order to mollify any ill-feeling that might there exist in regard to the neutrality of Egypt, consented to the proposed meeting, so far as he was concerned, and in due course it was arranged. The Turkish prince who was sent over to Port Said had lived for so many years as a prisoner in Constantinople during the reign of the deposed Sultan that his manners are said to have been astonishingly inelegant, and his natural awkwardness was accentuated by the fact that he could only speak Turkish. Coming across the Mediterranean he was terribly sea-sick, and thus his appearance on his arrival was not of the kind which was likely to inspire respect in the minds of the critical Egyptians. On board the yacht *Medina* at Port Said he is said, perhaps on doubtful authority, to have sat in the sun contentedly picking his teeth, or playing with the buttons of his trousers, while the very smart and absolutely European Khedive—vassal of the Porte — discussed high affairs of State with the King.

Very soon it was apparent to educated Egyptians that, far from the Turkish prince honouring the Khedive with his presence, the Khedive was involuntarily placed in the position of patron to this ill-educated young man; and the effect caused by this reversed status was more far-reaching than was generally supposed. The unfortunate prince seems to have had a somewhat unpleasant time during the three days in which he was the Khedive's guest in Cairo; for, owing to the determination of Lord Kitchener to avoid all risk of the Turkish prince's appearance in public acting as an incentive to anti-Italian rioting, his Imperial Highness was obliged to make all his movements at a different hour from that which had been announced. Instead of travelling from Port Said to Cairo by day, according to the official programme, he was bundled into the special train at dead of night, arriving in the biting cold of daybreak, and being met only by a few sleepy officials. When it was announced that he would visit the Zoo or the Pyramids he was whisked away in a small motor-brougham to the Museum or to Heliopolis; and when the crowds had

gathered to see him as he entered the front gate
of the palace, the unprepared loiterers at the back
door were permitted to gaze for a brief moment on
the hurrying little figure.

Thus the Imperial visit passed off without com-
motion, Turkish confidence in English friendship,
and Egyptian confidence in their own superiority
to the Turks, being at one and the same time
assured.

Shortly after this, however, the Italian Government seems to have made representations to England with regard to the gun-running which was
being practised along the western borders of
Egypt, and already in December it was rumoured
that a detachment of the 21st Lancers was to
be sent to the frontier to check this. "You see,"
said the officers' mess, "we must play fair to
Italy"; but the question as to why they were
to do so does not seem to have been put. On
the face of it, our friendship to Turkey would
seem to have been more urgent politically than
our friendship to Italy. The effect on our vast
Mohammedan possessions of an *entente* with the
Porte at that time would have been great; and
in Egypt it must be admitted that our easiest
hours have been those in which we were on friendly
terms with Turkey, and our most anxious hours
those in which our relations with that country
were bad. The Sultan was recognised as the head
of the Mohammedan faith, and since there is no

nationality in Islam, all race-differences being lost in the community of religion, an insult to Turkey was, at that time, likely to be regarded as an insult to every one of the ninety - four million Moslem subjects of our King. Yet, in spite of this recognised fact, we took the strongest steps to prevent any aid passing from Egypt to the Turks in Tripoli, and we sternly suppressed the little breaches of neutrality at which we might so easily have winked. And it is to be remembered that this neutrality itself was such a forced attitude that we might have been expected to have insisted upon it as quietly as possible, avoiding actions which were calculated to bring our attitude to public notice. If we had not been in Egypt there would have been a direct road for Turkish troops from Constantinople to the seat of war, and in all probability Italy, if she had been so rash as to attack Tripoli at all, would have been driven into the sea. Since we held Egypt really on behalf of the Egyptians, however, it is quite natural that we should have more or less disassociated the country from Turkish affairs, and until reminded by the Sultan, should silently have ignored the ancient statute which declared that the Egyptian army was at the disposal of the Porte in time of war, and that the highroad from Syria to Tripoli was open to the Turks. But surely there must have been some urgent reason for our conduct in boldly forcing this attitude on public attention by military propaganda.

During January, the Arabs of the Eastern desert which lies between Syria and Egypt began to show signs of restlessness, and there was some reason to suppose that they would attempt to slip across the Delta, either singly or in small bodies, in order to travel through to Tripoli for the defence of Islam. Lord Kitchener then built forts along the Suez Canal, and sent troops to hold them, thus once more demonstrating the uncompromising attitude of England to the Porte, and calling public attention to our vigilance in preventing the Turks from receiving any help whatsoever from that portion of their Empire which we held for them. In February certain well-known Turkish officers who were trying to cross Egypt disguised as Arabs were arrested, and were sent back to Constantinople in spite of all their protests.

Such occurrences as these show clearly enough that we had an understanding with Italy, based on our desire to wean her from the Triple Alliance. It was a contract forced from us at a time of great peril, when it was absolutely necessary that we should secure Italy's support in the great war which threatened us. It was England, and England alone, who gave Italy the opportunity of seizing her coveted portion of North Africa, and by giving this to her we won no less a prize than the breaking up of the Triple Alliance.

The attitude of Italy in the great European war came as a surprise to most people, and it was generally attributed to the traditional hatred of the Italians for their Austrian neighbours. Certainly this was one of the contributory causes for their attitude; but the facts here recounted suggest that it was largely due to the obligations to England contracted during the Turco-Italian War; for without our help the occupation of Tripoli could never have been sustained, notwithstanding the wonderful bravery and dash of the Italian troops. Thus the refusal of the Italian Government to take arms against us looks very much as though it were a practical application of the maxim that one good turn deserves another.

We may thus understand why Lord Kitchener was sent to Egypt, and we may now see the reason of our actions in that country. The risk which we took was twofold. Firstly there was that of a rupture with the Porte; but this was not a serious danger, for we could always say to Turkey: "If you make trouble with us we will take Egypt from you altogether." The second risk was that of a rising in Egypt. Lord Kitchener was the only man who, by his presence, could remove all chance of a serious outbreak, and very rightly he was chosen for the work. Had he not been available it is doubtful whether we could have accepted the arrangement with Italy; for a concentration of British troops in Egypt, which would have been the alternative method of insuring quiet there, would have been awkward for us and provocative to the Moslems.

No sooner was the Turco-Italian trouble ended than the outbreak of the Turco-Balkan war brought new anxieties to the Government of Egypt. The question again arose as to whether the Egyptians, as the subjects of the Sultan, would be called upon to send an army to the aid of the Turks; but fortunately the Porte did not wish to complicate the international situation by calling up the question of the position of England in Egypt. Thus Lord Kitchener was again enabled to advise the Khedive to declare his neutrality; and native opinion, though favouring the Ottomans, remained calm and outwardly indifferent. When the defeat of the Turks was assured, most of the European residents thought that the British Government would quietly annex Egypt; but actually no such step was contemplated. This restraint was due not only to our desire to avoid any action likely to add fuel to the smouldering fire of German and Austrian jealousy, and thus precipitate the European conflict which the Triple Entente were labouring so desperately to avoid; but it was also due to our inherent love of fair-play. We remembered that when we had come to Egypt in 1882 our declared policy was to maintain "the

rights of the sovereign and vassal as now established between the Sultan and the Khedive," and
that for thirty years we had honourably continued
to do so, in spite of all the difficulties involved.
We were pledged to uphold the Sultan's position
as overlord of Egypt, and though Egyptian
neutrality was declared, we still saw that the
tribute to Turkey was regularly paid, that the
Turkish flag was flown, and that the nominal
authority of the Sultan was maintained in the
many ways recorded in the Turco - Egyptian
Treaty. It would be hard to find a parallel
instance to such a contradictory situation; and
yet it was the only safe solution of the matter.

Lord Kitchener's task in Egypt was at all times
facilitated by his excellent personal relations with
the French. It is not generally remembered
that he fought on the side of France in the
Franco-Prussian War; and the recognised fact
that he would "like to have another smack at
the Germans" provided him with a common
basis of friendship with every Frenchman. It
was rumoured that the British attitude in the
summer of 1911 in so strongly supporting France
in Morocco was largely due to Lord Kitchener's
influence. In Egypt the French gave him every
assistance, and there was an atmosphere of com-
placency in this respect which did not fail to have
its effect on the native mind. Thus it was felt
that whatever the future of Turkey and Egypt,

R

and whatever changes the next few years might bring, we should have the support both of France and of Italy ; and there was already some hope of an alliance. The English, French, and Italians held between them the entire coast of North Africa, from the Atlantic along the Mediterranean and down the Red Sea to the Indian Ocean ; and, in fact, between them they possessed about seven-eighths of the whole of Africa this side of the Equator. With such interests in common an alliance seemed both natural and necessary.

We must now turn from the international aspect of Egyptian affairs to the internal organisation of the country. Lord Kitchener quickly effected many changes in the Government administration, and gave his attention at once to a surprisingly wide range of subjects. Sir Eldon Gorst, as was pointed out in the last chapter, was so occupied with the political aspect of Egyptian affairs that he could not find sufficient time to inquire into the workings of all the Government offices. But for Lord Kitchener there were no political troubles : nobody was bold enough to make them. His lordship well knew how to humour his Egyptian friends, and how to reduce his enemies by a word and a look. Those who saw the former leaving his study beaming with delight, and the latter crawling from The Presence with the cold sweat on their brow, describe the spectacle as truly wonderful. " He put his hands on my shoulders," cried

LORD KITCHENER OF KHARTOUM
(As Commander-in-Chief of the Egyptian Army).

an old Shêkh, "and said to me, 'Am I not your father? Will a father forget his children?'" "He said to me," declared a British civilian who had nursed a complaint for some years, 'Mr Blank, if there's anything else you want, I can always find time to see *you*.'" His cordiality astonished both English and Egyptians, for it was supposed that his manners would be somewhat severe; and this fact, combined with his occasional well-merited "shortness," at once created the opinion both in European and native circles that political tranquillity was the best policy. Thus he was free to look into the workings of the machine of government and to adjust that which was out of order.

There was hardly a department which was not speedily subjected to some degree of scrutiny; and not one of the Ministers, Advisers, or Directors-General continued to consider that the last word upon any subject rested with himself. Each one turned to Lord Kitchener for a final opinion. In the old days the head of an administration would address his subordinates with the words, "I propose to do so-and-so," or "I wish you to act in such-and-such a manner." But now he said: "Lord Kitchener proposes . . .," or "Lord Kitchener wishes . . ." Numerous stories were told in Cairo in this regard, and there was probably in most of them a certain degree of truth.

It was related that a land company which was

developing a certain suburb of Cairo wrote to his lordship to complain that, although they had offered very fair terms to the Ministry of Finance for co-operation in the making of a motor-road which should link them with the city, only evasive answers had been received, and the matter had now dragged on for three or four years. Lord Kitchener, having satisfied himself that the proposals were satisfactory, told the financial authorities simply that he wished to motor out to the suburb on a certain date, and that the road must then be finished. "But," they objected, "labour is expensive and difficult to obtain." "Turn the prisoners on to the work," said he. "That isn't possible," they replied; "we have not got a sufficient number of warders to keep them in hand along a straggling line of that kind." "Warders!" exclaimed Lord Kitchener. "What the devil is the Army of Occupation doing with itself? Let them act as warders. Please see that the work begins to-morrow."

On another occasion the work of building the new barracks for the Army of Occupation was held up owing to the fact that the Ministry of Finance did not feel able to supply any further funds at that moment. That able official, Sir Paul Harvey, the Financial Adviser, was inclined to keep a somewhat tight hand upon the purse-strings; and when he stated that money could not be found for a certain purpose the matter was immediately dropped. He was not accustomed to be contradicted. In regard to these barracks his inability to find the money was reported to Lord Kitchener, who sent a message to him asking why the funds were not forthcoming. In reply he sent a detailed statement explaining the reasons for his desire to postpone the work. Lord Kitchener read the statement carefully, and, so the story goes, returned it with the curt endorsement: "Money *must* be found immediately," thus establishing his right to control even this most autocratic Ministry.

A few days after his arrival in Egypt a rumour reached the Agency that a certain native official in Upper Egypt had been guilty of some small offence or other, and Lord Kitchener thought the matter worthy of inquiry. He therefore told the startled head of the Ministry concerned to send an English inspector post-haste to the spot—a journey of some twelve hours in the train—in order to ascertain the true facts. The inspector, being accustomed to settle matters of this kind out of court, and feeling that the case did not merit the public scolding of the offender, wrote a mild report upon the subject. This was forwarded to Lord Kitchener, who is said to have read it and returned it with the following words scribbled across the corner: "I asked you to find out the facts, not to whitewash the official."

At another time Lord Kitchener caused the

Ministry of Education much perturbation by demanding that a number of schoolboys should be expelled from one of the Government schools on account of their having incited the crowd to riot on a certain occasion. Both the Egyptian and English officials of the Ministry objected; but Lord Kitchener, knowing how necessary severity was, insisted on the expulsion, which was duly carried out.

Whether these stories are true or not, they serve to illustrate the manner in which Lord Kitchener took upon himself the whole burden of government in Egypt, and made the Agency the responsible and head office for every Ministry and department. Of course, this may be described as having put all our eggs into one basket, and it was argued that in the event of Lord Kitchener's transfer, retirement, or death, the chief men of the Government would be unprepared to assume responsibility once more. But it was this very fact of the probable shortness of his tenure of office in Egypt which made it essential that he should bring his mind to bear upon every detail, and should make things "hum," as the saying is, while he was there! He undoubtedly made some small mistakes, but in all successful work it must be remembered that to get things done is more important than always to do things right. Life is not a game of chess, and the players have no cause to sit for hours staring at their pieces. The greater game contains the greater possibilities of success; and, since there are always so many later opportunities for adjustment and rectification on broad lines, the first rule is not invariably to move correctly, but *to move*.

As actual ruler of Egypt Lord Kitchener resumed—to the mild extent prevalent in that country—the pomp and circumstance of power, which had been quite abandoned in recent years. The dull brown colour of the liveries of the native servants at the Agency were discarded in favour of scarlet and gold. A state ball-room was built on to the official residence. The dinner-parties and other functions were of an elaborate nature, and Lord Kitchener's own splendid service of gold plate was much admired by the Egyptian grandees, to whom a display of this kind means a very great deal. In the streets of Cairo he often drove in a well-turned-out carriage and pair, preceded by two *saises* or out-runners, who cried hoarsely to the people to clear the way, while the native pedestrians, duly impressed, nudged each other and pointed, saying, "Look, my brother, there is *El Lor-r-r-d*." The man in the street was very fond of Lord Kitchener, and his appearance in public was always the signal for the collection of a small crowd. To the blank amazement of all residents, when he first arrived in Cairo he was heartily cheered by the natives, who extremely rarely give expression to their feelings in this

manner; and on subsequent occasions of importance his reception was most cordial.

Lord Kitchener's attitude towards the natives,
and towards the question of their participation
in the government of the country, was in principle
the same as that of Sir Eldon Gorst. The opinion
of Egyptian Ministers and officials was scrupu-
lously consulted, and they were led to feel that
they had some voice in public affairs. Owing,
however, to the fact that the British Agent was
recognised to be such a very great man—a sort
of Grand Vizier and Commander-in-Chief and
King's Chief Favourite rolled into one—native
argumentativeness was wonderfully curtailed, and
that carping criticism to which Sir Eldon Gorst's
actions were always subjected was no longer
heard. The Egyptian is very quick to recognise
his master, and there can be little doubt that he
is most happy and contented when he is conscious
that he is ruled by a man whom it is no dishon-
our to serve. He is, in his own fashion, a proud
person, and he finds difficulty in giving allegiance
to any but a mighty man of valour. For such a
one, however, he is prepared to silence his natural
habit of talkativeness, and, conscious that he is
under the great man's eye, to work quietly for the
common good. Lord Kitchener, as was expected,
had very little difficulty in governing Egypt, and
so long as he remained in the country complete
tranquillity reigned.

During the two and a half years of his tenure of office in Cairo, all manner of reforms were instituted, especially in regard to agriculture and irrigation. A new Ministry of Agriculture was instituted, and many improvements were made in regard to cotton-growing, which is one of the chief sources of Egypt's wealth. Vast irrigation schemes were undertaken, which, incidentally, were freely criticised by engineers; but so ably were they carried out by the genius of Sir Murdoch Macdonald, the Under-Secretary of State to the Ministry of Public Works, who is one of the great engineers of the age, that confidence in their ultimate success was generally felt.

On the whole, Lord Kitchener was fortunate in the group of Englishmen and Egyptians who were associated with him, and who are now guiding the country through its present crisis. Sir Paul Harvey, unable, it is supposed, to approve of his lordship's useful but bold expenditure of public money, resigned his office as Financial Adviser, and Lord Edward Cecil, the son of the great Lord Salisbury, was chosen to take his place. The new Adviser had served the Egyptian Government for many years; and, as was expected, he proved to be a sound administrator of exceptionally acute perception. At the Ministry of the Interior Mr (now Sir) Ronald Graham successfully carried on the best traditions of Anglo-Egyptian administration, with the aid of a very notable group of high-principled and hard-working English inspectors. At Alexandria the complicated task of bringing cohesion into the work of the cosmopolitan and heterogeneous municipal councils was performed with astonishing tact by Dr Alexander Granville, to whom Egypt owes a very deep debt; and in Cairo, Harvey Pasha acted with ability as the Commandant of the City. At the British Agency Lord Kitchener was assisted by a very able staff: Mr (now Sir) Milne Cheetham, the First Secretary, being conspicuous for his diplomatic handling of the varied situations, and Mr Ronald Storrs, the widely talented Oriental Secretary, having a very masterly grasp of the complexities of native action and opinion.

When Lord Kitchener returned to England for his annual leave, in June 1914, there was not a cloud upon the horizon. He had successfully steered Egypt through the manifold difficulties of the two Turkish wars, and had raised British prestige there to perhaps its greatest height. Then suddenly, like a bolt from the blue, came the news of the Serbian complication; and in a moment Europe was plunged into war. Lord Kitchener at once prepared to return to Egypt to hold the country quiet; but as he stepped upon the vessel which was to carry him from England, he received the order to take charge of the War Office, and therewith he turned his back on the Land of the Pharaohs, probably for ever.

CHAPTER VIII.

THE PROTECTORATE.

WHILE the Protectorate of Egypt is still in its infancy it is very necessary for us to have in mind a general outline of the events which have brought about the present changes in Egypt, for there can be no doubt that a great many of our actions during the last few months are open to criticism on the grounds of irregular procedure. Since, however, our moral right has been so overwhelmingly great, we must be prepared to bear any such criticism undismayed, and must be fortified against the attacks on England's honour which are certain to be made, with apparent justification, by those who can only see the very obvious technical carelessnesses of the British Government, and who choose to be blind to the equally obvious high-mindedness of British action in general. England has not been called "Perfidious Albion" for nothing. As Professor Seeley once remarked, "we seem, as it were, to have conquered and peopled half the world in a fit of

absence of mind"; and in Egypt our actions lately
have constituted a very typical instance of this
cheery obliviousness to the letter of the law which
has earned for us from time to time the mistrust
of other nations.   When we know by a kind of
healthy instinct that we are doing good, and that
we have the force of moral right behind us, we are
apt to prance along with small regard for technical
niceties, and hence the nations with more phari-
saical tendencies find us a very rude people.

Let us review the development of the Egyptian
situation which I have endeavoured to outline in
the foregoing chapters.   When the Turks conquered the Egyptians in 1517 it was agreed that
Egypt should be governed by twenty-four native
Mameluke chieftains under the supervision of a
Turkish governor, that a considerable tribute should
be paid annually to the Porte, and that 12,000
Egyptian troops should be supplied to the Sultan
in time of war.   At the beginning of the nineteenth
century, Mohammed Ali, the Turkish Governor of
Egypt, made war on the Turks, and would probably
have dethroned the Sultan had not the Powers
intervened to preserve the *status quo*.   In 1842
England successfully urged Mohammed Ali to sign
a treaty with the Porte, in which it was agreed
that his descendants should hold the hereditary
governorship of Egypt, that a tribute of £412,000
should be paid annually to Turkey, that the
Egyptian army should have a maximum strength

of 18,000 men, who should be at the disposal of the Sultan in war time, and that the Egyptians should be regarded as Ottoman subjects. In 1867, Ismail Pasha, the grandson of Mohammed Ali, made a new treaty with the Sultan, in which it was agreed that the ruler of Egypt should no longer be called simply governor, but should have the hereditary title of Khedive. The tribute was raised to £682,000 per annum, but the clauses of the earlier agreement were more or less maintained.

In 1882 the Powers felt it necessary that some steps should be taken to restore order in Egypt, as the lives of foreigners were greatly endangered by the revolution led by Arabi Pasha. There was much delay, however, in deciding on a course of action, and at last England, having unsuccessfully invited the co-operation of France and, of course, of Turkey, invaded Egypt. Our avowed object was to maintain the Khedive upon his throne, to restore order, and to establish a sound administration in this province of the Turkish Empire, thereby encouraging native and foreign commerce, and also securing the safety of the Suez Canal. We undertook to uphold the integrity of the existing Turco-Egyptian treaties, and to continue to regard Egyptians as Ottoman subjects. Ten years later, in 1892, the recently deposed Khedive came to the throne, and the arrangement with the Porte was restated. In the decree dated

March 27 of that year, it was laid down that Egyptian territory was a part of the Turkish Empire, and that Egyptians were subjects of the Sultan, paying annual tribute to the Porte; that the Egyptian army was at the disposal of the Sultan, and was to use the Turkish flag and the Turkish military ranks, all appointments above the rank of colonel being made by the Sultan himself and not by the Khedive; that the coinage of Egypt was to be issued in the Sultan's name, and taxes collected in his name; and that the Khedive was not empowered to make peace or war, nor any political treaties with foreign Powers.   This decree was never revoked, and was, until the recent declaration of the Protectorate, officially acknowledged by us as the recognised basis of our position in Egypt.

The attitude of the British Government has always been, until recently, perfectly clear.   Lord Cromer emphatically stated that so long as the Turco-Egyptian Treaty, which it was thus our avowed object to uphold, was still in force, "there could be no such thing as an Egyptian state or an Egyptian nationality separate from Turkey."   Our Army of Occupation in Egypt was maintained simply and solely to prevent any disorders which might impair the prosperity of the country and injure native or European interests.   The Egyptian governmental departments remained under native Ministers, holding office by favour of the Sultan, to each of whom an English "Adviser" was assigned. British officials in Egypt were in no way connected with the British Government, but were simply private persons in the service of the Khedive. The British officers in the Egyptian army were seconded from their British regiments, and were lent to the Khedive for a certain number of years. The British interests were supervised, not by a High Commissioner or an Ambassador, but by a simple Consul-General (in turn Lord Cromer, Sir Eldon Gorst, and Lord Kitchener), whose actual rank was not above that of the Consuls-General of the other Powers. Thus, except for the presence of England's strong guiding hand and enforcement of internal peace, the relations between Egypt and Turkey were in no way affected, and the country still remained the dutiful vassal of the Porte. It was definitely stated by Lord Dufferin at the beginning of the Occupation that our object was to establish good government, and that we should evacuate the country as soon as a more or less permanent security was assured. In 1910 Sir Eldon Gorst repeated this interpretation of our position in Egypt, but explained that, so far as could be seen, the day of our departure was still a long way off.

Now, since we upheld the Turco-Egyptian agreement in such a very correct manner, the Sultan had little objection to our occupation of this pro-

vince of his. We maintained order and kept the
peace there; we upheld the Sultan's authority and
that of his Viceroy, the Khedive; we saw that the
tribute was paid with punctilious regularity; our
presence encouraged the investment of European
capital in the country; and, in a word, we saved
the Porte a great deal of trouble and expenditure.
On our part we had the advantage of having a
dominating influence in a country strategically
important to us; we there found noble employment for hundreds of our young men; and, really
above all, we had the immense pleasure of organ-
ising, developing, and bringing happiness and
prosperity to a most engaging nation. But there
was one point in the agreement with Turkey
which was a source of anxiety—namely, the undoubted Turkish right to demand Egyptian military
help in time of war. In 1768 the Sultan had asked
his Egyptian vassal for troops to help him against
Russia; during the Greek War of Independence
Egypt had been obliged to furnish an army; and
in the Crimean War the Egyptians had fought for
the Turks. It was therefore quite apparent that,
since we were pledged to maintain the existing
treaties, Egyptian troops would have to be supplied to the Sultan should he demand them at
any time. Fortunately, however, the Porte was
persuaded never to ask for them in her recent
wars; and thus England was saved from a very
awkward situation. But it must be remembered

that this hesitation on Turkey's part to cause complications with us by insisting on its rights, did not in any way invalidate those rights nor abrogate our pledge to maintain them. During the Turco - Italian and Turco - Balkan wars the Sultan's decision to refrain from demanding Egyptian help enabled Egypt to declare its neutrality —an attitude which, it seems, was not in opposition to the letter of the Turco-Egyptian Treaty, though it was to the spirit.

When war was declared between England and Germany, it at once became apparent that the Germans in Egypt would renew with vigour their everlasting efforts to upset our administration in that country. Legally, of course, no action against them could be taken, since Egypt was, according to our oft-repeated definition, an integral part of the neutral Turkish Empire, and we had no actual rights there. But it was fully realised that the Germans intended to stir up the natives against us, and it was necessary that steps should be taken to prevent them from involving both us and the innocent Egyptians in this further farrago of bloodshed and misery. The British authorities, therefore, persuaded the Egyptian Government to regard itself as in a state of war with Germany and Austria, and the people of those nationalities were either turned out of Egypt or were put under restraint, while their shipping was given forty-eight hours to leave Egyptian ports.

Technically this was as audacious an act of justifiable illegality as any ever committed by a British Government, for it really constituted an enforced act of rebellion on the part of Egypt against the suzerainty of the Sultan. It will be remembered that the Turco-Egyptian Treaty, the integrity of which we had emphatically stated our intention to maintain, clearly said that Egypt, being a vassal State, was not allowed to declare war on anybody, and that all its political relations with other nations were to be conducted through the Turkish sovereign. The British Government had laid down as one of the fundamental axioms of our occupation of Egypt that " the rights of the sovereign and vassal as now established between the Sultan and the Khedive should be maintained "; and Egypt's inability to make war or peace was recognised by us in documentary form as late as 1892. Now, however, in these days of excitement, when the authorities felt that at all costs bloodshed in Egypt must be prevented, I do not suppose that anybody remembered the clauses of the Turco - Egyptian Treaty which we were pledged to respect. The British Government did not deliberately ignore this particular clause : it literally forgot to consult the archives. Had this been done and the irregularity observed, the position could have been regularised with ease by means of a frank Egyptian announcement to the Porte, either (1) that Egypt was in a state of open rebellion against the Sultan, or (2) that it was not in revolt, that it had simply broken this one clause of the treaty in the exceptional circumstances, and that it craved the Sultan's indulgence. No such step was taken, however; and, hand in hand with the Egyptians, the British agents went boldly on their way, rounding up the Germans in this portion of the territory of Germany's friend, Turkey.

The wisdom of these precautions was soon made apparent. A German officer named Mors, who was employed in the Alexandria police, was proved to have incited the natives against us, to have acted as a spy in German interests, and to have planned to blow up the Suez Canal. He was publicly degraded and sentenced to penal servitude for life. Revelations in regard to the activities of a German political agent, named Dr Pruffer, also now came to light; and already in September it was perfectly obvious that Germany was urging Turkey to send an expedition to Egypt to turn the British troops out of the country and to reassert the sovereign rights of the Porte. Turkey was, somewhat unconsciously, within those rights in showing the intention of attempting to punish Egypt for its insubordination; but I do not think that many persons in England were well enough versed in Turco-Egyptian history to realise that we, first of all, had given the Sultan so very clear a technical *casus belli* against us. One thing, however, was quite obvious: Turkey would never have troubled to assert herself unless she had been urged to do so by Germany. The Porte had nothing to fear from England in Egypt. The British, as has been said, maintained order, upheld the Sultan's authority, and saw that the tribute was paid regularly. Moreover, as early as the first week in August, the home Government had definitely stated that if Turkey remained neutral they " did not propose to alter the status of Egypt," and had " emphatically contradicted the report that the annexation of Egypt was under consideration."

The Turks, however, were soon teased by the Germans to feelings of some anger at our actions on the Nile; and the French Ambassador reported a Turkish Minister as saying that " England was treating Egypt as if it belonged to her, whereas it formed part of the Ottoman dominions, and that . . . England should now sign a convention providing for the evacuation of Egypt by British troops at the end of the war." Meanwhile the Turkish newspapers were full of denunciations of what they called our high-handed proceedings; and the Mosul and Damascus army corps of the Turkish army were hurriedly massed on the Egyptian frontier, ostensibly with a view to chastising the insubordinate province if further acts of hostility to its overlord were committed. Roads were prepared and transport collected; mines were sent to the Gulf of Akaba to protect the Turkish forces there from naval attack; many German officers were hurried into Syria; and the Hedjaz railway was seized for military purposes. On one occasion some Bedouîn levies actually crossed the frontier, the ground here being more or less open desert.

The anomaly of the situation rapidly increased. Not a word had yet been uttered by England to indicate that the Sultan's authority in Egypt had ceased to be recognised, or that the country was no longer regarded as part of the Turkish Empire; and yet circumstances were forcing the British authorities to act as though they did not admit these very points which England was in Egypt to emphasise. When the Foreign Office asked the Sultan why the Turkish troops were massed on the Egyptian frontier, he replied by asking us what on earth many thousands of our troops were doing in his province of Egypt. When, later, Sir Edward Grey insisted on knowing whether the Sultan intended to invade Egypt, he replied that, "as Egypt was one of his own provinces, how could he dream of invading it?" These queries and answers were at first exchanged in the most sprightly spirit, and the Turkish play upon the intricacies of the situation must have caused real amusement in the British chanceries. England felt no enmity to Turkey. We hoped sincerely that the Porte would keep out of the mess, and we had every intention of holding

Egypt intact on the Sultan's behalf. The British mind, obtuse in its inherent humanity, cared only for the welfare of the Egyptians and the confining of the sufferings of the war to their then limits. But as time passed a growing sense of irritation was felt on both sides. Egypt was found to be full of Turkish and German spies, and on more than one occasion weak-minded Egyptians were persuaded to cause local disturbances. One night a native whose emotions had thus been worked upon aroused his neighbours by rushing madly round and round the cemetery of his district shouting "War! war!" until he was taken in charge. Two men, dressed like Turks, and professing to be Persians, were found tampering with a railway line in the Delta, but when interrogated they gave the ominous names of Goldstein and Goldberger. A well-known Turkish senator was discovered to be in Egypt, engaged in inciting the natives; and shortly afterwards three prominent Turkish officers were arrested while similarly occupied.

At last, three months after the outbreak of hostilities in Europe, war was declared between England and Turkey; and thereby the political situation in Egypt was made more anomalous than ever. Legally, war between England and the Porte meant that we were also at war with Egypt, for the British Government had not yet advised Egypt to declare itself in revolt against the Sultan. The British officers serving in the Egyptian army had been merely lent to the Khedive for short terms of years; and it had always been fully recognised that they were thus for the time being in the service of the Sultan, since the Egyptian forces were, according to treaty, a part of the Turkish army. These officers were now, therefore, in the pay of our enemy; and similarly all British officials in the Egyptian Government were under certain obligations to the Sultan. The native Ministers and high officials found themselves in a still more delicate and awkward situation, for they held their office by mandate of the Khedive as Vassal of Turkey, and they naturally regarded the measures which they were required to take as totally inconsistent with that mandate. Nobody, however, seems to have been very deeply troubled by these technical irregularities, and no Englishman dreamed of resigning his office. All the precautionary measures exercised against the Germans were now extended to the Turks; all suspicious Ottomans were arrested, and Turkish shipping was ordered to leave Egyptian waters immediately. These actions were totally illegal, for a state of war between Turkey and England did not in any way nullify the terms of the unrevoked agreement between Turkey and Egypt. The situation could have been regularised by an Egyptian declaration of independence from Turkey, but none was made.

Egyptians were still officially regarded as Turkish subjects, and in London and Paris they were obliged to register themselves as alien enemies, and were prevented from returning to their own country, in case they should there act in favour of the Turks. At the same time those of military age in Egypt were prevented from going abroad, in case they should be required to serve against the Turks!

During these anxious times the Khedive remained in Constantinople as a willing prisoner of his overlord. He was on his annual visit to that city when the European war broke out; and, realising the difficult position in which his country might find itself, he chose to remain at a safe distance from his Ministers and advisers. Soon after war was declared between Turkey and England, however, he definitely took sides with the Sultan. In adopting this attitude he was acting in the most correct manner and strictly in accordance with the Turco-Egyptian Treaties which England supported; but nevertheless there is no doubt that he was inspired by nothing more or less than hostility to the whole British race. He had always disliked us. He had been educated in Vienna and had there learnt to sneer at the British army; and soon after his accession he passed such disparaging comments upon our troops that Lord Kitchener, who was then Sirdar, or Commander-in-Chief of the Egyptian forces,

THE EX-KHEDIVE.

ABBAS PASHA HILMI.

threatened to resign unless an apology was forth-coming. A story is related which tells how one night at the opera in Cairo Lord Cromer visited the Khedive in his box and requested him to make the necessary apology on the instant. The Khedive refused, and thereupon Lord Cromer invited him to step out on to the balcony which overlooked the Place de l'Opera. The Khedive did so, and Lord Cromer then directed his atten-tion to a closed brougham which stood below, surrounded by a small detachment of British Hussars, and coldly remarked that it was wait-ing to drive his Highness into exile should he feel unable to make amends to the Army. Whether this tale be true or not, the fact remains that the apology was not delayed. Throughout his reign the Khedive has intrigued against us, and though from time to time his relations with the British Agency have rightly been described as cordial, there has always been an undercurrent of political enmity. His friendship to Sir Eldon Gorst was quite sincere, and English people were much touched by his incognito visit to Sir Eldon when he lay dying at his home in England. He detested the bluff Lord Cromer, however, and thoroughly disliked Lord Kitchener. Thus, doubt-less, he welcomed the opportunity of being able to turn against England without placing himself legally in the wrong; and, certainly, had he simply protested his fidelity to the Sultan in the Turco-

British conflict, we could have had no case against him; but he chose to display his friendship for Germany and Austria before the Sultan became the ally of those countries, and thus he showed publicly and gratuitously his adherence to our enemies.

Soon after war was declared against Turkey, Mr Asquith, in his Guildhall speech, spoke of the Turkish violation of the frontier, mentioned above, as being an act of "lawless intrusion" on the part of the Porte; and he thus made confusion more confounded, for he issued this statement as the head of a Government which, on paper, still definitely recognised Turkey's suzerainty over Egypt, and therefore recognised the Sultan's right to take such steps to punish the insubordinate acts which Egypt had committed—for example, in treating the Germans as enemies without the consent of the Porte. Mr Asquith probably had never read the treaties, and, after all, they were now of little consequence, since Turkey had become the ally of our enemies; but nevertheless he could well have afforded to give the Turks their due, and to have described their incursion across the frontier as hostile but, under the circumstances, in no way lawless. England went to war with Turkey because the Sultan's Government had been intolerably provocative and because they obviously intended to go to war with us. That was reason enough. For more than thirty years the British

have honourably held Egypt for the Porte, and
have received the approbation of the world for
the punctilious correctness in continuing to recognise the Turkish rights there ; but by describing
the Sultan's proposed punitive expedition into his
own Egyptian province as "lawless," Mr Asquith
threw away the fruits of this correctness, for
his remarks implied that the British Government
had been unconscious of Turkish suzerainty over
Egypt.

The fact that Turkey heralded her entrance into
the war by bombarding certain points on the
Russian Black Sea coast led at first to the general
assumption that it was her main intention to
direct her attack against the Czar's forces. This
I believe to be incorrect. Turkey's main object
was from the first the conquest of Egypt. The
opening of hostilities in the Black Sea was due
to the inability of the Porte to make up her
mind to enter the conflict, an inability which
determined the Turkish war party to encourage
the German officers on board Turkish battleships
to force the Sultan's hand by committing acts of
aggression against Russia. Ever since the beginning of the war the Turkish imagination had been
filled with the dream of regaining her lost prestige ; but her thoughts were not turned to the
west or north : they were directed to the east and
south. She knew well enough that it was useless
to attempt to recover her lost possessions in

Europe; and, indeed, her German tutors carefully guided her attention away from the west. Her dream was to restore herself to a position of supremacy in the Mohammedan world; but, had it not been for the reckless methods of her war party and its Teutonic advisers, she would not have attempted to realise her desires until she was assured that the Allies, and especially England, had been beaten. Turkey, in fact, fell a victim to the enchantment of Germany's "Calais" war-cry. The wave of confident enthusiasm which drove the German hordes towards England at the end of October inflamed the minds of the war party, and gave the Prussian officers their opportunity. Acts of hostility were committed. Then came the news that the roads to Calais were not resounding with the thunder of the Kaiser's advancing armies, but were a silent shambles of his dead. The Grand Vizier attempted to apologise; but it was too late. The exasperated Russians would not accept the half-hearted and insincere apology; and England was willing enough to follow their lead in the good hope of giving the *coup-de-grâce* to the emaciated Turkish question. The Porte was thus committed to the undertaking of her wild projects, which, even at the outset, she must already have known to be doomed to utter failure.

In her plan of campaign, as it was first dreamed, her first object was to capture the Suez Canal, thus cutting direct communication between England and India; her second object was to take Cairo and Alexandria, thus establishing a base for the taking over of the Sudan, linking up ultimately with the German possessions in East Africa; her third was to assert herself in Arabia, to come to an agreement with the disaffected tribes of the Yemen, and to strengthen her prestige in the holy cities; and her final object was to use this strategic position in Egypt and this religious prestige to stir up trouble in Persia, Afghanistan, India, Tripoli, Algeria, Morocco, and other Mohammedan countries in which the Allies are interested. In Europe and in Asia Minor her efforts were intended to be purely defensive, her object being to hold her home territory intact while her expeditionary force went forth on its great adventure. On her western, or European, frontiers she had much reason to hope that Bulgaria would play a friendly part, if only by neutrality. In her past wars with Russia, the frontiers of the two countries met in the Balkans; but now neither nation could strike a blow at the other on this side of the Black Sea without the participation of both Bulgaria and Roumania. The only Turco-Russian frontier lies along some 200 miles of mountainous country between Armenia and the Caucasus; and here the Porte was well aware that offensive hostilities on her part could have little effect on Russia, and

none on the European storm centre.   Germany
never expected Turkish intervention to weaken
the Russian battle line, which was so great a
terror to her eastern provinces.   That was not
the Kaiser's reason for seeking the Sultan's aid.
His immediate object was to weaken the *British*
line in North France and Belgium, and our home
defences, by occupying the attention of large
bodies of our troops in the east; and this was
the original enterprise upon which Turkey was
made to set out.   Its complexion, of course, came
to be much changed by the strong Russian offensive in Armenia, and later by the attack on the
Dardanelles; but there can be no doubt that
at the outset the Turks and Germans had their
eyes on Egypt, and that the country around the
Suez Canal was intended to be by far the most
important field of operations.   Already in September a large army of Turkish troops, supported
by Arab and Bedouîn contingents, was massed
on the frontier between Syria and Egypt; but
the German defeat at the Marne restrained the
Porte from giving the order to march across
the desert to the Suez Canal.   This delay gave
the British Government time to concentrate a
very large army in Egypt; and the forces
ready for the defence of the Canal soon became
adequate.   Large tracts of desert near Port Said
were flooded, and outer trenches and fortifications
were constructed some thirty miles to the east

of the Canal. Battleships were held in readiness to patrol the waterway and to serve as floating batteries, while heavy guns were mounted at all strategic points. As a result of these great preparations the Turkish hopes of a successful invasion rapidly diminished, and this southern campaign, which was at first expected to be the main Ottoman enterprise, came to have only a secondary importance.

The Turks, of course, relied to a great extent on the loyalty of Egypt to its overlord. They thought that the Egyptians would be as ready to strike a blow at the British Occupation as was the Khedive; and they believed that all Mussulmans—that is to say, some five-sixths of the population of Egypt—would respond to the call of the Sultan in his capacity as Caliph of Islam. The temper of the Egyptian people was, indeed, a little uncertain at first, for the Turks had always been respected by them as the chief Mohammedan Power.

Moreover, the acute financial depression in Egypt at this time was causing a certain amount of distress and consequent unrest. Owing to the ravages of the boll-worm the cotton crop had been bad, and now, since the outbreak of the war, the market was very limited. (The total export of cotton in the year 1913 was over £26,000,000, of which 43 per cent went to the United Kingdom, 20 per cent to countries neutral in the present war, and the remaining 37 per cent mostly to

Germany and Austria.) There was also a great falling off in general trade, which was seriously felt in Alexandria and Cairo. The imports for October 1914, the month preceding the declaration of war with Turkey, were £2,000,000 less than in October 1913, and the exports £3,500,000 less. The British Government, however, very wisely lent the Egyptian Government £5,000,000 with which to purchase the unsold cotton from small growers ; and thus the distress and irritation of the peasants were eased, and consequently they were in no mood to engage in a revolution.

The air was further clarified by a proclamation issued by Sir John Maxwell, the Commander-in-Chief of the British forces in Egypt, in which he stated that the British Government would not call upon the Egyptians to fight against the Turks, or to bear the expenses of the campaign, but that England would shoulder the entire burden, and would fight without the assistance of the Egyptian army, "to protect the rights and liberties of Egypt, which were originally won by Mohammed Ali."

The declaration was probably induced by a combination of circumstances. It was doubtless felt that the Egyptian troops would not fight with any enthusiasm against fellow Mohammedans, and therefore might as well stand out. Then the disconnection of the Egyptian army with the war, and the absence of additional taxes, would tend to create a certain supineness in the nation, and would lessen the danger of those sporadic outbursts of excitement which, in a neurotic country like Egypt, are so liable to develop into serious disturbances. And certainly the forces at our disposal must have been thought to be quite sufficient to check the Turkish invasion, without the assistance of the 18,000 Egyptians.

The proclamation, of course, had much the same sense as the establishment of a British Protectorate, for it meant that England would literally *protect* this portion of the Turkish Empire against the big stick of its overlord. But technically it was astonishingly irregular, since no declaration had yet been made that Egypt had ceased to be the Sultan's vassal province, and England's reason for being in Egypt at all was still the original "maintenance of the treaties established between the Sultan and the Khedive." With their usual absent-mindedness, the British authorities forgot that "the rights and liberties won by Mohammed Ali," referred to in General Maxwell's proclamation, were granted in 1840 at England's special request, on the explicit understanding that Egyptians should be regarded as Ottoman subjects, that Egyptian troops should be at the disposal of the Sultan, and that the Egyptian Government should make neither peace nor war with any nation without Turkish consent. Thus, like characters in 'Alice in Wonderland,' we now

stated that we were making war on the Turkish
Empire on behalf of Egypt, which we admitted
was part of the Turkish Empire; and we further
declared that we were fighting in defence of a
treaty which we broke in fighting in defence of it.
In supporting Mohammed Ali's treaty rights we
were upholding the position of Egypt as vassal of
the Sultan, and, mad though it sounds, we were
presumably fighting to uphold the Sultan's right
to fight us for allowing the Egyptians to allow us
to fight the Sultan on the Sultan's own territory!
Moreover, although we already knew that the
Khedive had sided against England, we still
recognised that the Sultan was his overlord, and
we therefore technically supported his action in
attacking us.

A pretty muddle indeed! The British Government could have set matters right with ease had
it now issued a declaration of some kind to show
that it regarded Turkish suzerainty as at an end;
but no such statement was issued. Yet there was
nothing to hide, or of which to be ashamed. England's work in Egypt since 1882 formed one of the
most noble pages of our history. A band of
Englishmen had toiled there for over thirty years,
not consciously for national gain and not at all for
personal profit; and a nation which we found
starving and oppressed had been transformed into
one of the most prosperous and contented peoples
in the whole world. Moreover, for thirty years

we had honourably held Egypt for the Turks; and
even when Austria seized the two Balkan provinces from Turkey and Italy laid hands on Tripoli,
we not only refrained from annexing Egypt, but
actually restated our expectation to evacuate the
country ultimately. Our action in taking steps
against Germans in Egypt was justified by the
fact that it prevented bloodshed; for the agents
of Germany were determined to stir up the natives
against us. Why, then, did we give the impression that we were attempting to blind ourselves to the hard facts of the case? What ill
counsel prompted us to deny the Turkish rights
which for thirty years it had been our pride to
uphold, and thus to endanger the respect which
our punctiliousness in Egypt had earned for us?
It was sheer carelessness. We knew that we were
in the right, that every dictate of God and man
demanded that we should not let the Egyptians
fall back into that utter misery from which England, and England alone, had rescued them. And
in the single resolve to save twelve million human
beings from the ruthlessness of Turkish domination, the Government did not bother to think
about technicalities. That is the only explanation. The hostile critic will doubtless remark
that England, then, is shown to have as little regard for the sanctity of treaties as has Germany;
and in reply one can only say in all sincerity that
whereas Germany disregarded a treaty for the

sake of self-aggrandisement, England did so, not for British gain, but for another nation's happiness—not as an aggressor, but as a protector.

The reward of our labours in Egypt was soon abundantly offered by the Egyptians and Sudanese. Prince Hussein Kamel (now Sultan of Egypt) clearly showed his devotion to the British cause. Prince Said Halîm, the Khedive's cousin, stated in the English press that "every true Egyptian will remain loyal to the great Mother Country who civilised and enriched the Egyptians." The Khedive's poet-laureate published a set of Arabic verses, from which the following lines deserve to be quoted :—

"What is Thy judgment, O Lord, what is Thy opinion of the Kaiser's tremendously expansive dream ?

"The Emperor of Germany has delivered a speech, decreeing that in the Great Kingdom he will appropriate the larger part himself, and will leave the smaller part to Thee.

"Which sword, O Lord, is sharper—Thine or his ?

"Should his dream be realised, the calamity to Islam would indeed be great.

"O God, forget not Thy flock because it appears to be the humbler side.

"We are the victims of a reckless band of men" (i.e., the Turkish war party).

Another well-known Arabic poet dedicated an

ode to "Tommy Atkins," and bade him to crush German militarism which had ruined Turkey, and to "return the Prussian's arrow into his own neck."

The Egyptian newspapers unanimously denounced the Turkish action, and 'El Moayad,' the leading organ, published an article showing that the Arab world had always been badly treated by the Porte. The Grand Sheikh of the Senoussi proclaimed his friendliness to Egypt and to the British. The chief ulemas of El Azhar University in Cairo issued instructions to the people, in the name of the Prophet, to keep the peace. The ulemas and sheikhs of the Sudan declared that they were "with the British Government heart and soul, having no bond with Turkey." A distinguished Arabic writer, formerly editor of an Alexandrian newspaper, published an appeal to Ottomans to realise that England has always been Turkey's good friend. Hundreds of letters were received by the Government and the British Agency protesting the writers' devotion, and large numbers of natives sent subscriptions to the Prince of Wales' Fund. But perhaps the attitude of the Egyptians in general towards the English was rather one of kindly toleration than of warm friendship, while their relationship to the Turks had more in it of indifference than of liking or dislike. "*Auzinhum taiyib min bayid,*" said the peasants in regard to the Ottomans: "We wish them well—from afar."

It will be as well to review here some of the factors which influenced Egyptian opinion in regard to Turkey. In the first place, let it be clearly understood that the articulate portion of the nation has no great liking for the English. The *fellahîn*, or peasants, are not particularly grateful for all that we have done for them, but to some extent they realise the value of the law and order which we have established; and, on the whole, it may be said that the rural population is well satisfied. The *effendi*, or educated classes, however, think that they have been somewhat sat upon. They have always clamoured for self-government, which has not yet been given to them; and a large number of young Egyptians of the upper and middle classes regard the British official as a cold, stern, unsympathetic school-master. Perhaps one in every ten British officials is popular with the natives; the others are re-spected, and sometimes mildly liked, but not loved. The Egyptians, generally speaking, neither understand nor appreciate incorruptibility, high-mindedness, and activity; and what we call sterling qualities are detested by them. A large number of Egyptians loathed Lord Cromer, who is one of the most high-principled, the most just, and the most honourable men England has ever bred. On the other hand, they loved Lord Kitchener, whose real high-mindedness they had little op-portunity of observing, owing to the shortness of his tenure of office as Consul-General, but whose shrewdness and supposed unscrupulousness were commonly discussed. Lord Kitchener's influence with the natives was enormous ; they feared him, thought they understood him, and loved him ; and the fact of his supreme command in his own country had a very quieting effect upon them. In spite of the goodwill of the Press and of certain individuals, as recorded above, one may say that on the whole the Egyptians did not much care whether we remained in Egypt or not. On the other hand, all better-class Egyptians regarded France as the pattern of what a nation should be. They nearly all speak French, dress as much as possible in the French style, and emulate the manners of Paris. If the war had been simply a Franco-German contest the Egyptians would have been enthusiastically on the side of the French ; but as far as they are concerned the fight was mainly Turco-British. Speaking generally, it may be said that the fact that France and England were allies had an appreciable effect on native opinion in the direction we desired.

As regards Egypt's relations with Turkey, the question had two distinct aspects—civil and religious. As to the former, history shows that the Egyptians were never notably loyal to their Ottoman overlords, and were always ready enough to come to blows with them. The new situation was somewhat akin to that of 1769, when Ali Bey, of Egypt, was ordered by the Sultan to join in the war against Russia. This led to his revolt against Turkey and his conquest of Syria. He then proclaimed himself Sultan of Egypt, and lent his aid to the Russians. The incidents recorded in this volume suffice to show that there has been much old enmity between the Sultan and his Egyptian vassal; and, if the matter were purely political, the Egyptians would have had no objection to a fight with Turkey.

As regards the religious aspect of the question, there can be no doubt that the Egyptians regard the Sultan with much reverence as the head of their faith. He is the Caliph of Islam, and is therefore to them what an Italian Pope is, let us say, to a French Catholic. But, at the same time, this reverence for the Sultan as Caliph does not seem to be so potent a factor in Egypt's attitude as is the respect entertained for him as the head of the leading Mohammedan nation. Turkey is, to the Egyptians, the hope of Islam; and they felt that a demonstration of the Sultan's power was a matter of good cheer to all Mussulmans. Egyptians have for some years entertained the hope that Turkey, as a Mohammedan nation, would increase its influence in Europe, and would thereby prove to the world that Mohammedans were as capable as Christians. They looked always to Turkey as the representative of Islam, and any Turkish success against Christians was hailed with genuine delight, not for fanatical reasons, but simply as a vindication of their own creed. The Egyptians have suffered a great many slights at the hands of the very arrogant lower - class Greeks and Italians who reside in their country and who have been protected by the Capitulations; and they have consoled themselves with the hope that one day these objectionable Christians would be well punished by the Mohammedan champion, Turkey. Since the Balkan war, however, this hope was much diminished, though it has not yet been wholly dispelled; and now the Sultan's entrance into the fray at the earnest appeal of the Christian nation of Germans, was regarded as a fine tribute to Mohammedan worth. The Egyptians have forgotten in what manner the Sultans of Turkey became Caliphs and obtained the right to speak in the name of Islam; but it will be as well if the facts are recalled.

The Caliph is the representative of the Prophet and the temporal sovereign of all Mohammedans. Originally the office was not hereditary, but each Caliph nominated his successor. The descendants of Abbas, the uncle of the Prophet, reigned as Caliphs over large possessions, of which Egypt was a part, from A.D. 750 to 868, and again from 905 to 969. In 1258 a descendant of this line was established as Caliph upon the throne of Egypt, and his successors nominally held office after him until the Turkish conquest of 1517.

The victorious Sultan Selim I. then stated that Mutawakkil, the last of these Abbaside Caliphs, had handed the office over to him; and though it is now impossible to ascertain whether this was a fabrication or not, it may certainly be said that, if the Caliphate was really handed over, the transaction was made under compulsion. Selim was not a descendant of the Prophet, and he had no claim to the office. Yet he stripped Egypt of its religious dominion; seized the Prophet's banner and other sacred relics which were preserved in Cairo, and took them to Constantinople; and sent the fallen Egyptian Caliph to die in exile. To this day the Shiites do not admit the Sultan's right to the Caliphate, and many of the Sunnites regard the Sherîf of Mecca, who is a descendant of the Prophet, as the true head of the Faith. The Egyptians, however, trained by many years of tribulation to a ready subserviency, acknowledge the Sultan's claim to the sacred office; and, unless their religious leaders are wise enough at this juncture to raise the question of his right to speak as Caliph, the contemplated fall of Turkey will appear to the native mind more in the aspect of a menace to Islam in general than in that of a benefit to Egypt in particular.

Nevertheless there are a few Egyptians. who have considered this question, and have asked themselves whether it would be possible to restore the Caliphate to Cairo in the person of the new

Sultan of Egypt; or, failing that, to acknowledge the rights of the Sherif of Mecca, and to bolster up the Egyptian sovereign into a kind of Defender of the Faith. Egypt being so close to the holy cities of Islam, he certainly ought to be their natural protector, whether as Caliph or not; and it is to be hoped that the subject will now be openly discussed in Cairo, in order that the Egyptians may realise that the fall of Turkey does not mean a blow to Islam, but rather an adjustment which will infuse new life and new hope into the Mohammedan religion.

The anomalous and utterly irregular situation in Egypt was at last brought to an end on December 18, 1914, by a proclamation which stated that "the suzerainty of Turkey over Egypt is terminated," and that "Egypt is placed under the Protection of His Majesty, and will henceforth constitute a British Protectorate." On the next day another proclamation was issued, stating that "in view of the action of His Highness Abbas Hilmi Pasha, lately Khedive of Egypt, who has adhered to the King's enemies, His Majesty's Government have seen fit to depose him from the Khedivate, and that high dignity has been offered, with the title of Sultan of Egypt, to His Highness Prince Hussein Kamel Pasha, eldest living prince of the family of Mohammed Ali, and has been accepted by him."

A very general tribute was paid both by natives

and Europeans to the unselfish restraint of England in refraining from taking forcible possession of Egypt at this time, when such a movement could have been backed by an irresistible army. In refraining from annexing Egypt and in declaring a simple Protectorate, England has given the best answer to those who would criticise our recent irregular actions on the Nile; for it is thus clearly shown, beyond all dispute, that the British Government has been actuated throughout by the most disinterested desire for the welfare of the Egyptian nation, without regard to the aggrandisement of our own Empire. England still adheres to the original policy of training the Egyptians to govern themselves, and the fact that no advantage whatsoever has been taken of the helplessness of Egypt has given the greatest satisfaction to the natives, and has raised British prestige to a height never before attained.

The attitude of the British troops to the populace is exemplary. In one of his first speeches the new Sultan stated that the behaviour of officers and men since the beginning of the Occupation had been "perfect." "There has been," he said, "no swaggering and no sabre-rattling in their relations with the inhabitants of this country." As an example of this spirit, which is so happily in contrast with German militarism, I may relate an incident which occurred at a grand march-past in connection with the new Sultan's accession. As the procession was passing the saluting point, a native funeral came into sight along a side-street, and was, of course, stopped by the police. Seeing this, Sir John Maxwell, who was taking the salute, instantly intervened. He ordered the band of the Rifles, which was just passing, to cease playing, and he directed the troops to halt. He then moved aside, and allowed the simple native *cortège* to proceed through the British lines. The incident, though trifling in itself, caused a deep impression, and demonstrated in a noteworthy manner the policy of the protecting Power.

The Egyptians received the announcement of the Protectorate without emotion. They showed no frothy enthusiasm which might afterwards have given way to a revulsion of feeling in our disfavour; but their relief and general approval was manifest. The deposition of the Khedive was, on the whole, popular. One cannot help a feeling of sorrow in recalling to mind the short, rotund, double-chinned figure, who for so many years waddled through the halls of Abdin Palace, with amiable expression and shifty eye; for in many ways he was a kindly and pleasant personage, having something of the inherent charm of his great house. Had he played the game in his dealings with England, he would now be Sultan of Egypt, and in the future he might possibly have become Caliph of Islam, an office which for many centuries was vested in Egypt, and which, as we have seen, was seized by the Turkish sovereign in 1517. Now, owing to his personal dislike of Englishmen, and to his erroneous belief that the German cause would triumph, he has been led to turn against us, and therefore has been sent to join the sad little company of exiled rulers whose lives must necessarily be shadowed by vain ambitions and bitter remorse.

The new sovereign is a man of very different stamp. He possesses a manner of perfect royalty, is as honest as the day, and is admirable from every point of view. He has been called the "Father of the *fellah*"—the Egyptian peasant; and his dealings both with the working men and with the upper classes have been always marked by kindliness, justice, and sound sense. In an interview granted to a press representative shortly after his accession, he expressed sentiments which none but a high-minded statesman could have uttered. "If I can succeed," he said, "in inspiring the people of Egypt with some of that civic spirit which the young nations of the British Empire have displayed, I shall be content. To reach that goal education is required—not mere book-learning, but social and moral training which men learn first from their mothers. Female education is what the country greatly needs, and if I am in some things a Conservative, I am a Liberal in this. I believe there is a great future for my country. Once the disturbance caused by the war has ceased, Egypt will be a centre of intensive cultivation, moral as well as material. Remember we have three great assets—the Nile, the Egyptian sun, and, above all, the *fellahîn* who till the fruitful soil of Egypt. I know them well and love them. You will not find a race of men more accessible to progress, better tempered, or harder working. . . . I trust entirely in England, and hope she trusts me. I have always worked for a good understanding between England and Egypt."

His Highness has been most ably supported throughout these trying times by the ex-Regent and present Prime Minister of Egypt, Hussein Rushdy Pasha, to whom British thanks are due. He is an honest, bluff, and very intelligent man, of somewhat Bohemian habits. He has helped to steer his country round one of the most awkward corners in its career, and he merits the greatest credit for his tactful interpretation of a most difficult *rôle*.

Amongst Englishmen, mention should be made of the good work accomplished by Sir Milne Cheetham, the British Chargé d'Affaires, whose tactful handling of the situation has been much admired. Sir Ronald Graham, the Adviser to the Ministry of the Interior, showed most conspicuous good sense and cool judgment, and the internal quietude of the country during these most anxious days was largely due to his influence. At the

British Agency Mr Ronald Storrs acted with great circumspection, and may be said to have contributed in no small measure to the successful solution of Egypt's difficulties. Sir Murdoch Macdonald, of the Ministry of Public Works, Lord Edward Cecil, the Financial Adviser, and Sir George Macauley, the Director of the State Railways, will also be long remembered for their able work under very trying circumstances.

The future of Egypt is still somewhat uncertain; for, although the corner has been turned, the road is still difficult and full of pitfalls. The new form of government does not bring with it many changes in the actual methods of administration. The main difference will be noticed in the abolition of the Capitulations, which have always been such a thorn in the flesh of the Government. These Capitulations have given foreigners in Egypt certain privileges which have been very greatly abused. A foreign subject, let us say, committed a crime against an Egyptian; but, by the capitulatory rights, he could not be tried by an Egyptian court; although an English judge was seated upon the bench. He had to be taken in custody by his Consulate, and tried in the Mixed Courts, or deported to his own country for trial. Again, when a reform was to be instituted in Egyptian administration which had some vague bearing upon foreign interests, the consent of innumerable foreign Governments had to be obtained, a process often occupying many years. The establishment of one law both for Egyptians and for foreigners will remove a drag upon the Government which has been most seriously felt in recent years, and which has very rightly been resented by the natives and their British colleagues. As regards the tribute of £682,000 paid annually to Turkey, no final arrangements have yet been made. The whole of this sum is hypothecated for the payment of a Turkish debt; and, of course, the interests of the Allies' bondholders have to be safeguarded.

As heretofore, the Egyptians will play a large part in their own government, and England will exert only a guiding pressure upon the administration. A small Army of Occupation will remain in the country after the establishment of peace, to serve as a kind of police force for the maintenance of order; but it is still a question whether the native army will be increased beyond the 18,000 men which was the maximum authorised by the Turco-Egyptian Treaties. The British Consul-General is replaced by a High Commissioner, and to this office Sir Arthur M'Mahon, late Foreign Secretary to the Government of India, has been appointed, but the actual activities of the earlier office will not be greatly altered.

For the moment the contemplated invasion of Egypt by a Turkish army occupies public attention; for, in spite of the great difficulties of crossing the desert, the scheme has not yet been abandoned. Djemal Pasha, the Turkish commander, is said to have been superseded by General von Falkenberg, an able German officer, who believes the task of successfully attacking the Suez Canal to be practicable. This officer has been instructed to effect the arrest of the new Sultan of Egypt, and to try him by court-martial for his insubordination to the Turkish Sultan. The very large British Imperial forces now assembled in Egypt, however, are confident of their ability to defeat these designs, and little fear is felt of a native rising in favour of the Porte. It is to be hoped, as has been said above, that in future years Egypt will be able to re-establish its protective influence over the Hedjaz, where the sacred cities of Mecca and Medina are situated; and Mr Asquith has recently reminded the world that it is England's determination "to defend against all invaders, and to maintain inviolate, the Holy Places of Islam."

The relationship of Egypt to Syria is as yet undecided; but it is to be remembered that in the past the latter country has usually been a dependence of the Egyptian dominions. If, as is expected, the Turkish overthrow is complete, Syria will certainly come under the protection of either England or France. Meanwhile German East Africa, which adjoins the Sudan, will probably pass into our hands; and thus the valley of the

Nile will be surrounded by friendly territory, and will become, as the dynasty of Mohammed Ali has always wished, the centre of Near South-Eastern civilisation.

Thus we have brought to a close the first period of our great work in the ancient land of the Pharaohs, and have opened in all happiness and with all good auguries the clean page upon which we are about to write the mighty story of the new Egypt.

INDEX.

at Salhiel, 30; history of, 52;
attacked by the Turks, 53;
ambushed by Mohammed Ali, 56;
massacre of the Mamelukes, 58
Marchant, Major, 196
Matchell, Major, 208
Maxwell, Sir John, Commander-
in-Chief of the British forces in
Egypt, 288
Menou, General, 31, 50
Murad Bey, Mameluke chief, 4, 7;
at the battle of the Pyramids, 26
Mustapha Kamel Pasha, 213
Mustapha Pasha Fehmy, 209
Macauley, Sir George, 304
Macdonald, Sir Murdoch, 265, 304
M'Mahon, Sir Arthur, High Com-
missioner in Egypt, 305

Nationalist Party in Egypt, 202,
208
Navarino, battle of, 65
Nelson's chase after the French
Fleet, 14
Neutrality, Egyptian, 273
Nubar Pasha, 114

Palmer, Sir Elwin, 209
Porte and Egypt, 193
Porte and the Sudan, 197
Protectorate: Egypt proclaimed a
British, 299
Pyramids, battle of the, 26

Rifki, Osman, Minister of War,
127, 129
Roosevelt, Colonel, 206
Royle, Charles, English judge, 143

Sadyk, Ismail, Minister of Finance
to Ismail Pasha, 107, 109, 110
Said Pasha, Viceroy of Egypt, 84
Selim I., Sultan of Turkey, declared
Sultan of Egypt, 3
Seymour, Admiral, commanding
British Fleet, 147, 152

Sherif Pasha, 135, 183
Smith, Sir Sidney, 36, 40
Storrs, Mr Roland, 234, 266, 304
Sudan, the, 174, 183; recon-
quered, 193, 196
Suez Canal, guests at opening of,
102; opening of, 103
Sultan of Egypt, 299
Syria: Bonaparte's expedition
into, 36; revolts against
Mohammed Ali, 68, 76; future
of, 306

Tel-el-Kebir, battle of, 159
Tewfik Pasha: succeeds as
Khedive, 117; browbeaten by
discontented officers, 129; interview with disaffected army, 132;
quarrel with Arabi and the
army, 137; at Ramleh during
the bombardment of Alexandria,
149; made prisoner by Arabi,
151; places himself under British
protection, 152; makes state
entry into Cairo, 163; com-
mutes Arabi's death sentence,
163, 177
Tripoli, the seizure of, by Italy,
239
Turco-Egyptian Treaty, 77, 270,
274
Turks: conquer Egypt, 3; defeated by Bonaparte at Aboukir,
40; defeated by the Egyptians
at Konia, 67; defeated at
Nezib, 73; rights of, in Egypt,
243; war declared between England and the, 278; their plan
of campaign against Egypt, 284

Watson, Sir Charles, 161
Wingate, Sir Reginald, 196
Wolff, Sir Henry, 193
Wolseley, Sir Garnet, commanding
British troops in Egypt, 155,
156, 159, 163

PRINTED BY WILLIAM BLACKWOOD AND SONS.

REVIEWS OF
WORKS BY THE SAME AUTHOR.

SECOND IMPRESSION.

THE LIFE AND TIMES OF AKHNATON, PHARAOH OF EGYPT.

WM. BLACKWOOD & SONS. 10s. 6d. net.

Arthur C. Benson writes in the 'Church Family Newspaper': "Here is a strange and sad story of old and forgotten things. . . . I can hardly describe with what wonder and amazement I have read this book. . . . What a marvellous outlook into the remotest past it all is ! What a reconstruction of the life and spirit of a man ! There can hardly be a stranger episode in all human history."

Manchester Courier.—"Mr Weigall's new book provides the best of good reading. He makes the dead to live. He has to deal with a great, a magnificent subject, . . . and we think that he has risen to the occasion. It is a theme . . . to move a writer to express every quality at his command, and it is well that a writer in command of so many qualities as Mr Weigall should have the opportunity given him. He shows imagination, an eye for beauty, feeling for the high spiritual significance of a prophet's ardours, warmth of sympathy for the prophet's heart ; and, perhaps above all else, a sense for the rhythm and melody of prose. . . . Akhnaton, Pharaoh of Egypt, was a great mind ; and in Mr Weigall's pages he becomes a lovable spirit. . . . Akhnaton lived and died three thousand years ago. To-day, in Mr Weigall's book, he lives again. This seems to us a memorable achievement. The labour that has gone to effect it is great, and the knowledge is great."

Irish Times.—"Mr Weigall has written Akhnaton's history, and given us a very great book."

The World.—"It is no mean feat of scholarship and research which Mr Weigall has accomplished. . . . The character, genius, and philosophy of this 'the world's first idealist,' will for ever repay such study as Mr Weigall has devoted to them in an admirably researchful volume."

Daily News.—"Mr Weigall has given much more than a bare record of historical facts. . . . Closely intimate with the scenes amid which the Pharaohs moved, steeped in the atmosphere created by the study of temples, pictures, and inscriptions, he has very brilliantly . . . filled out the portrait of this most remarkable of Egyptian kings. . . . In the result he has produced a fascinating study. . . . The story, as Mr Weigall has written it, reads like a romance. . . . It is a relief to find a scholar so well versed in his subject who is able to treat it in so luminous a manner."

Manchester Daily Guardian.—"Mr Weigall's book is eminently readable. . . . He utilises the scanty records so effectively that the · · · general reader should be glad to be thus introduced to a boy-reformer who in the fourteenth century B.C. anticipated the Psalms of Judaism and taught the loving fatherhood of the one God."

Pall Mall Gazette.—"The career of a man with such lofty conceptions (as Akhnaton) was well worth telling. Mr Weigall has dealt with his material in masterly fashion, and he makes his hero as much a reality to us as is the most familiar character in history. . . . He writes with equal enthusiasm and scholarship."

Daily Telegraph.—"Over 3000 years after his death the young Pharaoh's story is newly pieced together, and the biographer for whom he has so long waited has made real for us the dim past in a remarkable fashion. . . . It is a deeply interesting book that Mr Weigall has given us, and a personality of surprising vigour and amazing originality to whom he has introduced us."

The Literary Post.—"The historical value of the explorations now being carried on in Egypt is fully exemplified in the work before us, in which the remote past is conjured up with a vividness that is as rare as it is exhilarating. The veil of thirty-four centuries is lifted, and we see the Egypt of the Eighteenth Dynasty, in all its power and magnificence, as clearly as if we were indeed living in that splendid age. But it is more than a mere picture of a past civilisation that Mr Weigall brings before us; for the picture, fine as it is, is but the setting for the study of a temperament, of the development of a mind curiously in advance of its age. . . . One of the most fascinating books it has ever been our privilege to read."

Egyptian Gazette.—"The most remarkable figure in the early history of the world is Akhnaton. . . . The life and times of this Pharaoh is the subject of a new work by Mr Weigall, and he has made good use of his material. . . . No more sympathetic writer could have been found for the task than this young English Egyptologist."

Observer.—"It is a strange and pathetic story, and nothing is more strange about it than that it should be told at all, and that after these ages it should be possible to reconstruct, with so much accuracy and detail, the character of one who has . . . been called 'the first individual in human history.'"

Glasgow Evening News.—"A fascinating record of one of the most striking figures in history."

Scotsman.—"The aim of Mr Weigall's new volume is . . . to rouse the interest of the general reader in Egyptology, by introducing him to what is perhaps the most picturesque episode in the whole of Egyptian history. This is a useful purpose, and one which the book is excellently calculated to fulfil. . . . Mr Weigall has cast his net widely, so that nothing escapes him. . . . We cannot help wondering whether Mr Weigall has the Pharaoh's private diary up his sleeve. . . . His style is vivid and forcible. . . . The translations that are given are of astonishing interest, and will whet the appetite of students of religion. . . . The illustrations have been admirably chosen."

The Academy.—"Mr Weigall has given an interesting and picturesque sketch of this solitary . . . figure in history."

The Bookman.—"Mr Weigall's work is just as good reading for those who know nothing whatever about Egypt as for those who are experts in the subject. So clearly and untechnically does the author write, that he is easily to be understood. . . . This book is really the extraordinarily interesting biography of the 'first individual in human history.'"

Truth.—"Mr Weigall's extremely interesting . . . 'Life and Times of Akhnaton' presents a portrait of a Christ more than a thousand years before Christ."

Aberdeen Free Press.—"The author might have described this book by the title . . . 'Christianity in the Fourteenth Century B.C.,' for he sets before him, and well accomplishes, the task of giving an . . . account of . . . the establishment of the Aton-worship by Akhnaton, about B.C. 1375. . . . The book is on the right lines, and should do much to popularise the subject, and awaken a greatly needed interest in the great work of exploration in Egypt."

Birmingham Daily Post.—"The task which Mr Weigall has undertaken . . . was well worth the labour. . . . Mr Weigall has a fine gift of style, and a singularly attractive subject, of which he shows himself entirely worthy."

Athenæum.—"Mr Weigall writes well and easily, while his enthusiasm for his subject carries the reader along with him, and will doubtless cause his book to be read by hundreds."

Glasgow Daily Herald.—"As an Egyptologist of considerable distinction, Mr Weigall is eminently qualified to write such a book as this. . . . To clothe the bones of Akhnaton with flesh and blood is the purpose of this remarkable volume. It is . . . a daring book, undeniably clever, marked by great learning, and displaying unmistakable touches of genius. . . . The reader . . . will find much in this volume that will profoundly impress him."

Christian Commonwealth.—"A book of most absorbing interest. It has all the charm of a novel, and . . . nothing is wanting to make it one of the most notable that has been issued from the Press for a long time."

Times.—"The author of this singularly beautiful book—at once a reconstruction from the original sources by a scholar deeply versed in Egyptian archæology and history and himself a partner in many discoveries, and also an eloquent and illuminating exposition of a learned subject by one who is himself an idealist gifted with insight and sympathy—has done much to set 'the world's first idealist' in his true place as the voice of God in a barren land. No one, we think, can read Mr Weigall's volume without being inspired with the enthusiasm which he makes no effort to disguise."

Saturday Review.—"Mr Weigall has written a fascinating book. . . . He has the historical imagination and the power of picturesque expression which enable him . . . to present a general picture that is at once lifelike and satisfying."

Liverpool Daily Courier.—"A fascinating . . . and delightful book."

Guardian.—"The biographer of the heretic king has done his work extremely well. He has a power of description and of visualising the events he describes that is used with great profit and pleasure to the reader, and his book will interest all who care for the history of religion."

Reynolds's Newspaper.—"A truly wonderful story."

Yorkshire Daily Post.—"A singularly readable book."

Daily Chronicle.—"Mr Weigall has written a remarkable book. Seldom does a reviewer, having read a volume through, at once re-read it because of the pleasure it has given. Yet such was the fact on this occasion. The story of Akhnaton is strengthening and beautiful : it would perhaps be pitiful—it is in some respects so human—if it were not remembered that since it happened ages have drifted by ; and, with the intervention of centuries, abolition of sorrow comes. Nevertheless, the spirit of its message lingers ; and men will be wise to remember the facts and the moral of the efforts Akhnaton made."

Morrison Davidson, in 'Everyman.'—"A truly wonderful story. . . . We are enabled to look right into the soul of an Imperial Egyptian idealist."

SECOND IMPRESSION.

TRAVELS IN
THE UPPER EGYPTIAN DESERTS.

WM. BLACKWOOD & SONS. 7s. 6d. net.

Aberdeen Free Press.—"Antiquities rather than incidents are the chief characteristics of these 'Travels.' Yet on this account they are none the less, but indeed much the more, interesting. They take the reader back to long past ages and tell him many marvellous things. . . . We heartily commend this pleasantly written volume to thoughtful readers."

Pall Mall Gazette.—"Mr Weigall reveals to us the secrets of the Eastern desert, that stony waste which stretches from the Nile to the Red Sea. . . . Next to visiting the desert itself we can imagine nothing so delightful as reading Mr Weigall's fascinating story."

Irish Times.—"Mr Weigall has succeeded in making us realise the desert. What the others (Pierre Loti, &c.) effect by a delicate art, he accomplishes by simple . . . talk about things which he knows and loves. This is the real secret of the success of his book, for it is a success. . . . We hope that he will publish more of these papers soon."

Newcastle Chronicle.—"The reader will not need to be an enthusiastic Egyptologist in order to fully enjoy Mr Weigall's company. . . . It is not easy to overpraise the chapter on 'A Nubian Highway,' full of spirited pictures of the past."

Westminster Gazette.—"Since the days of Eliot, Warburton, and Kinglake, many writers have celebrated the delights of travel in the desert. None, I think, has realised the fascination of the desert more fully than Mr Weigall. . . . The sights, the sounds, the very air of the desert, visit the senses of the reader with a keenness that is almost painful. . . . Altogether, Mr Weigall's 'Travels' reveal the extraordinary variety of interest these eastern deserts possess for the intelligent European. His delightful book is most efficiently illustrated."

Observer.—"A graphic and human narrative of a deserted land."

Scotsman.—"Mr Weigall has felt the desert, and he is quite competent to transfer his feelings to paper. If the reading of his book does not induce freckles on the reader's nose . . . it can only be for physiological reasons."

Liverpool Daily Post.—"Few writers have given more admirable pictures of the desert than Mr Weigall. . . . His hope is, though he disclaims the power, to hold his readers so entranced . . . that they shall feel the sunlight streaming over the desert plains, and imagine the glow of the sun and the wind upon their cheeks, till they hold their hands to their eyes as a shelter from the glare. We can sincerely congratulate him upon his success. . . . He not only leads us through a strange country, but he peoples it with bygone races, and to the charm of a landscape painting he adds the erudition of an Egyptologist."

Liverpool Courier.—"The Upper Egyptian deserts . . . were in remote days the scene of extraordinary activities, and Mr Weigall, in a very fascinating way, reveals to us some of the interest they still possess. . . . Mr Weigall's literary power is very notable, and we have not for a long time read a more interesting and suggestive book of travel than this."

Manchester Courier.—"There are many delightful descriptions of days and nights in the desert, graphic in their sense of sight and sound, many brightly recorded incidents of journeys over wastes of sand that have long remained untrodden. . . . The style of the author is at all times attractive and admirably adapted to the theme he is discussing."

Glasgow Evening News.—"It is a book which recalls, without much obvious effort to recall, all the wonder and mystery with which the name of Egypt has always been associated."

Belfast News Letter.—"One of the most interesting books of travel published in recent years."

Yorkshire Daily Post.—"Mr Weigall's account of the quarries (in the Eastern desert) is fascinating."

Spectator.—"Mr Weigall gives us here what we may call the private side of some of his official journeys. . . . The book has many interesting things in it, things both old and new."

Homiletic Review.—"This alluring treatise . . . abounds in graphic illustrations and quaint inscriptions."

Manchester Guardian.—"Mr Weigall's book gives some vivid pictures of a civilisation that is no more, and of a region which is practically unknown to modern travellers. . . . He traces in a most graphic manner the history of the (mining and quarrying) industry."

Daily Chronicle.—"The book breathes of the desert. It brings back the glow of the hot sun on the yellow sands stretching to the horizon, and the long camel-roads from oasis to oasis. It is full of the zeal of exploration and research, touched with the true spirit of wonder and mystery which ought to be in the mind of every explorer. We recommend it as one of the best products of recent Egyptian exploration."

The Times.—"Mr Weigall is the scholar-sportsman, and the game, of whose hunting he writes, was found chiefly in the Eastern Egyptian desert. . . . He describes it in a clear, agreeable English, and with a fine sensitiveness to the mystery and romance of ancient things and to the natural beauties of a desert land. . . . The description of Kossair, so rarely visited, and especially of the midnight fishery on its reefs, is the bright particular gem of a book which contains many passages of very great literary merit. Mr Weigall writes with so much distinction (not to mention his power of observation and his knowledge) that one of these days he should give us a travel-book which may take rank in the small company of the very best."

The Guardian.—"Every one who reads Mr Weigall's book will envy the author's experiences. . . . Whether following the Nubian road to Abu Simbel, the highway to the 'dream town' of Kossair, or exploring temples or Roman stations, Mr Weigall carries the reader with him; in his company the dead past lives again."

The Nation.—" Mr Weigall is an archæologist of repute, but he is also a great deal more. The book he has given us includes the results of archæological research; but it is pre-eminently a book of the desert, and the atmosphere thereof. Its word-painting makes one think of Fromentin in Algeria, or Mr Robert Hichens in Biskra. . . . An altogether delightful book."

The Sphinx.—"This is a work which every lover of Egypt should possess. The author has discovered the soul of the desert and has painted it in beautiful language. . . . We are compelled to admit that the result is the greatest work on the desert that has ever been written. . . . Apart from exquisite descriptions and word-paintings which only emphasise the chiaroscuro of his conception, and which carry us beyond the ken of touristland into 'The Garden of Allah,' Mr Weigall gives some interesting accounts of temples and ruins which add considerably to the value of the book."

Saturday Review.—"'Travels in the Upper Egyptian Deserts' is really interesting and well worth reading. . . . We think the author has attained his desire, of carrying away his readers on the fabled magic carpet. For in this book we are really brought face to face with facts and past history, with which are interwoven the incidents of exceedingly interesting but arduous journeyings. . . . The tale is well told, and the reader will not weary of it."

Athenæum.—"It is a book to be read again. . . . Its main purpose is to give the impressions of life in the Eastern Egyptian desert, on the old trade-routes which led from the Nile to the Red Sea. . . . Mr Weigall describes all this excellently. . . . There is much in the book that will delight all desert travellers, and the photographs will help those who are so unfortunate as to know the desert only in their dreams."

Douglas Sladen (author of 'Egypt and the English,' &c.)—"The style is extraordinarily felicitous; such a wonderful mixture of esprit and erudition."

John Ward (author of 'Pyramids and Progress,' &c.)—"The very best book of travel in Egypt that I have seen. . . . The language is so clear, the descriptive portions so graphic, and yet the style so simple, that the work is, in its way, a masterpiece."

THE TREASURY OF ANCIENT EGYPT.

MISCELLANEOUS CHAPTERS ON ANCIENT EGYPTIAN HISTORY AND ARCHÆOLOGY.

WM. BLACKWOOD & SONS. 7s. 6d. net.

The Earl of Cromer, writing to Mr Weigall, says: "I have read your book with great pleasure and interest. You have, I think, done excellent service in many respects. In the first place, you have brought out very clearly the value of archæology, which is really only another name for history, to the practical politician of the present day. I may remark that, to the modern Egyptian politician, the career of Akhnaton appears to me to be full of solemn warning. . . . In the second place, let me congratulate you, and also thank you, for the masterly defence which you have made of the Engineers (in connection with the flooding of Philæ). . . . You have also given a most interesting list of the survival of the ancient customs. There can be no doubt, as you very truly say, that the Egyptians have preserved both their ancient national characteristics and their customs in a very singular degree."

Theodore Roosevelt, writing in the 'Outlook' of September 30, 1911, says: "This is a thoroughly delightful book. The chapters . . . are admirable, because they combine the virtues of accuracy and charm. . . . The chapter headed 'The Misfortunes of Wenamon' is not only of extreme interest, but is most amusing as well; and it could be told, as Mr Weigall tells it, only by a man who, in addition to being thoroughly grounded in the skeletal parts of his profession, is also intimately acquainted with the Egyptian of to-day, and, moreover, possesses the priceless gift of historic imagination. . . . Chapters such as that which tells of the 'Shipwrecked Sailor' are very interesting; and still more so such a chapter as that treating of the 'Temperament of the Ancient Egyptians.' . . . But, after all, the best chapters are those in which Mr Weigall preaches the codes which he himself so admirably practises. His doctrine is that archæology should be studied as much as possible in the open; that archæologists, in order to reach the highest point in their profession, should be not merely antiquarians but out-of-door men; and above all, gifted with that supreme quality of the best type of historian, the quality of seeing the living body through the dry bones, and then making others see it also. . . . The man who has such vision has in him the stuff out of which great historians, and therefore great archæologists, are made. . . . Incidentally, we should all be in hearty agreement with what Mr Weigall says as to the proper function of museums. . . . Mr Weigall's book is exceedingly interesting: it is the work of a thorough scholar,—not merely accurate, but truthful with the truth that comes only from insight and broad-minded grasp of essential facts, added to exhaustive study and wide learning; and it teaches certain lessons which it is of capital importance to learn and apply."

Athenæum.—"Will be read with pleasure. . . . Mr Weigall's views are both reasonable and well expressed."

Times.—"Mr Weigall has a very keen sense of the romance of a digger's life and a very pretty touch in describing it. . . . He has done a real service to historical truth."

Cape Times.—"Mr Weigall is the true archæologist who 'has turned to the Past because he is in love with the Present.' . . . Every page of his volume is of extraordinary interest."

Saturday Review.—"The charm of style is added to the knowledge of the expert. . . . Full of good things excellently expressed."

Pall Mall Gazette.—"Mr Weigall is the key to one of the richest storehouses the world contains—the whole range of Egyptology. . . . Readers will find delight in his reconstruction of the everyday life of the ancient Egyptians. . . . The chapters are full of humour and romance."

Spectator.—"Mr Weigall has made excellent use of the unusual opportunities which have come in his way. . . . Highly interesting."

Bookman.—"A brilliant and faithful study of the temperament of the ancient Egyptians."

Glasgow Daily Herald.—"Mr Weigall's flowing and almost breezy pages will at once attract the reader. . . . Nothing seems to pass the author's penetrating glance "

Truth.—"Extraordinarily interesting and suggestive."

Westminster Gazette.—"Certain to interest many readers. . . . We have an admirable account of the actual conditions of work set forth by one who is an expert excavator and a master of the art of description."

Newcastle Chronicle.—"No Egyptologist has made a more favourable impression on what may be termed the aristocracy of the reading public than Mr Weigall. He writes from a knowledge of his subject that is as wide as it is deep."

Times of India.—"Mr Weigall's eloquent narrative shows him to be at once scholar, poet, and sportsman."

Egyptian Observer.—"Mr Weigall is at his best in the world of Ancient Egypt, where his brilliant imagination and intimate knowledge introduces us to his friends of long ago. . . . The book is deeply interesting, and couched in a rich, polished, and brilliant style."

Rudyard Kipling, writing to Mr Weigall, says: "A fascinating book. I very much enjoyed your defence of History. The chapter on the 'Misfortunes of Wenamon' is delicious."

THE LIFE AND TIMES OF CLEOPATRA, QUEEN OF EGYPT.

A STUDY IN THE ORIGIN OF THE ROMAN EMPIRE.

WM. BLACKWOOD & SONS. 16s. net.

John Beattie Crozier, LL.D., the philosopher and historian, writing to Mr Weigall, says: "I can check nearly every statement you make *separately*, but the *unification* which you have given is a new and real acquisition. In every way the book is most admirable, and in itself would dispense any ordinary reader from resorting to any other books. . . . For me it has been the one great event within the last two years."

Saturday Review.—"Historic Cleopatra may well have been a great politician. Mr Weigall, in this brilliant . . . record of her life, gives excellent reasons for believing it. . . . Mr Weigall's imagination—it is imagination of the natural historian—is best when politically active. Never once is probability outraged. . . . We can unreservedly praise his portraits of Cæsar, Antony, and Octavian; and we receive his political fancies as inspired history."

Athenæum.—"Mr Weigall has made himself a high reputation not only as an explorer, but also as a writer on things Egyptian. He is probably one of the best living authorities on Upper Egypt, and his delightful travels in the deserts around it are justly admired. Now he attacks a far more serious task, where it is not merely necessary to be an explorer and observer, but where the qualities of an historian are taxed to the utmost. . . . In the book before us the author has written many attractive and even brilliant pages. His analysis and explanation of the complicated action of the period is able and generally convincing. . . . We recommend the work to our readers as an interesting and stimulating volume."

Times of India.—"Mr Weigall has acquired a catholic knowledge of the history of the Nile Valley. What is more rare, he links with this encyclopædic knowledge a fine and vigorous literary style. These remarkable qualities combined have produced the book of the year. . . . The ancient world has been made to live as it lives in no other published volume."

Sheffield Daily Telegraph.—"An entrancing historical study. . . . Rarely has an author brought so much undisguised and yet unobtruded learning to bear upon a subject of such marvellous interest. Mr Weigall must feel a delightful satisfaction in the result of his painstaking and brilliant apology for a much-traduced woman."

Daily News.—"Mr Weigall seems to get as near the truth as one can in estimating so infinite a thing as such a spirit (as that of Cleopatra). . . . His account of Antony is an excellent piece of shrewd and vivid analysis."

Observer.—"The general reader will welcome **Mr Weigall's** book with delight ; yielding to the fascination of this wonderful story of wonderful events, as told simply and effectively by a scholar who has let learning quicken and not dull his wits. . . . It is a fascinating and valuable book.".

Glasgow Daily Herald.—"The book presents an interesting description of a great epoch. . . . The picture of ancient Alexandria is masterly and illuminating."

Daily Telegraph.—"There has not been an English biography or study of the fascinating Queen of Egypt that can compare with this full volume. . . . A deeply interesting narrative. . . . He makes Cleopatra a real woman. . . . He succeeds in putting before us a very striking chapter of history in an impressive and thoroughly interesting fashion."

Belfast News Letter.—"Of the first historical importance. . . . A fascinating study."

Liverpool Courier.—"A really monumental treatise on this fascinating subject. . . . As clear-cut as any cameo is the presentation of Antony which Mr Weigall has given us."

Liverpool Daily Post and Mercury.—"It may immediately be stated that never before have Mr Weigall's admittedly great gifts of narration been more proficiently set forth than in this his latest book. . . . Certainly Mr Weigall's 'Life of Cleopatra' lifts her immeasurably above her former position in the popular estimate. . . . Not before has the complete story of one of the world's most striking personalities been more concisely told. . . . The charm of style and of narration is as attractive as the subject."

Scotsman.—"An admirable volume. . . . Mr Weigall's deductions from the able historical analysis he presents will appeal to all as at least exceedingly plausible. . . . The book is one which will repay the careful attention of the reader. It is lucidly and picturesquely written."

Birmingham Daily Post.—"Brilliantly written. . . . History is brought into vivid relation with the present. . . . We accept thankfully his brilliant account of Alexandria in the days of Cleopatra."

Standard.—"A wonderful picture of one of the most bewitching women of antiquity, told as only a scholar who has studied closely the patriotic but baffled ambition of Cleopatra could have told it. . . . Mr Weigall handles his scholarship with independent judgment and imagination. . . . The book deserves to be widely read."

Guardian.—"We have thoroughly enjoyed Mr Weigall's book. It is excellently written, and will enable a good many people vividly to realise the kind of world in which the Queen moved. The sketch of the Alexandria of Cleopatra's day is particularly admirable. . . . In Mr Weigall's pages the Queen is very much alive."

Manchester Courier.—"An admirable volume. . . . Mr Weigall has had unrivalled opportunities for compiling matter for his volume, and he has set it forward with skill."